JUST AS
I AM

A
Practical Guide
to Being Out, Proud,
and Christian

THE REV. ROBERT WILLIAMS

HarperPerennial
A Division of HarperCollins*Publishers*

Library of Congress Cataloging-in-Publication Data
  Williams, Robert, 1955 July 21–
    Just as I am : a practical guide to being out, proud, and
  Christian / Robert Williams. — 1st HarperPerennial ed.
      p.   cm.
    Reprint. Originally published: New York : Crown Publishers, c1992.
    ISBN 0-06-097555-5
    1. Gays—Religious life.   2. Sex—Religious aspects—Christianity.
  I. Williams, Robert, 1955 July 21– . II. Title.
  [BV4596.G38W55   1993]
  208′.664—dc20   92-54862

93 94 95 96 97 **CW** 10 9 8 7 6 5 4 3 2 1

To the members of ACT UP and Queer Nation, whose courage and relentless passion for justice lead them, it seems to me, to follow closely in the footsteps of Jesus the Christ.

CONTENTS

INTRODUCTION

My Own Journey

Just as I am, without one plea
But that Thy blood was shed for me,
And that Thou bidd'st me come to Thee,
O Lamb of God, I come; I come!

I had sung the song dozens, perhaps hundreds of times, for it was used at least once a month as the final hymn, the "Hymn of Invitation," and I had been regularly attending church for all of my eleven years. But suddenly, that Thursday night, "Junior Night" of the week-long revival at Pioneer Drive Baptist Church in Abilene, Texas, the words of the hymn came alive. They were sung for *me*. Jesus was calling *me*. I had a mental image of being out in a field, hearing God call to me from far away, and I was rushing toward the voice, crossing barbed-wire fences to get there. There was a compelling urgency to this vision—I wanted to go—but at the same time, there was a slight sense of dread. I felt that the call I was attempting to answer was also a call away from something.

Feeling almost as if I were pulled by an unseen hand, I stepped into the aisle. Halfway down, Brother Jack met me, shook my hand, then put his arm around my shoulder and guided me in praying that

Jesus would come into my heart at that moment. A few minutes later, he presented me to the congregation as having just "accepted Jesus Christ as his personal Lord and Savior." He called my mother, who was in the congregation, to come and stand with me at the front of the church, as people filed by to shake my hand or hug me. At about the third such greeting, without fully understanding why, I broke into tears and sobbed throughout the rest of the process. Mostly, I felt happy, loved, and supported, but that vague sense of dread lingered. *What have I gotten myself into?*

From that moment, Jesus the Christ has been the primary passion of my life. I have continued to follow him, through dozens of different churches in at least four denominations, through New Age study groups and gay religious caucuses, through the most Byzantine expressions of anglo-catholic worship and piety, to the enthusiasm of the charismatic renewal movement, to the most politically radical expressions of faith. My religion has taken on many forms, but the goal of seeking and serving Christ has never changed.

By the time I was in high school, the fervor of my devotion to religion had begun to frighten my parents and irritate my teachers. The summer before my senior year, at another church service that ended with the singing of "Just As I Am," I again walked down the aisle to make public the fact that I felt God was calling me to "full-time Christian service." I attended a Southern Baptist college and intended to enroll in a Southern Baptist seminary. But I couldn't. I just couldn't imagine myself in the role of a Fundamentalist minister. I began to feel that my religion and my intellectual development were on a collision course, that I was being forced to choose between them.

I decided to resolve the conflict by searching for a church that encouraged, rather than denigrated, intellectual exploration. Jeanette Clift-George, the Christian actor and dramatist who was a mentor to me at the time, once told me, "You are a very angry young man. I think you'd be a much more loving person if you were, say, a Presbyterian or an Episcopalian." I tried being a Presbyterian first. Over twenty years of fierce indoctrination that equated anything remotely catholic or ceremonial with the satanic had made me literally afraid of the Episcopal Church. Still, I had always been a closet catholic. As a child I was fascinated with the images of catholicism I saw on television and used to play at such pious actions as making the sign of the cross. I found the Presbyterian church offered only half of what I was looking for. It certainly did value intelligence, but in the long run, the worship service was too similar to what I was leaving behind. It was still too protestant.

Finally, I got up the courage to visit an Episcopal church. I felt compelled to whisper to the usher who handed me a bulletin, "I've never been in an Episcopal church before. I don't know what to do." He told me to just do what everyone else did. On the one hand, I felt lost. I felt like a fool because I didn't know when to sit, kneel, or stand, and I had no idea what the other manual actions were about (though I found them fascinating). At the same time, I had an overwhelming feeling that I had come home. I thought to myself, *This is where I belong. This is where I was born to be.*

A psychic once told me I had a guardian angel who had been with me since I was twenty-three years old. God knows I needed an angel that year! Within a space of a few weeks, I moved from my small hometown to a major city, acquired my first apartment alone, started a new career, left the Baptist Church to become an Episcopalian, and came out. When I visited my first gay bar, I felt exactly the same as when I had visited the Episcopal church: On the one hand, I was afraid, unsure of myself, lost; but on the other, I knew, *This is where I belong.*

On my second or third visit to a gay bar, I ran into the priest of my newfound Episcopal church. Sensing this was all new to me, he said, "If you need to talk, give me a call." A few days later, I had an attack of guilt and self-loathing, culminating in my burning about $75 worth of gay pornography. I called my priest and told him I did need to talk. He spent an entire day with me, loading me down with books to read, and walking me through a crash course on what I now call "The Bible and Homosexuality 101." It took a while for my heart to catch up, but at least on an intellectual level, all my negative religious upbringing was set aside in one sweep. Not only did I no longer feel a conflict between my sexuality and my spirituality, they were now inextricably intertwined.

My passion for handsome and intelligent men runs a close second to my passion for Christ, and the major project of my entire adult life has been weaving those two passions more and more closely together. In Dallas, I met a group of gay men who shared my two passions, and we founded a chapter of Integrity, the lesbian/gay caucus within the Episcopal Church. We all lived in the heart of Oak Lawn, Dallas's gay ghetto, and we were so serious about our anglo-catholic religion we were thought of by most of our neighbors as being positively weird. More than one potential lover told me he just didn't feel he could compete with the church for my affection. In the meantime, with the community around me, I was becoming more and more out and more and more politically radical.

I was working in the fields of advertising and fund-raising, but every moment of my spare time and every ounce of my spare energy was devoted to something religious. I read everything I could get my hands on about catholic piety, theology, and the intersection of sex and spirit. I went to Mass at both Episcopal and Roman Catholic churches several times a week and spent hours alone in churches, praying the Rosary, making the Stations of the Cross, or lighting candles before the statue of Mary. I began to resent my job because it cut into the time I could be attending Mass, reading and arguing theology, or planning an Integrity liturgy. My high school experience of "surrendering for special service" began to rear its head again. Yet being ordained was out of the question. The Diocese of Dallas wouldn't even allow women to be ordained, although the rest of the church had been doing so for years. The bishop would not entertain the idea of ordaining a "practicing homosexual."

I enrolled in a diocesan program that was a sort of part-time seminary. We attended classes from Friday afternoon through Sunday afternoon one weekend a month (like the army reserves). The entire program, which would take five years, would culminate in a master of divinity degree. Most Saturday and Sunday mornings of the school, I would drag myself bleary-eyed from bed (usually from another man's bed), hung over from a late night at a bar, and barely make it in time for my first class—but when I got there, I was blissfully happy. Nothing felt more right than to be reading, studying, discussing, and writing about theology. I only stayed one semester in that program because it convinced me once and for all that I wanted to go to seminary, a real, full-time seminary. If I couldn't be ordained, I thought, then at least I could get a job teaching. The important thing was to be able to "do theology" on a full-time basis.

Almost by accident (or the movement of the Holy Spirit), I found myself at Episcopal Divinity School in Cambridge, Massachusetts. EDS happens to be one of the most politically and theologically progressive seminaries in the world, as well as a leading center of feminist theology and a very gay-positive environment—but I didn't know any of that. In fact, I told the EDS recruiter I was reluctant to go there because, since it was an Episcopal seminary, I was afraid it would be too conservative for me. Instead, I found myself, for the first time in my life, as a conservative in a liberal-to-radical environment.

Had you asked me when I lived in Dallas, I would have said I was definitely in sympathy with feminist ideology, but at EDS, I found myself at odds with, actually frightened of, the feminist rhetoric. Since I had fled from evangelicalism to anglo-catholicism, I found the catholic tradition freeing and life-giving, and I was dismayed to hear angry feminists trashing catholic worship as anti-woman. When they suggested tampering with the Prayer Book, the book I had grown to love more than I could ever love the Bible, I literally panicked.

After one semester, however, I came to realize that feminist Christian concerns and gay Christian concerns are, at root, the same. We are both marginalized by a church that is run as an ecclesiastical country club for straight (or closeted) white men. Just as men at the top of the power pyramids fear and loathe women who won't submit to their control, they fear and loathe gay men who show no interest in controlling women. Once I made the connections, EDS became the perfect place for my education. Not only did I get a solid grounding in the Christian tradition, I also learned to do constructive liberation theology, and I was once and for all "radicalized."

A seminary, even a liberal seminary, is a fairly intimate community environment, and EDS is a rather small community. Being so closely surrounded by so many men and women who intended to become priests, my own longing to fulfill my old vocation to "special service" returned with a vengeance. About that time my lover clipped and brought me a newspaper article about an Episcopal bishop I had never heard of, John Spong of the Diocese of Newark. The article quoted the bishop as saying that since the Episcopal Church is willing to bless the hounds at a fox hunt, he couldn't understand why they couldn't bless committed same-sex couples. Bishop Spong, I decided, was my chance to be ordained.

I wrote to him, explaining my situation and asking him to adopt me into the ordination process in his diocese. He did almost literally adopt me. I became his golden boy protégé, making appearances at his side at various diocesan functions. I developed something close to a crush on this charismatic man who seemed to be so much like me—flamboyant, rebellious, outspoken, and irreverent. After two years, passing a week of academic testing not unlike the bar exams for the legal profession, three days of psychological screening, twenty-three group interviews, and two physical exams in less than two months (the second due to unspoken fears about my HIV status), I was finally ordained, fulfilling my fifteen-year-old vocation.

Bishop Spong decided, with my full permission, that my ordination should be touted as a very public event, a sort of gauntlet thrown down in the growing debate about sexuality within the church. Since he already had the attention of the media, since gay religious issues in all churches are such a hot item, and since we happened to be located next to one of the world's most important media centers, the diocesan press release about the ordination brought as much media coverage as any event in the history of the

Episcopal Church. All the major television networks, *The New York Times, Time,* and *Newsweek* sent reporters to the ceremony.

Bishop Spong had urged me to personalize the ordination liturgy, and I took full advantage of that permission. Although set in the framework of the traditional liturgy (which the diocesan press release described as "a 2,000-year-old ceremony"), the ordination was unmistakably a gay-and-proud event. One of the readings was an essay by lesbian poet Audre Lorde. The offertory-hymn text began, "What love is this, dare speak its name . . . ?" and during Communion, we sang, "We are a gentle, angry people." I included a litany of the saints featuring the canon of gay saints, Aelred of Rievaulx, Joan of Arc, the male couple Sergius and Bacchus, and the Beloved Disciple; and it was my lover who chanted the litany. I took a line from one of the Prayer Book ordination prayers as a central theme for the ceremony: *Let the whole world see and know that things which had been cast down are being raised up.*

In another way, Bishop Spong regretted telling me to make the ceremony my own. He and the Diocese of Newark in general are on the more protestant end of the Episcopal liturgical scale, while I am an enthusiastic liturgy queen. I designed a ceremony that may well have been the most elaborate liturgy the diocese had ever experienced. We had not one but three acolytes swinging pots of incense. During the prayer invoking the Holy Spirit on the ordinand, I didn't just kneel, but prostrated myself on the floor before the altar, according to the ancient practice. The media loved that image, and the cameras zoomed in. Because we were on opposite sides of the altar, Bishop Spong, who doesn't approve of such catholic gestures, didn't know I had assumed the full prostration position until he saw it that night on the news. As an homage to my religious roots, I had a number of evangelical hymns, including "Just As I Am," sung during the administration of Communion.

One of the barriers to ordination in the Episcopal Church for queer candidates is employability. The church canons do not allow a bishop to ordain someone who doesn't have a place to practice the priesthood. We solved that problem by creating a job for me. I founded and became executive director of The Oasis, a diocesan-sponsored ministry to the lesbian and gay community. The intensive media coverage that began with the ordination never let up. Nearly every time I preached, celebrated the Eucharist, or spoke at a public gathering, there were reporters present.

Six weeks after my ordination, I was invited to make a presentation on the theology of same-sex marriage at a symposium sponsored by the Episcopal Diocese of Michigan. A priest who was in the audience directed several hostile questions to me. "You seem to be disparaging the church's tradition of celibacy," he said. "Yes," I said. "I am. I can't think of anything positive to say about celibacy. I have spent most of my career trying to promote a sex-positive philosophy within the church, and I don't see how celibacy can possibly be justified apart from an inherently sex-negative stance."

The priest refused to drop it, and our exchange dragged on for about twenty minutes. Finally he demanded, "Do you really think Mother Teresa's life would be significantly enhanced—"

Exasperated, I cut him off. "If she got laid? Yes! I am saying that everyone's life is significantly enhanced by sexual activity, and significantly diminished by the lack of it."

When I returned to my office, I received a call from a reporter with Religious News Service. "Did you really say Mother Teresa should have sex?" he asked. I told him I had and tried to explain the context. Then I called Les Smith, the press officer for the Diocese of Newark. I told him about the Mother Teresa incident and asked what I should do. He laughed and said to do nothing: "Just let it blow over."

It was not, however, the first or last time I would find that Bishop Spong's staff is not particularly skillful in predicting his often irrational and violent reactions to crises. The next day, I found on my answering machine a diatribe from the bishop, his voice trembling with rage. It was followed by an equally angry letter, in which he told me I should apologize to the Roman Catholic Church. I countered that asking a self-affirming gay man to "apologize" to the Roman Catholic Church is like asking a Jew to "apologize" to the

Nazis. I have never seen or talked to Bishop Spong since. He told the board of directors of The Oasis that he demanded my resignation, and they agreed with him. Never in my life had I experienced such a feeling of betrayal. Bishop Spong, my trusted mentor and friend, whose relationship to me was almost that of a father figure, not only tossed me aside, but seemed, for a few months, to be on a personal vendetta to discredit and destroy me. At one point, my lover and I warned the diocese we would sue the bishop for libel if he continued issuing the sort of statements that were being reported by the press.

My relationship with my lover, Jim, had been strained for a while. When I first met him, he had been largely in the closet. After three years with me, he was definitely out (his picture ran, along with mine, in *The New York Times*). Still, it was all new to him, and several months of accusations and bickering between the bishop and me, with every new detail resulting in newspaper headlines, coupled with the financial pressure on us, having gone overnight from two incomes to one, was the last straw to destroy our relationship. Although lately our friendship has been restored, we ended our romantic relationship on very bad terms.

Although I was still, technically, a priest in good standing, for all practical purposes, I had been deposed. Conservatives had always despised me, and now that I was at odds with the church's most liberal bishop, I was an ecclesiastical hot potato. No parish in the diocese (or in any other diocese) would dare to ask me to celebrate or preach. At the time of the Detroit symposium, I had been booked to speak to several Integrity chapters; afterward, they all rescinded the invitations.

When things began to calm down, I decided to go back to graduate school. I had, after all, always wanted to teach, and I knew I would have a better chance of doing so with a doctoral degree. I enrolled in a Ph.D. program in human sexuality at New York University, reasoning that the combination of a degree in theology and a degree in sexology would make me uniquely qualified in my chosen field of sexual theology. I spent two semesters at NYU, including a summer program in Sweden, comparing cultural attitudes toward sex. Although I don't regret the time I spent in the program, it was not really what I wanted. It was geared too heavily toward training sex educators for public schools and government agencies, while I was much more interested in academic research and writing, and it was, surprisingly, much too conservative for my tastes.

On Halloween 1990, I had a cold so severe I was having trouble breathing. The next morning, I was so short of breath my boyfriend made me promise to go straight to the health clinic. The doctor at the NYU clinic sent me immediately to the emergency room at Bellevue Hospital. I thought I was going for tests and would be released that afternoon. Instead, I was admitted and diagnosed with AIDS and pneumocystis. I was in the hospital exactly a month, then spent almost another month recuperating at home, unable to go outside. In January, when I had recovered from the pneumonia, I was diagnosed with Kaposi's sarcoma. I resigned myself to the fact that I would probably be dead within a couple of years.

Then I discovered the Manhattan Center for Living, an institute for holistic education. I attended several seminars there on health and nutrition, in an effort to learn to "manage my illness." The center offered a workshop by George Melton called "Beyond AIDS: A Journey into Healing," which brought about for me what, in seminary, I learned to call a "paradigm shift." Although my friends were supportive and rallied to my aid when I was sick, no one, not one person, had ever suggested to me that it was possible to get *well*. The fact that George Melton expected to recover, and had been well for several years after his diagnosis, led me to a major turning point. I began to experience a renewed sense of vocation. I felt God was telling me that I didn't have to die from AIDS, that I could be totally, physically healed, and that I was also being called to be a healer, to help renew and restore the almost-lost tradition of Christian healing. The press heard I had AIDS, and both my diagnosis and my holistic approach to healing made headlines. I dropped out of the NYU program in order to devote myself full time to the study and practice of healing. I began to feel that the fast-paced and cynical atmosphere of the New York area was counterproductive to my healing process, so I explored the possibility of moving to Provincetown, where I had lived for two summers and a winter in the past. In Provincetown, I thought, it would be easier to surround myself with people who believed in the possibility of healing, even the healing of AIDS. The local Episcopal vicar, George Welles, even invited me to develop a healing ministry within his parish, St. Mary of the Harbor.

For four months, things were wonderful. I was again allowed to perform priestly duties. Each week I preached and celebrated a healing Mass that featured the ancient sacraments of the laying on of hands and anointing with holy oil. I gathered a group of lay people who wanted to explore the concept of Christian healing and develop their own healing gifts. As we read, studied, and prayed about the scriptures on healing, taking literally the promises about the miraculous healing power of Christ, we found ourselves becoming almost charismatic. We became, so far as I know, the *only* Christian healing ministry anywhere to insist that there are no incurable diseases, that AIDS can be totally healed. Our ministry was truly unique and almost magic.

Then, in June 1991, Bishop Johnson of Massachusetts refused to grant me a license to function as a priest in his diocese. Since his refusal came a few days before his annual visit to the parish, my friends, mostly members of the healing group, planned to stage a protest at the bishop's arrival. At that moment, George Welles chickened out and began to publicly support the bishop. When we arrived at the church that Sunday, we were greeted by both state and local police, there because George had called them to control our protest.

At first, we moved the healing ministry out of the parish, setting it up as an independent organization called the Palma Christi Institute for Healing. However, due to the acrimony with the bishop and the vicar, the healing ministry went quickly downhill. Attendance, which had averaged twenty-five to thirty per week, dropped to less than five. The study group became a constant source of negativity, argument, and discord.

The lesson I learned from the St. Mary's incident was that I was a fool for believing that there was any parish in the Episcopal Church (or for that matter, any hierarchically structured church) where I could exercise my vocation as a queer priest. Once more, I had been betrayed and lied to by clergy whom I had trusted and had counted as friends. Wanting to get over the sense of rage I felt at Bishop Johnson, George Welles, Bishop Spong, and the Episcopal Church in general, I decided the time had come to do what I should have done a long time ago. At the last healing Mass of the Palma Christi Institute, during my homily, I announced that I had "renounced the doctrine, discipline, and worship of the Episcopal Church."

When the Mother Teresa scandal broke, I entertained the idea of transferring my ministerial credentials to the mostly gay Metropolitan Community Church. A few days after the symposium in Detroit, I preached at the tiny Metropolitan Community Church in my hometown of Abilene, Texas. The contrast between the negativity I had received from Episcopalians, including gay and lesbian Episcopalians, and the enthusiastic acceptance I felt from the clergy and people of that MCC parish was striking. In fact, whenever I have had any contact with MCC clergy, or whenever the press has called on an MCC minister for comments on my situation, they have been impeccable. Two MCC ministers even took it upon themselves to actively recruit me for their church.

My Episcopalian friends, however, kept counseling me to "not give up on" the Episcopal Church, but to hang in there and try to make changes. Plus, my most serious reservation about the MCC was that its roots were largely evangelical and pentecostal—the tradition I had left behind over ten years before. I doubted I would feel comfortable with the generally protestant worship style of the MCC. Then, at the General Conference of the Metropolitan Community Church in the summer of 1991, the Rev. Elder Troy Perry, founder of the church, made an appalling speech in which he launched into a diatribe against the dangers of "goddess worship." I knew then I would be no happier in the MCC than I had been in the Episcopal Church.

Today, I describe myself as "a Christian priest who was originally ordained in the Episcopal Church." I have not renounced the priesthood, Christianity, or my Lord Jesus Christ—only the institutional church. I still perform priestly duties, especially same-sex weddings, and I remain firm in my conviction that Christ is healing AIDS now, and that along with thousands of my queer sisters and brothers, I am called to be a healer. Today, I understand that my primary vocation is to help recover the ancient office of our people, the gay priest/shaman/healer. I like to think of myself as a priest of the Queer Catholic Church.

This book might be described as a manual on how to live as a member of this nonhierarchical queer-positive church, even as a call to form local parishes of the Queer Catholic Church. It is a call to you to join in this process of recovery and renewal of our tribal spirituality, to be a queer Christian shaman.

An important part of the shamanic vocation is to journey through the realm of the spirit, then return to lead others on the same journey. This book is my way of doing that for you, my sisters and brothers. I truly believe that, as the hymn says, God calls us *just as we are*. My personality traits, including my "gayness," my passion, my enthusiastic celebration of the pleasures of sex, my political radicalism, and even my brash, outspoken style of communication, which gets me into hot water occasionally, are all gifts of God, to be used in the service of Christ. I call on you, as you read this book, to come with me on this journey just as *you* are, bringing along your sexuality, your passion, your personality, and your queerness as you answer the call of the Christ who loves you and desires you just as you are.

Notes on the Queer Use of Language in This Book

In the Genesis myth, God gives humanity the power to name things as an important sacred trust. I believe language is sacred, and the control of language is one of the patriarchy's most powerful tools for oppression, so we must be extremely careful and intentional about its use.

For years, I dutifully used the cumbersome phrase *lesbian and gay* to refer to anything related to our community. On the one hand, I heard the protest of lesbians who said *gay* is a male word and cannot include them; on the other hand, I longed for one word that described our entire community, that didn't separate us into two camps.

Then, radical activists began to redeem the pejorative word *queer* for positive uses. Although I am aware *queer* is still a highly controversial and strident word, I happily adopt it as the perfect word to describe the lesbian and gay community as a unified whole. (To be totally honest, the very fact that *queer* is controversial and strident is a large part of its appeal for me.) Besides its inclusiveness, the word has marvelous connotations. Being queer is the opposite of being normal and conventional, and so the word implies a radical self-acceptance. Yoav Shernock of Queer Nation in Los Angeles says *queer* and *gay* are not interchangeable terms, but have radically different meanings. *Queer,* Shernock says, is "a word of pride":

It tells people that we're opposed to assimilating. Those who believe that they're just like anyone else except for who they sleep with aren't Queer, they're Gay. Being Queer is more than who you sleep with. We don't want to fit into the strait world like Gays do.[1]

When I made the decision to use the word *queer* in this book, I had already completed the drafts of several chapters. Going back through those chapters (with, thank God, the help of computerized word processing) and replacing the words *gay* or *gay and lesbian* with *queer* transformed the tone of the entire manuscript. It suddenly felt more radical and more alive. I am reminded that the word *Christian* was originally a negative epithet used against the followers of Jesus, until they adopted it and turned it into a proud self-description. We should be proud to be queer Christians.

The delightful phrase *queer nation* is much more than just the name of a creative protest group; it has become an inspirational replacement for the rather arid term *lesbian/gay community*. Happily, the phrase reminds us we *are* a nation, an *ethne,* a people, a cross-cultural tribe with sisters and brothers in every part of the earth and in every historical period.

I have retained the words *gay* and *lesbian* to refer to queer men and women individually, and I have used these words at times when speaking of specific community organizations and activities. It is, after all, still officially called *gay* pride week, not queer pride week. The rather clinical word *homosexual* is used when it is appropriate—when the context deals specifically with queer sexuality; and also to describe a person of same-sex orientation who isn't out and proud enough to be called queer, gay, or lesbian.

Then there is the question of the use of pronouns in reference to God. Clearly, the consistent use of male pronouns for God reinforces the erroneous and dangerous notion that God is male, and I certainly affirm, to borrow a slogan coined by the Episcopal Women's Caucus, "God is not a boy's name." On the other hand,

---

[1] Quoted in Lilian Faderman, "Queer: A Slur That Some Gays Now Speak with Pride," *Boston Globe* (Sunday, July 28, 1991): 67, 70.

most examples of what is usually called "inclusive language" reinforce an equally dangerous notion—that God is an impersonal force, rather than a personal being. Like it or not, we are saddled with a language whose only neuter pronouns have inanimate connotations. I am profoundly uncomfortable with the idea that God is "neither male nor female," which translates as sexless. I prefer to think of God as *both* male and female, or androgynous. When the context makes it possible, I have simply avoided pronouns for God; but when the personality of God is at stake (and to avoid tortured sentence structures), I have chosen to use conventional pronouns, alternating between male and female.

Except when otherwise noted, all biblical quotations in this book are from the Revised Standard Version of the Bible. When the footnote says "rendered inclusive," it means any gender-specific language referring to God or to humanity has been changed. Occasionally, citations from the Book of Common Prayer have also been rendered inclusive.

PART ONE

Who Says? Sources of the Truth

1

FAITH

The Starting Point

Who are you?

I'm assuming, since you're reading this book, that you are:

1. A lesbian or a gay man—and one who is more or less out and proud.
2. Either on a spiritual journey, or wanting to begin one.

Perhaps you are a lesbian, pregnant with your first child. You have begun to read about and think about various theories of child rearing, and you have suddenly realized you have to make some decisions about what to tell your child about ultimate values and about God—and that means making some decisions about what *you* believe.

Perhaps you are a gay man and have just been told either that you have AIDS, or that you are HIV-positive. You know better than to see it as a certain death sentence, but still, it does make you stop and take stock—where you've been, where you're going, what you want for the rest of your life. You may also be doing some thinking about what, if anything, comes after this life.

Perhaps you're in recovery from a substance addiction. You've

3

been in the program for a while now, you've worked the program well. You've learned to live one day at a time, and it has worked well for you. But now you sense a need to concentrate on your spirituality, to give your "Higher Power" a name.

Maybe you're a veteran in the battle against AIDS. You've volunteered, you've protested, you've lobbied, you've raised funds, you've raised hell. You've also seen a lot of your comrades fall in the battle. You've been to a lot a funerals over the past few years, and it's beginning to raise some questions for you about life and death and what it all means.

Chances are, you were raised in a household that was at least nominally Christian. You may have been sent off to Sunday school or catechism classes as a child, and that is still the basis of your knowledge about the Bible and Christian doctrine. As you got older, you stopped going to church—either you made a conscious, angry decision to reject the negative teachings you were hearing, or maybe you just drifted away because the church wasn't speaking to what was going on in your life.

At any rate, you're back now—tentatively. You have begun to realize some approaches to Christianity are not negative or homophobic. You know some feminists and some queers find a source of meaning, strength, and power in Christianity, and you are curious whether it might work for you. You certainly know there are other ways of looking at the Bible and at basic Christian teachings than what you learned in Sunday school, and you'd like to know more about them.

But where do you begin?

When I was in seminary, I did a sort of specialization in the Christian traditions of spirituality. I trained to be a spiritual director, or what some people prefer to call, less hierarchically, a "spiritual friend"—one who helps others discern the movement of the Spirit in their lives and make informed choices about their spiritual journeys.

Since I knew I wanted to do spiritual direction primarily for queer Christians, I began to develop some specialized techniques. I used to believe that the first step for most of us lesbians and gay men who want to develop spirituality is to heal our image of God, to replace the negative, condemning "god" image deep within our psyche with a positive, loving image of God. I still believe that process is of central importance, but I have come to realize it is not, for many of our people, the *first* step.

One day a man came to see me for a first session of spiritual direction. I had assumed he was of a rather conventional religious bent, or he wouldn't have sought spiritual direction from a Christian priest. I was prepared to begin to explore his deep-seated images of God. This man caught me short, though. He told me that AIDS was the catalyst for his seeking spiritual direction. Like well over half the people who came to my office, he had grown up Roman Catholic, but had come out and left the church. He had also buried nine friends in the past five years, and he had recently found out that he was HIV-positive, so he had begun to think about mortality and, by extension, about spirituality.

All of that made him fairly typical of the gay men I had known who sought spiritual direction. My experience is that AIDS is a powerful catalyst that has forced gay men (and the lesbians who are friends of gay men) into the task of meaning making, into asking those "ultimate questions" about the meaning of life and death that are the starting point for any sort of spirituality.

But what this man said next made him less typical of the gay seekers I had met before. He told me that he *wasn't* a person of faith at all. He said he just couldn't believe in an afterlife because there didn't seem to be any evidence that it was true; and he wasn't sure he could believe in God either. He was not angry or bitter, he just was plainly *not* a believer. And he said, "Look, I don't have faith, but I *want* to. How do you get it in the first place?"

Faith as a Gift

How do you acquire faith? I find that a particularly difficult question to answer because it is a question I never had to ask for myself. A lot of it, of course, has to do with my upbringing. I was born into a religious household, and certainly the experience of growing up homosexual and Fundamentalist produced many emotional and spiritual scars. But prior to the wounds, there was also a profound gift I received from it: My early religious training instilled in me an unshakable faith in a loving, caring, and very personal God. Southern Baptists place great emphasis on memorizing scripture, and the first Bible verse I ever memorized, at about age four, was a portion of I John 4:16: "God is love." I heard and repeated that phrase so many times as a preschooler that I internalized it completely. Our Sunday school teacher told us a story of a little boy who was afraid of storms, but his mother taught him to banish the fear by repeating to himself, like a mantra, "Be not afraid. God is near." That simple mantra got me through my childhood night terrors—and I continue to use it to face my adult fears.

Today, when I am present at a celebration of the Eucharist, and we sing the ancient words of the Sanctus, which are introduced:

> *Therefore we praise you, joining our voices with Angels and Archangels and with all the company of heaven, who for ever sing this hymn to proclaim the glory of your Name . . .*[1]

I mean it quite literally. I *believe* in angels and archangels and demons. (In fact, I think it would be dishonest to continue to say those words in public worship if I *didn't* believe them.) Likewise, when, as a Christian priest, I celebrate the Holy Eucharist, I *believe* the Holy Spirit transforms the bread and wine into the Body and Blood of Christ. Wouldn't it show an appalling lack of integrity for me to say those words in the liturgy if I thought they were just nice pious poetry?

Maybe, if you're lucky, you have the gift of faith, too. But what if you don't? How can I answer you if what you want to know is how you acquire faith in the first place? What *is* faith, and how do you get it?

Faith as a Choice

The same week my spiritual-direction client confronted me with this question, I was called on to officiate a funeral for a young

[1] Book of Common Prayer, 362.

man who had died of complications related to AIDS. Planning that liturgy was a little unusual because the father of the man who died is an Episcopal priest, and he and his large family would be present. On the other hand, most of the man's friends were among the great host of the queer unchurched or "postchurched," those who have left the Christian church behind in bitterness. In that context, I had to come up with some words to say about faith in the resurrection and, in fact, about what it means to believe in God at all in the age of AIDS—and that really required me to get down to the basics. (And on top of that, I had the text of the homily written out, but the person who gave the eulogy, just before the homily, picked up my homily with his papers, so when I got into the pulpit, it wasn't there—I had to wing it.) So I had to preach about faith in the resurrection to a sophisticated, postchurched audience—extemporaneously.

I believe these two experiences in the same week were sent into my life by the Spirit for a purpose. They forced me to formulate an answer to a question that I now realize many lesbians and gay men are asking: *How do you* become *a person of faith?*

Ultimately, I believe faith is largely a matter of making certain choices. The ultimate questions, the religious questions, are *never* subject to the scientific method. Although from time to time, philosophical theologians still write books and essays attempting to "prove" the existence of God, it simply cannot be done. Questions like

Is there a God?

Is there life after death?

Does human life have any real meaning or purpose?

Is life basically good or basically bad?

can never be conclusively answered. You can mount up all sorts of so-called "evidence" on either side of any of these questions, but the bottom line is still that you have to make a choice.

No Proof

The work of Dr. Raymond Moody (discussed at some length in Chapter 20) comes as close as anything I have ever encountered to

7

offering conclusive "proof" of the afterlife. Moody is the physician who interviewed hundreds of people who had had "near-death experiences," who had been officially, clinically dead and then were finally revived. He has written about their experiences in a series of books, the first and most popular being *Life After Life*.[2] These people told remarkable stories about leaving their bodies, about looking down on the scene of their own death as an outside observer, of meeting loving "beings of light" who were there to be their guides to the other side, and, ultimately, about making a conscious choice to return to their bodies for a little longer. One thing that makes Moody's evidence so compelling is that it is so consistent—almost everyone reported the same type of experience, regardless of their culture or religious background (or whether or not they professed any religious belief).

I once facilitated a workshop in Provincetown on preparing for death. We had an attorney talk about wills and legal instruments, a counselor talk about helping the dying person let go, and I talked about the theology of death and afterlife. I used Moody's material because to me, it presented overwhelming *proof* that human existence continues after death. But in the evaluation sheets after the workshop, one of the participants wrote, "This is all very interesting, but I don't think it proves anything." And, you know, that person was right. You can read Moody's books (and there are now several of them) and say, "Wow! Here's proof of the afterlife," or you can read Moody's books and say, "Isn't it interesting that when people are dying, and their normal sensory data are blocked, they tend to hallucinate?"

I have a friend, a gay Episcopal priest who was trained as an anthropologist, who has done research into the physiological aspects of spirituality. Just as there seem to be particular neurochemical configurations that tend to produce homosexuality in a human being, there also seem to be specific neurochemical causes for what we would call religious faith, and especially "mysticism." (In fact, a fertile field for future research would be to examine the cor-

[2]Raymond A. Moody, *Life After Life: The Investigation of a Phenomenon—Survival of Bodily Death* (New York: Bantam Books, 1976/1977).

relations between these two—are people who tend to be homosexual especially likely to have mystical experiences?) There is a particular cerebral phenomenon, a lesion of the frontal lobe of the brain, that is present in most people who have the experience we would describe as "visions." You can evaluate that data cynically and say, yeah, you always knew mystics were crazy; or you can evaluate the same data from a faith perspective and say, perhaps God *uses* a lesion of the frontal lobe in order to "call" certain people into the special, intimate relationship of the mystic. It is, in the final analysis, a matter of *making a choice*.

Making Believe

Some of us grew up under such conditions that these choices were made quite early, and largely unconsciously—in our experience, it feels as if we have always had faith. Other people have had conversions, overwhelming experiences of the presence of the holy that have convinced them of the existence of God. But in either case, such circumstances are not within our control. For others, for those who *want* to believe but don't know how, the only option is to *choose* to believe. John Westerhoff III, an unconventional and outspoken Christian educator, says faith is literally a matter of "making believe." We need to "make believe" in order to believe, he says, just as we need to "make love" in order to love. In other words, to have faith is to choose to live your life *as though* God existed—or more radically still, to structure your life in such a way that it would be meaningless if God did not exist.

The centuries of the catholic tradition of spirituality understood this concept, which is summed up in a phrase that used to be common in catholic teaching: *making an act of faith*. What this language implies is that faith is not a matter of being intellectually convinced by amassing enough data, but rather an *act*, a choice, literally *making believe*.

The choices we make about these "ultimate questions" will shape our other choices. Most queers understand this because we have suffered the consequences of other people's religious beliefs. A case in point is that most of the states in the United States that still have "sodomy laws" are in the South, where the Fundamentalist religions are the strongest. (The very word *sodomy* was invented by the translators of the King James Bible.) James Watt, the incredibly inappropriate secretary of the interior a few years ago, was able to have such blatant disregard for environmental issues because he truly believed the world was going to end soon. John Cardinal O'Connor of New York continues to preach against the use of condoms and masturbation because of his religious belief that nonprocreative sex is contrary to the will of God.

In a more subtle way, the choices we make about questions of faith affect our other decisions, and therefore, our choices carry responsibilities, too. If I choose to believe the universe is basically hostile, then I can see human suffering—poverty and hunger and sickness—and shrug it off: *Well, that's just the way life is.* But if I believe the universe is a basically *good* place, that it is a garden of delights created for the enjoyment of God's creatures, then when I encounter poverty or hunger or sickness, I'm compelled to notice, *There's something wrong here,* and to do something about it.

Holy Atheism

This is not to imply that only Christians, or only those aligned with conventional faith communities, make moral choices—as we know only too well, perhaps more often the opposite is true. John J. McNeill, the gay Roman Catholic priest who was expelled from the Jesuit order, writes of the integrity and honesty of queer atheists, even suggesting a stage of atheism may be a necessary step in the development of a healthy lesbian or gay spirituality. In addition, he suggests, the witness of gay atheists may serve to remind gay believers that "God, too, may well be scandalized by the church."[3]

There is a popular saying about the religious climate of contemporary Spain: *Spaniards believe there is no God—and Mary is his mother.* I think many queers believe, "There is no God—and he hates me." Whether we have aligned ourselves with a more queer-positive, sex-positive spiritual community, or whether we have

[3]John J. McNeill, *Taking a Chance on God: Liberating Theology for Gays, Lesbians, and Their Lovers, Families, and Friends* (Boston: Beacon Press, 1988), 13.

eschewed belief in any sort of religious or spiritual system, we all grew up in a powerfully oppressive homophobic society—and that homophobia is largely fueled by religious belief. The bottom-line reasoning for any sort of homophobic attitude is always that to be queer is, somehow, a sin, an abomination, or a "crime against nature." Even nonreligious legislators appeal to what are essentially *theological* reasons for oppressing our people.

The legacy of growing up in a religiously homophobic culture is that we carry, deep down within our souls, an image of an angry, judging Father God who disapproves not only of what we *do,* but of who we *are* by our very nature. The act of renouncing such a (false) god is an act of psychological and spiritual health. Many of us need to "fire" the god of our childhood and replace him (it almost always is a *male* image) with alternative images of God. (In Chapter 6, you will find some specific ways to do this.) Choosing "atheism," rejecting this false and negative God image, may, ironically, be the first step on the spiritual path for a self-affirming queer.

Making Meaning

While atheism is healthier than believing in a stern and judgmental God, I do not find it a viable position to hold—especially in today's world. What I said in the AIDS funeral sermon I mentioned earlier is that I don't know how we can make any sense of life at all in the age of AIDS if we *don't* believe in God and *do* believe that death is the final answer. Instead of saying, "How can we believe in an afterlife, since it can't be proven?" I prefer to say, "How could we cope with so many untimely deaths if we *didn't* believe in an afterlife?"

If you want to take the pulse of the real beliefs and philosophy of our society (or any society), you need to look at popular culture—what TV shows are popular, what music is popular, and what the lyrics of that music say—but one of the shortcuts is to read the bumper stickers people choose to put on their cars or the T-shirts they put across their hearts. There's a T-shirt that's very popular today that literally makes me cringe whenever I see it. It is the slogan of the person who has made the opposite choices, that life is no good, that God does not exist, that death is the end: *Life's a bitch, and then you die.* Whenever I see people wearing that T-shirt, I want to run over to them, risking being labeled as another religious crazy, and say, "No! No, it's not! Life can be wonderful! Life is a gift, and death is just a doorway to even greater gifts!"

You must heal your negative God image, because while rejecting belief in God is healthier than believing in a vindictive, punishing God, a total rejection of belief in God, or at least in the overall benevolence of the universe, results in a meaningless life—a life lived as though on the stage of an absurdist drama.

The Risk of Spirituality

Spirituality, at least in the Christian tradition, is about *relationship*—it is to enter into an ever deepening, ever more intimate relationship with the Holy One. A relationship with God, just like a relationship with any other person, is a matter of trust. In order to begin a new relationship, whether with a lover or a friend, you must be willing to take risks. You must trust the other person as you gradually reveal more and more about yourself—your opinions and ideas, your wishes, hopes, dreams, and fears.

Beginning the spiritual path, which is beginning an intentional and intimate relationship with God, requires the same sort of trust. You must *trust* God as you gradually make yourself more and more vulnerable and open to God. Remember John McNeill's instructive title: *Taking a Chance on God,* emphasizing the importance of this *trust* in the spiritual journey.

In the early stages of a romantic relationship, one way you learn to trust this new and intriguing person is by meeting her or his friends. When you see your new acquaintance in the company of older friends, and you begin to get a sense of how they trust and love this person, you begin to relax a little. As the relationship progresses, your new lover's friends continue to be a resource to help you better understand and love her or him.

When you are beginning to risk a relationship with God, it is also helpful to put yourself in the company of others who already know and trust God. A community of faith, a group of other believers who are also seeking to deepen their relationship with God, is a central element of the Christian tradition of spirituality. It's not a "me and Jesus" approach; authentic Christian spirituality is practiced only in community. Classically, this community was understood to be the church, although for lesbian and gay people, the institutional church often drives us away from rather than closer to God. In Chapter 5, we'll explore the possibility of finding or building alternative communities of faith, groups of other seekers—especially other queer seekers—who can be companions on our journey.

All these things, though, are secondary steps. If you are really beginning at square one, if you are asking as did the man in my office, "How do I have faith?" then step one is to make a choice, make an act of faith. Ask yourself, *What if?* What if it is all true? How would I live if there is in fact a God who wants a relationship with me? Westerhoff's words are so powerful that I think they bear repeating: *Just as we make love in order to love, we make believe in order to believe.*

Being a spiritual person in any sense requires one act of faith—that there is a God, an intelligence and order behind the universe. Being a Christian requires a double act of faith—that there is a God, and that Jesus is the Christ, the "Son of God." Being a queer Christian requires a triple act of faith—that there is a God, that Jesus is the Christ, and that God created you queer and has special plans for you.

If you are like the man who came to see me asking how to acquire faith—if you are really starting at square one with this Christianity business—then I have a proposition for you. Make a deal with yourself and with me: Play the "what if" game just for the amount of time it takes you to read this book. Then, when you have finished, you can reevaluate and decide what you do or don't want to believe. But now, for the time being, try "making believe" with this triple act of faith:

1. There is a God, a loving, personal God, who desires to have a relationship with you.

2. Jesus the Christ is a unique manifestation of the will of God, our "elder brother" whose life can serve as an especially clear picture to us of what it means to be in a relationship with God.

3. Being queer is a wonderful, special gift, God's unique plan for your life.

Try to put your cynicism on hold long enough to play "what if," to proceed *as though* these three statements were true, just long enough to work your way through this book.

The Ship of Fools

One thing I can promise you about beginning a pilgrimage of Christian spirituality: It is a life of uncertainty and adventure. As a banner in a Methodist church in southern California proclaims, "A sure sign of the Spirit is that you will find yourself led into places you never dreamed."

While it may be human nature to want easy answers, clear-cut rules, and certainty, it seems to be the nature of God to refuse to give us that kind of certainty. The archetypical image of the spiritual pilgrimage in the Judeo-Christian tradition is God's call to Abraham to become the father of a new nation. When Abraham receives this call from God, God does not give him a specific path to follow:

> *Now the Lord said to Abraham, "Go from your country and your kindred and your father's house to the land that I will show you. And I will make of you a great nation, and I will bless you . . ."*[4]

Abraham's call is more a call *away* from something than *to* something. God asks him to leave behind everything that is familiar, to give up his security, and to start on a journey to a place that is only vaguely described as "the land that I will show you." That is why coming out is such a powerful metaphor for spirituality: God always calls you to give up what is safe and secure, calling you to un-

[4]Genesis 12:1–2.

certainty and adventure. Imagine God's call to Mary, the moment Christian artists and iconographers have captured as "The Annunciation." An angel, the messenger of God, comes to Mary and asks her whether she is willing to be the mother of the Messiah, God's specially anointed one. Imagine responding to a proposition like that in five minutes or less! But Mary, according to tradition, did just that. She told the angel, "Let it be to me according to your word."[5] When Jesus began his teaching and healing career, he recruited his disciples by walking up to them, total strangers, and saying, "Follow me." He never told them where they were going; he didn't seem to know himself. They went wherever they felt the Spirit leading them at the moment.

In the medieval church, a favorite image of the Christian path was the coracle, a round boat without rudders or sails. Sailing in such a boat, it would be impossible to control your destination. You would have to go wherever the wind and the waves carried you. This same theme is echoed in a common form of church architecture. From the inside, many Christian churches, with their pitched roof and exposed beams, look like upside-down ships. If you look up, it is as though you are standing on the underside of the deck, looking at the inside of the hull. The message is that living the Christian life is like setting sail in an upside-down boat, a "ship of fools."

Fundamentalists always seem to think they know exactly what God wants them—and you—to do at any given moment; and they are eager to tell you what it is. Those who have followed an authentic Christian spirituality, on the other hand, have typically found it a path of almost unbearable uncertainty. Thomas Merton, a contemporary Christian monk, spent his entire lifetime pursuing the spiritual path, and yet late in his career, he wrote:

My Lord God, I have no idea where I am going. I do not see the road ahead of me. I cannot know for certain where it will end. Nor do I really know myself, and the fact that I

[5]Luke 1:38.

think I am following your will does not mean that I am actually doing so.[6]

Just before his arrest and crucifixion, Jesus went alone to a private place to pray. His prayer, as recorded in the gospels, is full of the pain and anguish of not knowing for certain, even at this late stage of the game, whether he was doing the right thing. If Jesus, our Elder Brother, followed his path without ever being certain of his destination, then does it make any sense for you to expect your own spiritual path to be any clearer?

Authentic Christianity is not so much a source of peace and security as it is an adventure and a challenge. If what you want is to be taken care of, to have someone make important decisions for you, to follow a path someone else has carefully defined for you, you'll find it in Fundamentalism. If you are ready to be challenged, goaded, and led into places you never dreamed of, Christianity is the path for you. Let your adventure begin!

[6]Thomas Merton, *Thoughts in Solitude* (New York: Farrar, Straus and Giroux, 1956), 83.

2
PRAYER AND MEDITATION

Trusting Your Inner Voice

If you are fortunate enough to have been baptized as an adult, you made a promise, during the ceremony, to follow and obey Jesus Christ. Sounds okay, right? But wait a minute—how do you know what Jesus Christ wants you to do?

A Fundamentalist would tell you to read the Bible; but there are about as many ways to interpret the Bible as there are people who read it. A Roman Catholic would tell you to follow the teachings of the Church—but those, too, are open to various interpretations, and if you closely followed the current pronouncements of the Church hierarchy, you would probably not be reading this book, because you would believe homosexuality is "an intrinsic moral disorder." A liberal and much berated Christian ethicist, Joseph Fletcher, popularized what is known as situation ethics, suggesting that the Christian responsibility, in any given situation, is to do the most loving thing: *Whatever love requires.*[1] I happen to agree with Fletcher, but how do you *know* what is the most loving thing to do in any given situation?

Let's say you work as a nurse, dispensing medications. A friend of yours is gravely ill with cancer and in terrible pain. She asks you

[1]Joseph Fletcher, *Situation Ethics: The New Morality* (Philadelphia: Westminster Press, 1966).

17

to help her obtain a lethal dose of a medication so she can end her life. What's the most loving course of action? What would Christ have you do? .

Or let's say you're pregnant. You've just learned that you have AIDS. Would the most loving thing be to go full term and bear a child who may also have AIDS? Or would it be more loving to abort the pregnancy? What would Christ have you do?

Or, if you are male, imagine that several years ago you had an intense love affair with a man who you knew was a politician. Now he is running for a powerful public office, on a very conservative ticket. In the course of his campaign he has made many homophobic statements. Should you speak up and "out" him, or should you keep quiet? Which would be the more loving thing to do? What would Christ want you to do?

How do you *ever* know what Christ wants you to do?

In a work situation, if you don't understand exactly what it is your boss wants you to do, how do you find out? Don't you just go to your boss and ask? Why not do the same with Christ?

"Because," you might say, "Christ hasn't talked to me lately."

Then it's time you learned to listen to Christ.

The Christian literature is full of references to God or Christ or the Holy Spirit being within us. The prophet Jeremiah reports God as saying of the Israelites, "I will put my law within them and I will write it upon their hearts."[2] "We have the mind of Christ,"[3] Paul wrote to the Christians at Corinth. To the Philippians, he wrote, "Have this mind among yourselves, which is yours in Christ Jesus."[4] The letter to the Church at Colossae speaks of "Christ in you, the hope of glory."[5] Jesus himself repeatedly taught his disciples, "To you it has been given to know the secrets of the kingdom of God."[6]

If Christ is within you, then it is through the techniques of prayer and meditation that you are able to communicate with God

[2] Jeremiah 31:33.
[3] 1 Corinthians 2:16.
[4] Philippians 2:5.
[5] Colossians 1:27.
[6] See, for instance, Luke 8:10.

and, if you are a Christian, with Christ. (Without stirring up the hornet's nest of exactly what the doctrine of the Trinity means here, let's just say that for Christians, God speaks to us primarily *through* Christ.)

There are several different types of prayer and meditation, some of them variations on a theme, some of them mutually exclusive. In general, prayer means talking to God, while meditation allows God to talk to you. It's meditation, then, that we are really more concerned with here, but for the sake of completeness, let's start with prayer.

Prayer

How do you pray? Good question. The disciples asked Jesus the same question. According to the story in the gospel of Luke, after watching Jesus in prayer, one of his disciples said, "Lord, teach us to pray."[7]

Instead of giving them a discourse on prayer, what it means and how it works, Jesus simply gave them an example, a model prayer. It is what we know as the Lord's Prayer, the one that is used in nearly all Christian liturgies and every Twelve Step meeting in the world:

> *Our Father who art in heaven,*
> *hallowed be thy Name,*
> *thy kingdom come,*
> *thy will be done,*
> *on earth as it is in heaven.*
> *Give us this day our daily bread.*
> *And forgive us our trespasses*
> *as we forgive those*
> *who trespass against us.*
> *And lead us not into temptation,*
> *but deliver us from evil.*
> *For thine is the kingdom,*

[7]Luke 11:1.

*and the power, and the glory,
for ever and ever. Amen.*[8]

I don't believe Jesus necessarily meant for his followers to always pray *this* prayer, word for word, and we certainly don't have to retain the archaic pronouns such as *thy* and *thine*—though there is certainly nothing wrong with using these exact words. The point, however, was that Jesus was giving the disciples an example, an outline of how to pray. Let's look at the parts of this prayer in that light.

Our Father, who art in heaven

We'll go into more detail on this topic in Chapter 6, but for the time being, let it suffice to say, don't get hung up on the *Father* part here. If you prefer to image God as feminine, go right ahead. If your relationship with your natal family is such that *father* is a negative word for you, then don't use it. When Jesus used the word *father* to refer to God, he did not intend to convey either masculinity or dominance. What he did imply was intimacy.

In fact, the word Jesus actually used, the Aramaic word *abba,* is an affectionate, intimate word for father. It might more correctly be translated as "daddy." Jesus was making a radical departure from the religious tradition of his day, which conceived of God as being generally distant, remote, and fearful. By referring to God, whom other rabbis would have called "the Ruler of the Universe," as "daddy," Jesus was making a startling claim—that we can be in intimate, affectionate relationship with God. Jesus probably had no intention of reinforcing the erroneous concept that God is male; but he had every intention of saying that God is *personal*—not some remote force such as we might imply by "the Universe" or "a higher power," or even "love," but rather a loving, doting parent. In

[8]There are several slightly different versions of the Lord's Prayer, including three in the Bible. This one is the "traditional" version from the Book of Common Prayer, which is largely taken from the sixth chapter of Matthew in the Revised Standard Version—although the Matthew text does not have the concluding doxology ("For thine is the kingdom . . ."), and the punctuation is a little different.

the model prayer, then, the first step is to remember and reflect upon the awesome intimacy you can have with God.

hallowed be thy Name

This is a simple but profound act of praise and worship, and by including it here at the beginning of his model prayer, Jesus is telling us to begin our prayer session with a moment of worship and adoration. I mean, come on, didn't you learn this when you were in high school? You didn't greet your father at the door with, "Hi, Dad, can I have twenty dollars?" You probably said something more like, "Hi, Dad. Great tie. How was your day? Can I have twenty dollars?" Not that God needs the flattery, but it is helpful for *us* to spend a moment simply expressing our love for God before we begin asking for favors, focusing on God before we focus on ourselves.

thy kingdom come,
thy will be done,
on earth as it is in heaven

In another place, Jesus makes a rather astounding promise to his disciples: "Whatever you ask in prayer, you will receive, if you have faith."[9] The catch, of course, is "if you have faith." I don't believe that what Jesus means is "if you pray hard enough," but rather "if you are truly my follower." Jesus is not presenting God as a genie who will grant our every whim. He is not suggesting you pray, as Janis Joplin sang, "O Lord, won't you buy me a color TV?" What Jesus does promise you is, if you are centered in him, if you have conformed your will to the will of God, *then* your prayers will be answered. To pray "thy will be done on earth as it is in heaven" (which is essentially the same as the aphorism in many forms of the esoteric sciences, "as above, so also below") is to put yourself in alignment with the will of God. It is to affirm that what you are about is creating the realm of God here on earth. That is, you cannot

[9] Matthew 21:22.

21

pray, for instance, "O God, wipe my enemies off the face of the earth," because God simply does not work that way—our God is not a God of destruction.

Give us this day our daily bread

Now comes the part we've all been waiting for: the asking part. Jesus doesn't beat around the bush here. He doesn't pray "if it is okay with you" or "if it's not too much trouble"; he simply states what he needs. What's interesting, though, is the word *daily*. Jesus doesn't tell us to pray for all the bread we will need for the rest of our lives, or even for this month or this week, but *just for today*. There is an account in the Book of Exodus of God's literally providing bread for the People of God on a daily basis. In this story, each morning, the ground of the Israelites' encampment was covered with manna. The people could gather up all this manna they needed to eat *for that day;* but if they tried to save some overnight, "it bred worms and became foul."[10] If you have a Twelve Step program, you are familiar with the concept of living "one day at a time." What Jesus is teaching us about prayer here is that God will indeed take care of us—one day at a time.

And forgive us our trespasses as we forgive those who trespass against us

This simple little prayer gets more and more complicated. Now Jesus is telling us to make a confession of our sins (shortcomings) a part of our prayer. Not only that, but he is also reminding us of our responsibility to forgive other people of their shortcomings. *Trespass* is one of those hopelessly archaic words—it sounds as if it deals with property rights. A more contemporary translation of this prayer says, "Forgive us our sins as we forgive those who sin against us."[11] The rather startling impli-

[10]Exodus 16:20.

[11]Book of Common Prayer, 97. This is the alternative, "contemporary" version of the Lord's Prayer.

cation is that God's forgiveness is dependent upon our forgiveness of other people. If I am holding a major grudge against someone, do I really want to pray that God will forgive me in the same way I have "forgiven" that person?

> *And lead us not into temptation,*
> *but deliver us from evil*

This is a lousy translation! Have you ever wondered why you should have to ask God to spare you from temptation? Isn't it a rather sadistic God whose teaching method is to "lead us into temptation" and then punish us for giving in to it? The contemporary version of the Lord's Prayer in the Book of Common Prayer translates this line as, "Save us from the time of trial, and deliver us from evil";[12] so we are asking God's protection from "trials"— frustrations, upsets, problems of our everyday lives—and protection against the forces of evil, which Jesus clearly saw as real and powerful. Contrary to what some New Age spiritualities such as *A Course in Miracles*[13] teach, the Christian position is that there is clearly evil in the world, but we have the gift of being able to call on God to protect us from it, help us steer clear of it.

> *For thine is the kingdom,*
> *and the power, and the glory,*
> *for ever and ever. Amen.*

Just as this model prayer began with the worship and praise of God, so does it end with praising God. Our natural tendency, I think, would be just to do the request part: Give us our daily bread. Yet framed this way, beginning and ending with words of praise to God, and with an examination of conscience and confession of sin implied in the middle, the prayer becomes much more than just a

---

[12]Book of Common Prayer, 97.
[13]Chapter 11 on queer ethics, sin, evil, and reconciliation speaks much more about *A Course in Miracles.*

request to God: It is a little liturgy, a miniature worship service—yet it takes all of twenty seconds. No wonder it's such a popular prayer.

The model Jesus gives us, then, for prayer, is this:

1. Begin by remembering who you are—a beloved child of a loving, personal, and intimate God.
2. Spend some time adoring and praising God.
3. Be willing to align yourself with the "will of God," the purpose and pattern of the universe.
4. Ask, without apology or timidity, for what you need, *one day at a time*.
5. Look into your conscience and acknowledge those occasions when you have given less than your best—and at the same time be willing to forgive other people for *their* screwups.
6. End by adoring and praising God again.

So that, essentially, is how you pray. Christian tradition has suggested there are two primary forms of prayer: personal prayer and intercessory prayer. In the first, you pray for what you need; in the second, you pray for other people. Both are important for a balanced spiritual life. The tradition also teaches that some people seem to have a special gift for intercessory prayer—these are the people to whom you would say, "Pray for me," when you are facing some difficulty. That, by the way, is the concept behind "the religious life," the monastic vocation. It is popular to be sarcastic about the truly contemplative religious orders because, by usual standards, they appear not to be "doing enough." But in fact what they are doing is intercessing—praying for our needs and those of the world. That is their full-time *job*.

Intercession, though, should be a part of the spiritual discipline of every Christian. And we, as a people, have a hell of a lot to pray for. We should pray for those we know who are sick (that's a long list for most of us, these days), for those who are in any sort of danger or trouble, for those who are imprisoned or oppressed (both ourselves and others), for those who travel (who, in the light of widespread terrorism, are in at least as much danger as medieval pilgrims), for those who have died (also a long list for most of us), and for peace and justice in the world.

Praying for the relief of the problems of the world does not excuse you from getting out and doing something about them—in fact, prayer ought to lead you into doing what you can to change things—but you need to do both. The times I find myself most driven to intercessory prayer are those times when I feel totally helpless—when there is nothing I personally can do for my friend who is in trouble. You may even find, as you begin a discipline of daily prayer, that others begin to ask you to pray for them and those they love. You may discover *you* have a gift for intercessory prayer. No need to run off to a monastery, but do accept it as an awesome and honorable responsibility.

If you get really serious about prayer, you may want to keep a prayer list. If you're one of those obsessive types, you might want to note the dates that you add items to your prayer list. Then you can have the satisfaction of crossing them off when they are answered. Remember what Jesus promised: "*Whatever* you ask in prayer, you will receive, if you have faith."

Meditation

I have a friend who talks incessantly. *Chatters* would be a better word. She can call me on the phone and chatter for forty minutes nonstop. What little I get to say, during those rare moments when she pauses to take a breath, is not really heard at all—she simply uses it as a departure point to free-associate, and she's off on the next topic. Whatever you might call our telephone times, they are certainly not conversations.

Unfortunately, that is how most of us attempt to communicate with God. We chatter constantly, but we never stop to listen. And that makes for a rather one-sided relationship. Meditation is the antidote to our ceaseless yammering. It is a discipline that allows us to obey God's command in Psalm 46, "Be still and know that I am God." Learning to truly "be still," in mind, body, and spirit, in fact, is the essence of meditation.

There are various types of meditation. The classic, and the most difficult, is to practice absolute silence; to learn to relax your body totally and to learn to tell your constantly chattering mind to shut up, so that you can truly "be still and know" God. That kind of silence is not easy to achieve. It is rewarding, but it takes practice.

Other forms of meditation are, however, more immediately accessible to you even when you are just beginning. These intermediate forms can eventually lead you into the practice of total silence. Though it is not within the scope of this book to give a detailed explanation of how to meditate, some excellent books on that topic are included in the bibliography for this chapter.[14] I do, however, want to introduce you to two specific techniques that are useful in dealing with much of the material in other chapters of this book.

Contemplation of Scripture

As we will see in the next two chapters, the Bible is open to a startling array of contradictory interpretations. It is especially important that we queer Christians develop the skills for interpreting the Bible for ourselves. Those skills include the techniques of biblical scholarship, applying sound historical and literary criticism to the biblical texts. At least an elementary grasp of those techniques would be useful for all Christians. There is, however, another way of "knowing" the Bible, and that is to meditate upon a passage of scripture, asking the Spirit within you to illuminate it for you. This is a form of "knowing" that is the opposite of the rational, scientific approach. It is what the Bible itself refers to as wisdom.

The technique is simply one of creative visualization. You select a biblical passage, read it carefully and thoughtfully, then close the Bible and allow yourself to *experience* the passage. It works best with narrative passages, such as those in the gospels, the

[14]I was taught to meditate by the Dallas members of the Association for Research and Enlightenment (the A.R.E.), the organization formed to study and promote the material channeled by trance medium Edgar Cayce. The A.R.E., which is the most Christian-centered New Age group I know of, offers a wide array of resources on meditation, from books and tapes to workshops and local study and prayer groups. For information on the A.R.E. chapter nearest you, write the national headquarters at P.O. Box 595, Virginia Beach, VA 23451.

historical books of the Hebrew scriptures, or the Book of Acts. It also works well with some of the more obscure apocalyptic books, such as the Revelation.

As with any visualization, the secret is to set the scene as vividly as possible. When you close your eyes and imagine the setting you just read about, imagine it in the most intense detail you can muster. Pay attention to colors, sounds, smells. Notice what people are wearing, what color their eyes and hair are, what their facial expressions are.

The other secret is to place yourself in the scene. If you are working with a passage in which Jesus is instructing a group of his disciples, then *be* one of the disciples. Imagine yourself sitting with them, listening to Jesus, seeing him and the other disciples in careful detail. At first, it is probably better to place yourself as a "minor" character, in the background. Later, you may want to return to the same passage and imagine yourself as one of the major characters. Once you have set the scene and made it vivid in your mind, and placed yourself within the scene, the last step is to let go of the controls. Don't try to *direct* the scene, but step aside and let it unfold on its own. If you are as stubborn and strong willed as I am, you may find it difficult to stand aside and let the scene play out on its own. But when you manage to achieve it, you will know it immediately. The quality of your insights into the passage will be quantitatively different.

Just in case you don't have a Bible handy, I will give you a passage to practice with:

Early the next morning, Jesus went back to the Temple. All the people gathered around him, and he sat down and began to teach them. The teachers of the Law and the Pharisees brought in a woman who had been caught committing adultery, and they made her stand before them all. "Teacher," they said to Jesus, "this woman was caught in the very act of committing adultery. In our Law, Moses commanded that such a woman must be stoned to death. Now, what do you say?" They said this to trap Jesus, so that they could accuse him.

But he bent over and wrote on the ground with his finger. As they stood there asking him questions, he straightened up and said to them, "Whichever one of you has committed no sin may throw the first stone at her." Then he bent over again and wrote on the ground. When they heard this, they all left, one by one, the older ones first. Jesus was left alone, with the woman still standing there. He straightened up and said to her, "Where are they? Is there no one left to condemn you?"

"No one, sir," she answered.

"Well, then," Jesus said, "I do not condemn you either. [Go, but do not sin again."][15]

Here's how to "enter" this passage for yourself:

1. Make yourself as comfortable as possible, but not so comfortable that you are likely to drift off to sleep. Sitting upright is probably best.
2. Read the passage slowly and carefully, preferably aloud.
3. Close the book. Ask the Holy Spirit to guide your imagination and help you enter into the scene.
4. Close your eyes and "set the scene" for the story you just read. Be specific about detail. Who is present? What are they wearing? What are the physical surroundings? Notice colors, textures, sounds, smells.
5. Place yourself in the story, as a "minor" character. You are part of the crowd watching and listening. (Remember, later, you can do the exercise again and be one of the "major" characters.)
6. When you have the scene in your mind in as much vivid detail as possible, when you feel you are really *there,* then let go. Don't try to direct the action, but stand back as an observer and watch. What happens?

[15]John 8:1–11 (Good News Bible). I put the last sentence, Jesus' instructions to "not sin again," in brackets, because there are various versions of this text in the oldest surviving manuscripts, and some omit this line. An interesting question would be to see (provided you are really observing and not directing) whether or not Jesus says those words in the scene in your imagination.

When you have completed the exercise, ask yourself what you have learned from it. What did you notice in your meditation that you did not notice when you read the text? Did the scene as it unfolded match the written text, or did it differ from it? Were you able to see details that are not in the text? What, for instance, did Jesus write in the sand?

The more you do this sort of meditation, the more you will learn to trust your imagination, and to trust the Holy Spirit to reveal the truth to you. The tricky part is knowing when you have intruded your conscious ego's interpretation on the scene—when you have made it turn out the way you want. But when you know you have *not* done that, you can trust the wisdom of your inner vision. If you really get into this form of meditation, you may want to keep a journal of the insights into scripture the Holy Spirit reveals to you in this way.

This form of meditation is not limited to biblical passages. You can use the same technique for another sort of narrative passage, such as an account of the life of one of the saints. You might try it with the text of a liturgy, or a poem or hymn. You can also use the technique to "enter into" an icon, a painting, a sculpture, or a stained-glass window.

The point of all this is to learn to trust your inner wisdom, the Holy Spirit within you. Then, when you encounter someone else's interpretation of scripture that is based upon homophobic assumptions, you will have the authority of your own inner experience to draw upon so you can challenge that incorrect interpretation. This form of knowing does not contradict, but is complementary to, the standard practices of biblical scholarship. Often, you can hit upon an insight about a scripture passage through this form of meditation, then go to the library and do the research that will confirm it and help you defend your interpretation to others.

My own insight about the relationship between Jesus and "the beloved disciple," discussed in Chapters 4 and 8, came about in this way. One day I was praying alone in a church, meditating on the "sorrowful mysteries" of the Rosary. I was using a liturgy for the Rosary that gives short biblical references for each of the mysteries.

The biblical account was of the crucifixion, with Mary, the mother of Jesus, and "the disciple Jesus loved" standing at the foot of the cross. When I read the reference to the last words of Jesus, "Woman, behold your son" and "Behold your mother," followed by "And afterwards, the disciple made a place for her in his home," it struck me: Standing at the foot of the cross were Jesus' mother and his lover![16] It was one of the most profound religious experiences of my life. I took my new understanding to the library, where I was able to find all sorts of data to support what I already "knew" through the Spirit. Yet I would never have known what to look for if I hadn't had this inner experience first.

Guided Meditation

If you have been involved with any sort of New Age spirituality group, such as a healing circle, or have participated in any sort of transformational workshop, such as est or The Experience or The AIDS Mastery Workshop, you have had ample experience with the technique called guided meditation.

In traditional Christian spirituality, the term *guided meditation* is not often used, but the technique is identical to what a retreat conductor does on what is called a guided retreat. Guided meditations can be designed for a variety of purposes, from self-healing to weight loss. You can buy cassette tapes of guided meditations. The most familiar of such meditations in the queer community are probably the self-healing tapes of Louise Hay. For the purposes of healing, I also commend to you the "applied meditations" by Margo Adair, which are published in *Psychoimmunity and the Healing Process.* Adair's meditations are also available on cassettes.[17] Sally Fisher, the creator of The AIDS Mastery Workshop, also offers an excellent series of visualization tapes.[18]

[16]John 19:25–27.
[17]Write for a catalogue to Tools for Change, P.O. Box 14141, San Francisco, CA 94114, or call (415) 861-6838. *Psychoimmunity and the Healing Process* includes a price list on page 317. If the meditation that follows here sounds similar to one of Adair's, it is because I have used her meditations so often they have become internalized.
[18]Write for a catalogue to Brotherhood Press, 279 S. Beverly Drive, Suite 185, Beverly Hills, CA 90212.

The guided meditation I want to offer here is for the purpose of discovering, getting in touch with, and learning to trust your own inner wisdom, the voice of the Holy Spirit within you. Ideally, you should outgrow this meditation; you should come to the point where you no longer need it, for you can go directly to that place of inner "knowingness" whenever you want. In the early stages, however, you may find the guidance helpful. The most effective way to use this meditation is to record it, in your own voice, then play it back to yourself. It doesn't work to read it and try to enter a meditation state at the same time. If for any reason you find your own voice distracting, you might get someone else to record it for you. If you are working with a study or prayer group, you might have one person read it for the others. If you suffer from a lack of privacy, earphones or a Walkman would be useful. As with the scripture meditation, I don't suggest you listen to it lying down— you are likely to fall asleep. Sitting cross-legged on the floor or upright in a straight-backed chair is preferable, or if you are in a church with kneelers, you might try kneeling.

Make yourself comfortable. Close your eyes and begin to pay attention to your breathing. Don't try to direct or control your breathing, just notice it.

Beginning with your feet and moving slowly up, relax every part of your body: first your feet and ankles, then your lower legs, then your knees. Just relax. Let the tension go . . . let it go. Let the relaxation move on up to your thighs, and then to your crotch and buttocks. Let it go . . . let it go . . . let it go. Continue moving up to your stomach and lower back. Focus on your lower back a moment and release any tension you may be carrying there. Let it go . . . let it go . . . let it go. Move the relaxation up to your chest and upper back. Feel a relaxing warmth between your shoulder blades, melting away any tension you may have there. Let it go . . . let it go . . . let it go. Now let the relaxation move up to your shoulders and down your arms. Relax your hands now. Now let your neck relax, and let your jaw go loose. Move on up to your face, letting all the little muscles there relax. Then relax your scalp. Let any tension just melt away. Let it go . . . let it go . . . let it go.

Now imagine your breath blowing through your body like a warm, gentle breeze. Let it fill and flow over your entire body. Wherever you notice any tension still hanging on, let the warm breeze of your breath gently blow it away. Let it go . . . let it go . . . let it go.

You are completely relaxed now. It feels good to relax. Tell your body it's okay to relax completely, to let all the tension go. Tell yourself your body is at peace, and fully ready to participate in this meditation.

Now I am going to count down from ten to one. At each number, you find yourself going deeper and deeper into yourself, more and more relaxed, more and more centered. As you follow the numbers from ten to one, you find yourself going deeper and deeper into the place of wisdom deep within yourself. The deeper inside you go, the more vivid and more detailed your imagination becomes.

Ten: Going deeper and deeper now, deep within yourself. Nine: You are more and more relaxed, more and more centered. Eight: Your imagination is becoming more vivid, more fluid, more creative. Seven: Deeper and deeper, further and further down into yourself. Six: You are coming closer and closer to the center of yourself. Five: Your imagination is more and more alive, more and more vivid, more and more detailed. Four: Deeper and deeper, into a safe and secure place. Three: More and more centered, more and more relaxed. Two: You are coming closer and closer now to the place of wisdom deep within your soul. One: Very relaxed, very centered, and your imagination is alive and vibrant.

Now use your gifted imagination to create for yourself your place of wisdom and power. Use your mind to build the temple of the Holy Spirit deep within you. Let this temple take any form you like. See it in your mind. Build it the way you like. Notice the details of the temple—the colors, the sounds, the smells. Be there now. Feel yourself standing in this special place, your own temple of the Holy Spirit, your own shrine to your inner wisdom. Hear the sounds around you. Feel the textures, the temperature. Notice the smells. This is your special place of power and wisdom, a place where you are safe and secure and whole. This is a place where you can come to know everything you need to know, the place where you can come to know yourself. This is the place where you can come to know the Holy Spirit that dwells within you.

Now use your imagination to build an altar in this special temple. Let it take any form you like. Notice the details—the material from which it is constructed, the textures, the colors. See yourself reach out your hand and touch this special altar of wisdom and power. Feel it now. Notice how it feels to your touch. Notice any smells or sounds.

On the altar are a beautiful chalice and a loaf of bread. See them now. Notice how they look, how they feel. Notice the colors, the textures. Imagine it now. See and feel the details.

This is your special place, your safe place, the temple of your body, and your own altar to wisdom. Feel the life-giving force of the Holy Spirit flowing through this place. See the light of divine wisdom illuminating this place. You feel very much at home in this special place. You feel safe and warm and secure and loved. You feel wise and strong. This temple is your place. You belong here. You can come here anytime you like.

Now, standing before the altar, give thanks for who you are. Give thanks to God for creating you just the way you are. Acknowledge yourself for having the courage to be different. Acknowledge yourself for having the courage to be queer. Acknowledge yourself for having the courage to be who God created you to be. Acknowledge yourself for being queer and out and proud. Praise God for your life, your queerness. Give thanks to God for who you are, for what you've done, for where you've been, for whom you've loved, for what you've learned. Praise God for your body. Praise God for your sex organs. Think of how good and natural and holy it is to love others of your own sex. Thank God for your capacity to love. Thank God for your sexuality.

Now be still and listen and hear the voice of God answering you. Hear God's loving voice vibrating through your body, your very being. Hear the voice of God saying to you, "You are my beloved child. I am very proud of you."

Now go to the altar and take the bread. Break off a piece and put it into your mouth. As you eat it, you see hundreds and thousands of other women and men, your queer sisters and brothers. They are not in your temple with you; they are all in their own temples; but they are all eating their bread as you eat yours. Through this act of eating the bread, you are joined together with them, with thousands of strong and proud lesbian women and gay men. Feel your communion with them. Feel your connection. Feel them support you. Feel them holding you up. Feel their collective strength, their collective wisdom. You know you can draw on that strength and that wisdom anytime you need to; and you know that together with them, you can do anything. Feel the love they have for you. Feel how proud they are of you.

Now go to the altar again and take the chalice. As you drink from it, you see hundreds and thousands of other women and men, your Christian sisters and brothers. They are from all countries and all cultures and all time periods. These are not the false Christians who would condemn you for being who you are; these are the true followers of Christ who support and uphold and love you. They are not in your temple with you; they are all in their own temples; but they are all drinking from their chalices at the same time you drink from yours. Through this act of drinking from the chalice, you are joined together with them, and with all the angels and saints. Feel your communion with them. Feel your connection. Feel them support you. Feel them holding you up. Feel their collective strength, their wisdom. You know you can draw on that strength and that wisdom anytime you need to; and you know together with them, you can do anything. Feel the love they have for you. Feel them praying for you. Feel how proud they are of you.

Now replace the chalice and stand before the altar in prayer. Ask the Holy Spirit, Holy Wisdom, to come to you now. Watch as wisdom takes shape and is revealed to you. Wisdom may take any form. It could be the form of Christ or it could be an angel or an animal. Spirit has no limits. Whatever shape it takes is right for you at this moment. See the embodiment of holy wisdom coming to you now. Greet wisdom. Greet your Spirit guide.

You know that this Spirit guide, this personified wisdom, is there to help you know anything you need to know. Holy wisdom knows all things and will reveal them to you as you ask. Whatever questions you have, whatever problems you need to solve, whatever dilemmas are troubling you— you can bring all these here to your temple, your special holy place, and lay them before your Spirit guide who knows all things.

If you have questions or problems, ask them now, confident that holy wisdom will reveal the answers to you. Ask your questions with confidence and without fear, knowing that you will receive the answers you need. Ask your questions now. . . .

Now be still and listen as holy wisdom reveals to you the answers you need to hear. . . .

Now as wisdom begins to return to the heart of God, you stand alone before the altar again. Give thanks to God that wisdom came to you. Give thanks to God for the answers you have received. Give thanks to God for this special place, this holy temple deep within yourself. Know that you can return to this place anytime you want, for it is not outside yourself, it is deep within you. Know that you can return here anytime you need to, and that you can consult with holy wisdom, in the form of your special Spirit guide, anytime you need to. Give thanks to God for these special gifts, then prepare to leave this temple.

Now I am going to count, forward, from one to five. With each count, you will return more and more to your surface consciousness. By the count of five, you will be fully awake, fully alert, feeling rested and peaceful and wise.

One: Beginning to detach yourself from your special place; you know you can return whenever you want. Two: Beginning to return to the surface now. Three: More and more awake, more and more alert. Four: Beginning to return to the room now, relaxed and alert and rested. Five: Opening your eyes now, you are awake and refreshed and wise.

You may want to use this meditation the first few times without having a specific question in mind—but if one comes up at the moment, don't hold it back. After you have become comfortable with the technique, you can enter this meditative state whenever you have a problem or a question you need to answer. Just as in the scripture meditation, the trick is making sure your conscious mind is out of the way—that you are not controlling the experience, orchestrating the outcome you want. The more you use this technique, the more confident you will become, and you will learn to tell the difference between when you are directing the outcome and when you are standing back and observing.

The importance of this meditation is to teach yourself to tap into your inner wisdom, the place where the Spirit of God dwells within your heart. When you are bombarded with religious homophobia, with negative words from the Apostle Paul or Jerry Falwell or Cardinal O'Connor, you need this reserve of inner wisdom to draw on, so you will have the confidence to know what is true and what is false. When you have learned to trust the wisdom of the Holy Spirit within yourself, you will have the courage to call the lie the lie—even if it comes from the bishop or the Bible—because you listen to a higher authority, your own faith in the God within you.

3
THE BIBLE

The Bad News

How do you feel about the Bible? Has it been, for you, a source of "good news" (which is what the word *gospel* means), or have you heard it more often as bad news? Or has it just been so obscure and hard to understand you haven't thought much about it at all?

"A Rather Grossly Overrated Book"

Norman Pittenger, the process theologian who also happens to be gay, is nearing eighty years old and has lived most of his adult life in England. The combination of his age, his charm, and his acquired British accent allow him to get away with saying things in public other people cannot. One of Pittenger's most memorable quips is "The Bible is a rather grossly overrated book!"

I have another friend, who works in a bishop's office, who, when someone said to him, by way of argument, "But the Bible says . . ." threw up his hands in exasperation and said, "Screw the Bible! The Church would be a lot better off if we declared a moratorium on the damned thing for ten years!"

Unfortunately, that's not really an option. The Bible is so central to Christianity that a religious approach that did not take it seriously could not be called Christian. On the other hand, there is a desperate need to correct the misuse and abuse of the Bible that has grown up over centuries of Christian tradition. As queer Christians, especially, we must know how to take a very sophisticated, critical approach to scripture, for the Bible has been and continues to be used as a weapon against us.

When I was growing up in West Texas, "the buckle on the Bible Belt," every summer in Vacation Bible School I used to participate in a particularly chilling ritual we called "the Pledge of Allegiance to the Bible." It came third, after the Pledge of Allegiance to the United States flag and the Pledge of Allegiance to the Christian flag. Someone would hold up a large, leather-bound King James Bible while we recited:

> *I pledge allegiance to the Bible, God's Holy Word; and will make it a lamp unto my feet, a light unto my path, and will hide its words in my heart, that I might not sin against God.*

Having grown up holding the Bible in such high esteem, it was particularly disturbing when, as a gay adolescent struggling through puberty and trying to understand my intense fascination with the male bodies in the locker room, I began to hear people read such things from the Bible as:

> *You shall not lie with a male as one lies with a female; it is an abomination.*[1]

Like most adolescents, I didn't really know what an abomination was, but it was clearly bad. Nor was I *exactly* clear about what "lying with a male as with a female" meant, but it sounded like something I wanted to do. Yet if I did, I'd be breaking my pledge of allegiance to "God's Holy Word"!

Evaluating the Bible: Separating the "Good News" from the Bad News

Before I was ordained as an Episcopal priest, I had to take a vow (and sign a document) declaring, "I do believe the Holy

---

[1] Leviticus 18:22.

Scriptures of the Old and New Testaments to be the Word of God, and to contain everything necessary to salvation."[2]

I could take that vow with integrity only by understanding it to mean that while the Bible might "contain everything necessary to salvation," it also contains a lot of other junk, some of it plainly destructive and dangerous. The Bible, for instance, contains justifications for slavery, for genocide, and for domestic violence.

There is certainly a need for a tremendous amount of explanation and interpretation before the Bible can be at all accessible to contemporary people. Irreverent Fundamentalists like to tell a story that illustrates the necessity for biblical interpretation: A devout man, convinced God would speak to him through the scripture, opened his Bible at random searching for a message of wisdom and read Matthew 27:5, "He went and hanged himself." Needing clarification of this message, he tried it again, opening his Bible randomly to Luke 10:37, where he read, "Go and do likewise." Trying one more time, he let his Bible fall open to John 13:27, "What you are going to do, do quickly."

The Gideons, a Fundamentalist organization, have made it their mission to place the King James translation of the Bible in hotel rooms and hospitals, and to distribute it to groups such as students, soldiers, and nurses. The Gideons are convinced someone in a state of despondency and spiritual bankruptcy will pick up the Gideon Bible in a hotel room or foxhole, turn to John 3:16, "For God so loved the world that He gave His only begotten Son, that whosoever believeth in Him should not perish, but have everlasting life," and have a sudden, miraculous conversion experience. Isn't it just as likely that someone who has rented a hotel room in order to suicide might open the Gideon Bible and turn to "He went and hanged himself"? I often wonder how many closeted and self-hating homosexuals have, through an uninformed private reading of the Bible, had their self-hatred confirmed by stumbling across Leviticus 18:22, where they read about "sodomites" and "abomination."

Without interpretation, without placing it in its cultural, historical, and literary context, the Bible can be used for evil—and it has

[2]Book of Common Prayer, 526.

been, often. The Bible has been misused against our people so often and so destructively it is difficult for us to celebrate it as "the Word of God." The clearest testimony to the destructive use of the Bible against us is the entry into our language of the word *sodomy* to describe queer sex, a reference to a very questionable interpretation of "the sin of Sodom" in Genesis 19.

Actually, it is impossible to read the Bible at all without imposing an interpretation on it. No one truly takes all of the Bible at face value, not even those who claim to do so. The simplest form of interpretation is to ignore or skip over those verses that don't suit the purposes of the reader. Fundamentalists accuse us of this practice, which they attribute to our "humanist" leanings, and yet they do it much more often themselves. When Anita Bryant was quoting passages from Leviticus to prove God hates homosexuality, she seldom wore a hat, so she was ignoring a New Testament passage, I Corinthians 11:5, which prohibits a woman from "proclaiming God's message in public" without a covering on her head; not to mention I Corinthians 14:35, which declares, "It is a disgraceful thing for a woman to speak in a church meeting." Jerry Falwell can preach that "men who lie with other men" are an "abomination to God"[3] only by ignoring the fact that those who eat shellfish are similarly condemned as "an abomination."[4] Roman Catholics or Anglo-Catholics who call their priests "Father" and claim to take the Bible literally must simply ignore Jesus' own words: "Call no man your father on earth, for you have one Father, who is in heaven."[5] There are biblical injunctions against women cutting their hair or men wearing their hair long, against wearing clothes made from blended fabrics, and against anyone with any sort of birth defect or a permanent injury being a priest. Let's not mince words: *Anyone who claims to believe every word in the Bible literally is lying*.

Other minority theologians of liberation, most notably the black and feminist theologians, have pointed out the need for a *revisionist* approach to scripture. Feminist biblical scholars have

---

[3]Leviticus 18:22.
[4]Leviticus 11:10.
[5]Matthew 23:9.

wrestled with this question for years, because the Bible has been used as demonically against women as it has against queers.

Elisabeth Schussler Fiorenza, a New Testament scholar, has developed techniques through which feminists can approach the Bible, including techniques of imaginative reconstruction. Schussler Fiorenza, however, insists the first step in dealing with biblical texts is a *hermeneutic of suspicion* (*hermeneutic* means the interpretive stance or viewpoint from which you approach the text). A hermeneutic of suspicion looks for the patriarchal bias in the Bible and rejects those texts that contain it. She writes:

> The litmus test for invoking scripture as the Word of God must be whether or not biblical texts and traditions seek to end relations of domination and exploitation.[6]

James Cone, the black theologian of liberation, generally holds the Bible in higher esteem than most feminist theologians do, largely because the biblical passages that support racism, although they are present, are considerably fewer than those that support the subordination of women. Yet because some passages in the Bible do justify slavery and encourage slaves to be content with their station in life, black theology, too, recognizes the need for a hermeneutic of suspicion. Cone, concerned with defending the central position of the scripture in black theology, places all the burden upon the interpreters of the texts, charging that any oppressive interpretation must be called heretical:

> Any interpretation of the gospel in any historical period that fails to see Jesus as the Liberator of the oppressed is heretical. Any view of the gospel that fails to understand the Church as that community whose work and consciousness are defined by the community of the oppressed is not Christian and is thus heretical.[7]

[6]Elisabeth Schussler Fiorenza, *Bread Not Stone: The Challenge of Feminist Biblical Interpretation* (Boston: Beacon Press, 1984), xiii.
[7]James H. Cone, *God of the Oppressed* (New York: Seabury Press, 1975), 37.

While I agree with Cone about heretical interpretation, I think he is a little too timid about rejecting the texts themselves. Feminist scholars are more willing to acknowledge that after all the work of reinterpretation has been done, we will still be left with a number of oppressive texts, because these texts are the products of an oppressive culture. Katharine Doob Sakenfeld, in an article describing various feminist approaches to the Bible, warns:

> No feminist use of biblical material is finally immune to the risk of finding the Bible hurtful, unhelpful, not revealing of God, and not worth the effort to come to grips with it. Regardless of approach, feminists may find that the Bible seems to drive them away from itself (and sometimes from God), rather than drawing them closer. At the heart of the problem lies the issue of biblical authority.[8]

Face it: Sometimes the homophobic interpretation of a biblical text is a *correct* reflection of the writer's original intention—so simply reinterpreting the Bible is not enough. We must also *reevaluate* the Bible. Some queers who grew up Fundamentalist have not let go of their childhood religion, and they strive to find creative reinterpretations that will let them hold on to the concept of biblical literalism; but I believe such an approach is inherently flawed and inevitably destructive to us (and, in fact, to all marginalized peoples). What is needed is a fundamental (pun intended) change in the way the Bible is treated, the way it is used. There are parts of the Bible that should *never* be read in public worship or used for private devotion. There are parts of the Bible that should be trashed, period.

As a queer Christian, you must be bold about saying, with Pittenger, "The Bible is a rather grossly overrated book!" The point is not really whether or not some passage in the Bible condemns homosexual acts; the point is that you cannot allow your moral and ethical decisions to be determined by the literature of a people

---

[8]Katharine Doob Sakenfeld, "Feminist Uses of Biblical Materials," in Letty M. Russell, ed., *Feminist Interpretation of the Bible* (Philadelphia: Westminster Press, 1985), 64.

whose culture and history are so far removed from your own. You must dare to be iconoclastic enough to say, "So what if the Bible does say it? Who cares?"

Biblical Truth and Biblical Trash:
The Test of Canonicity

If you are to find anything positive in the Bible, you need a way of determining what in it is truth and what is trash. In theological terms, this is the issue of *canon,* the question of which texts are authoritative for the faith community and which texts are not. Clearly, you cannot simply accept the traditional wisdom on this matter, for included in the scriptures considered canonical are a number of passages that are destructive to you. If you are to be able to redeem the Bible at all for your own study and devotion, you must have some sort of filter, some way of determining for yourself what is canon and what is not. If you believe God is all-loving, you simply cannot call certain violent and hate-filled passages in the Bible "the Word of God."

If, as Schussler Fiorenza points out, we proclaim any text that oppresses human beings as "the Word of God," we are proclaiming our God is a God of oppression. Another feminist biblical scholar, Margaret Farley, offers a way of separating the wheat from the chaff in approaching sacred texts:

It cannot be believed unless it rings true to our deepest capacity for truth and goodness. If it contradicts this, it cannot be believed. If it falsifies this, it cannot be accepted.[9]

Queer Christians would do well to adopt this test of canonicity.

The Bible and Homosexuality 101:
Our "Texts of Terror"

Feminist biblical scholar Phyllis Trible has listed the biblical passages she calls the "texts of terror" because of their approval and

[9]Margaret A. Farley, "Feminist Consciousness and the Interpretation of Scripture," in Letty M. Russell, ed., *Feminist Interpretation of the Bible* (Philadelphia: Westminster Press, 1985), 43.

glorification of violence against women.[10] For instance, in the eleventh chapter of the Book of Judges, Jephthah, a military leader of the Israelites, makes a barbarous promise to God: that if God will grant him victory over his enemies, then when he returns from battle, the first person who comes out of his house to greet him will be burned as a human sacrifice. Jephthah wins his battle, and the first person who comes to meet him is his daughter. The Bible says he "did with her according to the vow which he had made."[11]

In addition to the texts of terror against women Trible has documented, a number of biblical passages could be called texts of terror against our people, too—passages that are used to justify antigay hatred and violence. This handful of biblical texts has been referred to as "the clobber passages." For the most part, it is the *abuse* of a biblical text when it is used to justify homophobia, because there is very little in the Bible that speaks about homosexuality at all. But because this small handful of biblical excerpts continues to be used against us, and because we can't "declare a moratorium on the Bible," it is imperative that you, as a queer Christian, be familiar with them and their correct interpretations.

What follows is not new material, by any means. I have heard and read and taught this basic information so many times that I have come to refer to it as The Bible and Homosexuality 101. I am, in fact, a little tired of hearing it. It irritates me when a church organization puts on some sort of seminar on homosexuality, and they end up doing The Bible and Homosexuality 101 for the thousandth time—I want to move on to The Bible and Homosexuality 303. Dozens of books by serious and respected biblical scholars deal with this material brilliantly—and many of them have been published for over fifteen years.

Absolutely the best is John Boswell's *Christianity, Social Tolerance, and Homosexuality*.[12] The book spans the first thirteen

[10]Phyllis Trible, *Texts of Terror: Literary-Feminist Readings of Biblical Narratives* (Philadelphia: Fortress Press, 1984).
[11]Judges 11:39.
[12]John Boswell, *Christianity, Social Tolerance, and Homosexuality: Gay People in Western Europe from the Beginning of the Christian Era to the Fourteenth Century* (Chicago: University of Chicago Press, 1980).

centuries of Christian history, but its fourth chapter, "The Scriptures," presents The Bible and Homosexuality 101 in a concise and often witty style. There is a popular misconception that Boswell's book is dense, scholarly, and hard to read—I suppose because it is well documented with footnotes. In fact, Boswell's style is easily readable, interesting, and often funny. If you haven't read it, read it now! If you don't own it, buy it now! It is a basic textbook for practicing queer Christianity.

If you are a practicing queer Christian, you may find this chapter redundant and boring because you have already *done* The Bible and Homosexuality 101. If you already know it, please disregard this section. Skim quickly over it, if you want. Yet I am constantly amazed at how many queer Christians have not been exposed to this information, and since it is so foundational, I offer it here in the interest of completeness.

The Creation Accounts of Genesis 1 and 2

In the first chapter of Genesis, God tells the first human beings:

> *Be fruitful and multiply, and fill the earth and subdue it; and have dominion over the fish of the sea and over the birds of the air and over every living thing that moves upon the face of the earth.*[13]

In another account of the creation in the next chapter, a passage you've probably heard read at heterosexual weddings, a sort of editorial comment is inserted after the description of the creation of the first woman as a "helper" for the first man:

> *Therefore a man leaves his father and his mother and cleaves to his wife, and they become one flesh.*[14]

These two passages are often used against queers as a way of accusing us of not fulfilling God's plan for creation, not taking our

[13]Genesis 1:28.
[14]Genesis 2:24.

proper role in the created order. (I'm sure you've heard some version of "God created Adam and Eve, not Adam and Steve!")

Your response can be simply to take these passages in a less literal, less Fundamentalist way. First of all, a number of queers *do* reproduce, either through heterosexual couplings before coming out, or by choosing children through alternative reproductive technologies. Second, we cannot afford to believe God commands all people to "be fruitful and multiply" today. What might have been a sensible command to the first human beings would be a destructive order in an overpopulated world. Overpopulation is only one of the many evils that have been done to our planet by human beings who have taken literally the command to dominate and subdue the earth.

Finally, we can hear in the second passage from Genesis 2 an affirmation not of heterosexuality, but of companionship. If we replace *wife* with a more inclusive word, such as *companion* (which is implied by the fact the function of the "wife" was to be a "helper"), this becomes a very positive passage, proclaiming that our God, who knows it is not good for us to be alone, has created for us the wonderful gift of loving companionship.

Genesis 19: Sodom and Gomorrah

The famous Sodom and Gomorrah story in the King James Version is the origin of the word *sodomy* as a negative term for queer sex. In the story Lot, a Hebrew, is living in a foreign city that is characterized as sinful and wicked. In Christopher Durang's wonderful play *Sister Mary Ignatius Explains It All for You,* which is about a sadistic nun (if that's not redundant!) teaching in a Catholic elementary school, the sister presents a succinct account of Sodom that, while comic, is actually a very accurate description of what most people believe the story to be: "Sodom is where they committed acts of homosexuality and bestiality in the Old Testament." She goes on to list modern-day Sodoms, such as New York, San Francisco, Amsterdam, and any city with a population over fifty thousand.

In the biblical account, because Lot is so holy, God favors him by sending messengers, presumably "angels," to visit his house. Lot, acting according to the Hebrew laws of hospitality and concern for foreigners and travelers, invites the visitors into his home and entertains them lavishly, before he knows they are angels.

The men of Sodom come to Lot's door and demand to see the foreigners who have entered their city. "Bring them out to us," they order Lot, "that we may know them." The Hebrew verb transliterated *yadah*, "to know," is occasionally, but rarely, used in scripture as a euphemism for sex. It occurs in the Hebrew scriptures 943 times, and in only ten of those does it carry the sense of "carnal knowledge." Most of the time, it just means what it says.[15]

This story may very well be one of "xenophobia," of a KKK-style unreasonable fear and hatred of those who are different. The men of Sodom seem to be demanding that Lot hand over his visitors precisely because they are foreigners, and therefore suspect and hated. Whether or not the men intend to rape the strangers (which is a way of showing contempt for enemies), they obviously intend to do them harm—and the violence is the issue, not queer sex. Lot is horrified, for since the men are now guests in his house, under the code of Hebrew hospitality, they are his responsibility. As a matter of sacred honor, he must protect them.

What Lot proposes to the men of Sodom in lieu of turning over the strangers who are under his protection ought to horrify us: He offers to give them his two virgin daughters, telling them to "do to them as you please." (This is one of Trible's "texts of terror" for women, too.) Lot, to protect the honor of his male guests, thinks nothing of sacrificing the lives of his daughters. A footnote in the New Jerusalem Bible matter-of-factly states, "At that period the honour of a woman was of less account than the sacred duty of hospitality." It seems to me that regardless of what else might be contained in this text, Lot's lack of concern for his daughters ought to render this story useless as a moral and ethical model!

At any rate, virtually all mainstream biblical scholars, including

---

[15]These numbers are from John Boswell, who in turn got them from Derrick Sherwin Bailey's seminal work, *Homosexuality in the Western Christian Tradition,* 2–3. The Boswell citation is in *Christianity, Social Tolerance, and Homosexuality,* 94.

those who are somewhat conservative, agree that the point of the story, the "sin of Sodom," is not about sex, but about violence. Often, the sin is presented as "inhospitality," but that word is not strong enough, in our cultural context, to capture the meaning. The sin of Sodom was mistrust and intended violence against strangers and foreigners, who, according to the Law of Moses, were to be protected and honored; in a nomadic desert society, such acts of hospitality as sharing food and water were a matter of survival for the traveler.

The strongest evidence that the story of Sodom is not about sex is to be found within the Bible itself. Throughout the Hebrew and Christian scriptures, Sodom is used as a symbol of great evil, but whenever the writer elaborates upon the evil of Sodom, violence and inhospitality to strangers are mentioned. Sex seldom enters the picture, particularly in the Hebrew scriptures, and homosexuality specifically *never* does. Some of the Christian writers do begin to equate Sodom with sexual sin, but the Hebrew writers did not. For instance, Ezekiel 16:49 says:

> *Behold, this was the guilt of your sister Sodom: she and her daughters had pride, surfeit of food, and prosperous ease, but did not aid the poor and needy.*

Therefore, if you want to be really "biblical" about it, you could properly call Donald Trump and George Bush "sodomites." When a family or a church group disowns one of its members after discovering his or her homosexuality, *they* are committing the sin of sodomy. When Cardinal O'Connor preaches against gay rights, he is committing the sin of sodomy.

The translators of the New Jerusalem Bible, by the way, took it upon themselves to decide that the desire of the men of Sodom to "know" the strangers did in fact mean sexual desire. Worse still, they chose words that removed the suggestion of violence entirely. In this translation, the men say to Lot, "Send them out to us so that we can have intercourse with them." (Given that *intercourse* is supposed to mean "an interchange between two persons," doesn't it seem especially inappropriate to refer to an act of rape as "intercourse"?)

Ironically, the New Jerusalem Bible, concerned to be known as an "ecumenical" translation, carries the nihil obstat and imprimatur of Roman Catholic officials, signifying, to quote the explanatory note on the title page itself, that the book is "considered to be free from doctrinal or moral error." Yet such a blatant mistranslation is both an academic faux pas and a grave moral error. Whether or not the passage refers to sex is debatable; the fact that it refers to violence is *not* debatable, and yet this translation would allow the reader to totally miss the intended violence of the passage. Given that the interpretation of the Hebrew word *yadah* is in dispute among biblical scholars (this edition of the Bible was published in 1985, five years after Boswell's book), it seems the responsible course would have been at least to have listed alternative translations in a footnote.

I point this out because so many queer Christians have told me they prefer the rather poetic New Jerusalem Bible translation for their own study and devotion. (For years, I used the previous edition of the Jerusalem Bible for this purpose.) Instead, we should boycott it! We should write angry letters to the publisher, translators, editor, and to those who signed the imprimatur and nihil obstat![16] Until queer scholars have produced our own translation that is truly "free from doctrinal or moral error," I recommend the use of the Revised Standard Version, particularly the study version known as the New Oxford Annotated Bible.[17] While it is not perfect, it is a much more careful translation, and freer from such blatant intrusions of the translators' own agenda. In the meantime, the New Jerusalem Bible, with its characteristic thickness, makes a good doorstop.

[16]If you're in the mood for a flurry of letter writing, the general editor is Henry Wansbrough. Wansbrough says "credit for the skillful translation" of the Old Testament must go to Alan Neame. John Deehan is responsible for the nihil obstat; and the imprimatur was given by Cardinal George Basil Hume, OSB, the Archbishop of Westminster, England. You can write all of them through the American publisher, Doubleday & Company, 666 Fifth Ave., New York, NY 10103.

[17]*The New Oxford Annotated Bible with the Apocrypha, Expanded Edition* (Revised Standard Version) (New York: Oxford University Press, 1973/1977).

Deuteronomy 23:17–18: The Dog Priests

This text is one of the most blatant examples of a mistranslation serving the hidden agenda of the translators and editors. The Revised Standard Version (1946, 1971) has taken a step toward cleaning up the error that the King James Version propagated through the use of the artificial word *sodomite*. The subject of this passage is idolatry. The Hebrews, concerned with keeping their religion and bloodlines pure, are forbidden to take part in any of the religious practices of their neighbors. In this passage, specifically prohibited is the ritual sex associated with many of the indigenous religions of the region. The Revised Standard Version has made this quite clear in verse 17, by using the term *cult prostitute* to refer to both male and female temple votaries; but it has retained the slang term translated *dog* in verse 18. The Hebrews of this period did not keep dogs as pets, and dogs were not favorably regarded. *Dog* became a Hebrew term of contempt, especially for a particular type of cult prostitute, roughly equivalent to what we would call a transvestite prostitute: a man dressed and made up as a woman, a "soft" or "effeminate" man. Possibly, the term originated with the "dog priests" of the Great Mother Goddess, who participated in a sexual/religious ecstatic celebration to mark the rising of the "dog star," Sirius.[18] In any case, the sin involved is the practice of a competing religion, not the transvestitism or the sex. The Hebrews were forbidden from engaging in sex with the votaries of these religions, and especially from serving as temple sex workers themselves. The sex, whether homosexual, heterosexual, or transvestitism, was not the issue; the issue was idolatry.

Leviticus 18:22: Lying with Men

In this single verse, Hebrew men are forbidden "to lie with a man as with a woman." The operative and telling phrase here is *as with a woman*. The prohibition has less to do with sex than it does with class distinction. Sex was seen as something a man does *to,* not

---

[18]Robert Graves, *The White Goddess: An Historical Grammar of Poetic Myth* (1948; rev. ed., Farrar, Straus & Giroux, 1966), 53; cited by Tom Horner in *Jonathan Loved David: Homosexuality in Biblical Times* (Philadelphia, Westminster Press, 1978), 60.

with, a woman, who is always seen as his social inferior, simply by virtue of her gender. Therefore to force an adult man into the receptive role in insertive sex is to degrade him by "treating him like a woman." If you're a feminist, you've probably already gotten your back up about the sexism inherent in this idea. Intriguingly, it also suggests that standard heterosexual sex is viewed as an act of humiliation and degradation of women by men. Again, since raping one's enemies was (and still is) a common way of showing contempt and claiming dominance over them, there is also a prohibition against violence and coercive sex here; but it has nothing to say about mutual, consensual queer sex.

I Corinthians 6:9: No Perverts in the Kingdom

This reference in a letter of Paul to those who will not "inherit the Kingdom of God" is another example of a hidden-agenda translation. Again, the Revised Standard Version has cleaned up some of the damage, translating as "sexual perverts" the same word the King James called "sodomites." Fine. If "sexual perversion" is defined as those sexual acts that violate one's basic nature, then queer sex, for you, is not perversion—compulsory heterosexual sex is perverse.

There is, however, a larger issue at stake here. Paul, like most of us, had his good moments and his bad moments. At times, he was brilliant, and he could write passionate, poetic accounts of the overwhelming love of God. The celebrated "Love Chapter," I Corinthians 13, so often read at weddings, is an example of Paul at his best. But Paul also had his off days, when he seemed to slip into depression or cynicism or just plain nastiness and vindictiveness. One of the clearest examples is his argument with the Judaizers, the Jewish Christians who insisted all Christians must first be Jews and obey Jewish law. Paul argued that being a Christian was not dependent upon keeping Jewish customs, such as circumcision, and in a diatribe against his circumcising detractors, he snarls, "I wish that those who unsettle you would mutilate themselves!"[19]

Okay, so we all lose our temper and say things we perhaps

[19]Galatians 5:12.

should not. But do we read Paul's bitchy wish that his enemies castrate themselves with the circumcision knife and then say, "The Word of God," just because Paul wrote it and early catholic bishops decided to call it scripture? Of course not. We need to weigh carefully everything Paul says, using Farley's test of canonicity: *It cannot be believed unless it rings true to our deepest capacity for truth and goodness.*

The concept of the Realm of God that Jesus taught is wildly inclusive; it has room for anyone who wants to come in. Any discussion of the household of God, then, that degenerates into a list of those who will not get into the club should strike you as misguided. It does not ring true to our deepest capacity for truth and goodness. This passage, then, simply has no authority for you.

I Timothy 1:10: No Sodomites in Heaven

This is another list of those who are not worthy of God's love, and so your first reaction might be to dismiss it out of hand. But even for those who insist on a more conservative attitude toward scripture, this passage need not present a problem. There is a translation error here. The Revised Standard Version, for unfathomable reasons, chose to translate the original as "sodomite," which is at best an anachronism, since the association between Sodom and queer sex was not made until the Middle Ages. A more accurate translation would be "male cult prostitute," and again the point is idolatry, rather than homosexuality or prostitution.

Romans 1:26–27: No Lesbians, Either

This text is unique among the traditional "clobber passages" in that it is the only one that makes any mention of lesbian activity. Here we must quarrel not only with Paul's theology, but with his psychology. He seems to feel that homosexuality is the result of practicing idolatry, of worshiping "the creature rather than the Creator," a notion that is even more absurd than that ancient psychological canard of attributing homosexual orientation to a household with an "absent father, close-binding mother." Also, Paul sees homosexuality as "unnatural," as a corruption or perversion of one's true nature. The recent findings of behavioral biologists are helpful here, for their evidence seems to be converging toward seeing a "biological determinant" for homosexuality, for seeing homosexual orientation as a product of perinatal chemical configurations in utero.[20]

This passage is an example of how scripture must be held in tension with tradition and reason, and "reason" would include the data of the social and natural sciences. Mainstream Christianity accepts and honors truth from any source, whether the scriptures or a biology laboratory, and Christians are never called upon to believe anything that contradicts the truth.

Robin Scroggs, a biblical scholar whose area of expertise is Paul, tries to excuse Paul by saying the only form of homosexuality he would have encountered would have been the inherently unequal and coercive man-boy pairings that were common in the Rome of his day.[21] Aside from my insistence that mutual same-sex pair bonds have *always* occurred in *every* culture, I don't see a reference to unequal or cross-generational sex in this text. Paul is decrying the fact that men are having sex together and women are having sex together instead of with the opposite sex—mutuality and equality seem to be implied. In fact, a truly radical analysis of the passage might suggest it is precisely the social equality of the sexual partners that causes Paul to label same-sex relations "unnatural." Sex that was "natural," in Paul's view, necessarily involved males dominating females!

Whatever excuses we make for Paul, it seems to me most honest to say, yes, perhaps Paul is condemning homosexuality in this passage, or at least labeling it as "unnatural" (which is not *exactly* the same thing as calling it sinful). But the bottom line for you is: So what? Paul was wrong about a number of other things, too. Why should you take him any more seriously than you take Jerry Falwell or Anita Bryant or Cardinal O'Connor? Paul, remem-

---

[20]See, for instance, James Weinrich, *Sexual Landscapes: Why We Are Who We Are, Why We Love Whom We Love* (New York: Charles Scribner's Sons, 1987).
[21]Robin Scroggs, *The New Testament and Homosexuality: Contextual Background for Contemporary Debate* (Philadelphia: Fortress Press, 1983). See also Scroggs's *Paul for a New Day* (Philadelphia: Fortress Press, 1977).

ber, never met Jesus in his lifetime, and so you and he stand on equal footing when you make claims about what "the Spirit" has told you. If Paul thought the Holy Spirit told him homosexuality was "unnatural," you can counter that the Holy Spirit tells you your homosexuality is quite natural—heterosexual acts (and celibacy) might be "unnatural" for you. What the Holy Spirit tells you is a greater authority for *your* life than what the Holy Spirit may or may not have told Paul.

4

THE BIBLE

The Good News

Positive Images of Queer Love in the Bible

Does it startle you for me to suggest there might be *positive* images of homosexuality in the Bible? The history of queer people in scripture has been repressed by the patriarchy, just as much as the history of our people and our culture in general has been repressed. We can find traces of our people in the Bible only by employing approaches that are radical, revisionist, and reconstructionist.

Again, the work of feminist biblical scholars comes to our aid here. Recognizing that the history of women in the Bible has been largely repressed and hidden, scholars such as Elisabeth Schussler Fiorenza, Alison Cheek, and Dorothee Solle have developed methods for "reading between the lines" of the Bible and recovering the women who have been rendered invisible by centuries of patriarchal tradition. Their methods involve the use of imaginative data, the data of experience, the data of the heart. If we rely simply upon the tools of scholarship officially sanctioned by straight, white, male theology, we will get nowhere. As Audre Lorde says, "The master's tools will never dismantle the master's house."[1] We must sup-

[1] Audre Lorde, *Sister Outsider* (Trumansburg, New York: Crossing Press, 1984), 110.

plement what we can "know" through historic and scientific methods with what we "know" from our own religious experience, from the voice of the Holy Spirit speaking within our own souls. Solle calls this method *phantasie* (retaining the German spelling to distinguish it from the pejorative connotations of the English *fantasy*). *Phantasie* is a process of creative imagining—not escapism, but active, faithful imaging of possibilities.[2]

There is a long precedent for such a theological method. Again, Paul, the one writer who probably tells us more about the nature of Christ than anyone else, never *met* Jesus. But he certainly met the Risen Christ, in an encounter that turned his whole life upside down. This is the way in which we can *know* more about scripture than we could ever know by poring through dusty manuscripts or from the exegesis of Greek passages. This is the knowing of prayer and devotion, the knowing that can be intimate, erotic, and passionate. Supplementing traditional methods of biblical scholarship with *phantasie* and other revisionist methods, I offer five examples of positive images of homosexuality in scripture. This list is by no means comprehensive. As more queer scholars turn their attention to the sacred texts, we will discover more and more images of our people in scripture.

David and Jonathan

The story of the love between Jonathan, the son of the king of Israel, and David, the former shepherd hired as a court musician, is so powerful and moving I almost always encourage its use at a marriage ceremony for two men. These two young men, from distinctly different social classes, fall deeply in love with each other. "The soul of Jonathan was knit to the soul of David, and Jonathan loved him as his own soul," the scripture tells us.[3] Recognizing the gulf of class distinction between them, Jonathan makes an intentional covenant with David, sealed and symbolized by removing his own rich clothes, armor, and weapons, and bestowing them upon

[2]Dorothee Solle, *Beyond Mere Obedience*, translation of *Phantasie und Gehorsam*, Lawrence W. Denef, trans. (Minneapolis: Augsburg, 1970), 30ff.
[3]1 Samuel 18:1.

David. When Jonathan is killed in battle, David writes a poetic eulogy including the lines:

> *Your love to me was wonderful,*
> *passing the love of women.*[4]

The story even includes an account of the violent disapproval of Jonathan's father, Saul, of the intense friendship between David and his son, resulting in his attempt to kill David.[5]

Episcopal priest Tom Horner has carefully documented the homoeroticism of the story of David and Jonathan in his book *Jonathan Loved David: Homosexuality in Biblical Times.*[6] Yes, David does marry a woman in the story, but marrying and having children would have been expected of him in any case. With a sense of exasperation toward those who refuse to see an erotic element in the story, Horner writes:

> "But cannot two men be good friends," someone said to me recently, "without the issue of homosexuality being raised?" Yes, they can, but *when* the two men come from a society that for two hundred years lived in the shadow of the Philistine culture, which accepted homosexuality; *when* they find themselves in a social context that was thoroughly military in the Eastern sense; *when* one of them—who is the social superior of the two—publicly makes a display of his love; *when* the two of them make a lifetime pact openly; *when* they meet secretly and kiss each other and shed copious tears at parting; *when* one of them proclaims that his love for the other surpassed his love for women—and *all* this is present in the David-Jonathan liaison—we have every reason to believe that a homosexual relationship existed.[6]

[4] 2 Samuel 1:26.
[5] 1 Samuel 18:12, 19:1–10ff.
[6] Horner, *Jonathan Loved David,* 27–28.

Ruth and Naomi

Just as the David and Jonathan story is appropriate for a gay male wedding, so is the Ruth and Naomi story a highly appropriate reading for a lesbian wedding. In fact, you may well have heard the words of the covenant Ruth makes with Naomi read or sung, ironically enough, at *heterosexual* weddings:[7]

> *Entreat me not to leave you or to return from following you; for where you go I will go, and where you lodge I will lodge; your people shall be my people, and your God my God; where you die I will die, and there will I be buried.*[8]

Naomi had relocated in a foreign country with her husband. Their two sons had married women of that country, one of whom was Ruth. After all three of the husbands died, Naomi said good-bye to her daughters-in-law and set out to return to her homeland. Ruth, however, refused to leave Naomi and made a vow to stay with her for life. The two of them return to Naomi's native country. As women, and especially poor women, have always done, Ruth did what she needed to do to survive (and to provide for Naomi): Ruth eventually marries again.

Is there any indication in the scriptural account that the love between Ruth and Naomi was sexual? No. Is there any indication that it was *not* sexual? No. The so-called "factual" data include large gaps, which we must fill in with the data gleaned from prayer and meditation and *phantasie*. Utilizing such data, you can choose to see this story as the account of a deeply committed, intergenerational, lesbian love affair.

---

[7] I am indebted to the Rev. Larry Uhrig for pointing this out in his book *Sex Positive: A Gay Contribution to Sexual and Spiritual Union* (Boston: Alyson Publications, 1986), 60. Actually, the David/Jonathan and Ruth/Naomi covenants are the *only* accounts in the Bible of covenanted love between two people who are social equals, because men and women were *not* social equals in any of the cultures recorded in the Bible. Therefore David and Jonathan and Ruth and Naomi present a clearer picture of what we today expect from a Christian marriage than do any of the heterosexual couplings in scripture.

[8] Ruth 1:16–17.

Eunuchs for the Sake of the Kingdom

> Let not the eunuch say,
> "Behold, I am a dry tree."
> For thus says the Lord:
> "To the eunuchs who keep my sabbaths,
> who choose the things that please me
> and hold fast my covenant,
> I will give in my house and within my walls
> a monument and a name
> better than sons and daughters;
> I will give them an everlasting name
> which shall not be cut off."[9]

The inclusion of this reference may be surprising to you, especially if you are familiar with the Bible. There is nothing in this passage that specifically mentions homosexuality in any way, but it does suggest there are other ways to please God than by being married and having children—especially since it is found in the context of prophecies about the coming messianic paradise.

In the midst of a biblical tradition that constantly emphasizes and glorifies heterosexual reproduction, this passage is a welcome oasis. Throughout much of the Hebrew scripture, producing children is almost synonymous with God's blessing. Yet in this passage, the prophet says keeping the covenant is far more important than being a parent. It is an image of the total inclusiveness of the household of God—those of us who do not reproduce but do keep the commandments will have "a monument and a name better than sons and daughters."

Then, in the gospel of Matthew, Jesus makes a reference to eunuchs:

> Not all men can receive this saying, but only those to whom it is given. For there are eunuchs who have been so from birth, and there are eunuchs who have been made eunuchs by men, and there are eunuchs who have made themselves

[9]Isaiah 56:3–5.

*eunuchs for the sake of the kingdom of heaven. He who is able
to receive this, let him receive it.*[10]

This cryptic saying of Jesus' is often used to justify the practice of
celibacy as a Christian virtue. Some fanatical Christian men have
taken it as an order to castrate themselves.[11] But Larry Uhrig, a
minister of the Metropolitan Community Church, hears it very
differently:

> I believe that Jesus was speaking to those who, from birth,
> have been sexually different. Sexual minorities can receive
> this message. This is an acknowledgment of sexual minor-
> ities; an acknowledgment that not all people can receive the
> meaning of this saying.[12]

When I first read Uhrig's book, although I found it intriguing, I
thought his interpretation of this passage was somewhat esoteric, if
not farfetched. But then, when I took the General Ordination Exam-
inations, the intensive week-long academic tests roughly equivalent
to the bar exams, which are required of those seeking ordination in
the Episcopal Church, I was startled to find a reference to the Isaiah
passage about the inheritance of eunuchs in one of our test questions, in the specific context of a discussion of biblical references to
homosexuality. Either one of the preparers of the GOE questions
had read Uhrig's book or the Holy Spirit is moving in some very
mysterious ways.

The Centurion's *Pais*

In the seventh chapter of the Gospel of Luke and in the eighth
chapter of the Gospel of Matthew, there is a story of a Roman
centurion who sends word to Jesus, asking him to come and heal a

[10]Matthew 19:11–12.
[11]As something of a fan of the teachings of the early theologian Origen, I feel compelled to
say I do not believe he was among those who castrated themselves as a religious act, as is
popularly believed about him. The only evidence we have for believing he did is the account
of St. Jerome, who clearly hated Origen and supplied us with a great deal of false information,
which later scholarship has refuted, about him and his teaching.
[12]Uhrig, *Sex Positive,* 66.

young man who is called, in the English translation, his "slave." In the accounts in Luke and Matthew, the details are almost identical, but in the Gospel of John,[13] there is an account of a healing that is similar enough to sound like the same story but in which the young man who is healed is not called the centurion's "slave" or "servant," but rather his "son." Why the confusion?

The word that the Revised Standard Version of the Bible translates as "slave" is, in the original Greek (transliterated into our alphabet), *pais*. Most lexicons define *pais* as "boy." It was a term of affection. The word *could* be used to describe a young male servant, but such a usage was very rare; it was more often used by a parent to describe a son. If someone did call a servant *pais,* the word implied a very special relationship, much more intimate and loving than the usual master/slave relationship. In fact, when the centurion uses the word *slave* later in the same passage in Luke, in verse eight, "When I say to my slave 'do this,' and he does it," the Greek word there is not *pais,* but the more usual word for slave, *dulos.* In other words, when he gives an example of authority, of giving orders to a slave, it is not this young man he is speaking of.

When you consider the urgency of the centurion's request to Jesus (Matthew's Gospel uses the word *beseeching*), you can't help but be struck by the uniqueness and intimacy of the relationship. Luke says the young man was "very dear to him." When we read this passage through my queer-colored glasses, when we employ the techniques of *phantasie,* it becomes obvious: this *pais* was the centurion's *lover.* This is a story about an intergenerational gay couple. It's a type of pairing that was extremely common in that culture and is not at all uncommon today: a mature and powerful man coupled with a younger and less powerful man. (Just for the record, the sociologists Andrew Mattison and David McWhirter, authors of *The Male Couple,* found that same-sex relationships are more likely to last when there *is* a significant age difference.)[14] In fact, if you read queer personals ads (especially in leather maga-

---

[13]John 4:46–54.
[14]David P. McWhirter and Andrew M. Mattison, *The Male Couple: How Relationships Develop* (Englewood Cliffs, New Jersey: Prentice-Hall, 1984), 215.

zines) you know how often the words *daddy* and *boy* are used. The *pais,* the young man in this story, may or may not have been a *slave,* but he was clearly, in the twentieth-century urban gay male sense of the term, the centurion's "boy."

Homosexuality was not uncommon in the Roman Empire. As late as the sixth century of the Common Era, the Romans accorded legal status to same-sex marriages. Homosexuality in the Roman army was even more common. The Roman government saw the particularly intense form of male bonding that would inevitably exist among gay men as being very useful to the army. For a high-ranking Roman soldier to have a male lover would not be unusual. The Romans wouldn't even raise an eyebrow. The Jews, on the other hand, might raise an eyebrow or two, and the centurion seems to have been aware of the Jewish distaste for homosexuality. Perhaps because he was aware of the sex-negative tendency of the Hebrews,[15] the centurion was reluctant to invite them in too close, to share with them the true nature of his relationship with the young man he loved. He would probably have assumed that the rabbi would be appalled at his relationship with his beloved. He seems almost ashamed. He declines Jesus' offer to come to his house, saying, "Lord, do not trouble yourself, for I am not worthy to have you come under my roof."

But Jesus surprises him. There is absolutely no hint in any of the three gospel accounts of any sort of condemnation from Jesus. Jesus seems moved by the request, and he commends the centurion to his entourage: "Not even in Israel have I seen such faith." And he does heal the young man. (There isn't even a hint of his adding any disclaimer, like "Go and sin no more.")

Gay religious caucuses like to say Jesus said nothing about homosexuality. There is a popular brochure that reads on its cover, "What Jesus said about homosexuality," and inside it's blank. But in fact, perhaps this gospel story is the very compelling record of what Jesus *did* have to say about homosexuality: "Not even in Israel have I

[15]The anti-Semitic tendency of contemporary Christians is just as sinful and insidious as the sex-negative tendency of the Hebrews, and I am on thin ice when I make these sorts of statements. Please understand I am not contrasting Jewish and Christian thought here, but the Judeo-Christian tradition as a whole with the Greco-Roman tradition.

seen such faith." Jesus was, in effect, telling his entourage, who might have been whispering among themselves about the "scandal," that they could learn some lessons in faith from this Roman gay couple.

Was Paul Queer?

A book written by my former bishop, John Spong, has speculated that Paul, the apostle and formative Christian theologian, may have been homosexual.[16] As you have just witnessed, I am quite willing to find homosexuality wherever it may appear in the scripture, but I just don't see it with Paul.

Bishop Spong's speculation is based primarily upon Paul's self-description of his "thorn in the flesh":

> *A thorn was given me in the flesh, a messenger of Satan, to harass me, to keep me from being too elated. Three times I besought the Lord about this, but he said to me, "My grace is sufficient for you, for my power is made perfect in weakness." I will all the more gladly boast of my weakness, that the power of Christ may rest upon me.*[17]

Bishop Spong has said that Paul's account of his "thorn in the flesh" sounds very similar to the way many gay men have described their sexuality to him during pastoral counseling situations.

Some of the early Church theologians, as well as some of the Reformers, speculated that Paul's "thorn in the flesh" was a "spiritual affliction," perhaps having something to do with "sins of the flesh." However, both the early Church theologians and the Reformers had a rather morbid fixation upon "sins of the flesh." Contemporary biblical scholars, although they characteristically warn there is insufficient data to be very specific, generally agree that Paul's affliction was a *physical* condition, such as malaria, eye disease, a speech defect, or epilepsy. Using the scriptural evidence, a case

[16]John S. Spong, *Living in Sin: A Bishop Re-Thinks Human Sexuality* (San Francisco: Harper & Row, 1988), 151.
[17]2 Corinthians 12:7–9.

could be made for any of these—the fact that Paul's letters seemed often to have been written by a scribe, while he affixed only his signature to them, for instance, supports the idea that Paul had a visual deficiency; and the fact Paul often describes himself as "inarticulate" supports the idea of a speech defect.

For my money, the most compelling case is to be made for frontal-lobe epilepsy. This condition, which has been known to affect a number of artists and religious visionaries, is marked by hypergraphia (excessive writing) and by hyperreligiosity, as well as by hyposexuality (reduced sexual drive)—all traits Paul clearly exhibits. In addition, the seizures associated with epilepsy (often accompanied by hallucinations) could explain Paul's dramatic "Damascus Road" conversion experience, in which he was struck blind and heard the voice of God, as well as his comment to the Church at Galatia: "though my condition was a trial to you, you did not scorn or despise me."[18]

In fact, shortly after a story about Bishop Spong's book ran in *The New York Times,* Wallace K. Tomlinson, a medical historian, sent a letter to the editor protesting that there is a significant body of literature compiled by medical historians to support the idea that Paul's "thorn in the flesh" was frontal-lobe epilepsy, and questioning how Spong could have neglected to at least comment upon this data. "Overlooking significant medical literature speaks poorly for his scholarship," Tomlinson wrote.[19]

Aside from the fact that Bishop Spong hasn't learned the most basic lesson of liberation theology—what is technically called "epistemological privilege," which is the insistence that all people, especially oppressed people, should be allowed to speak for themselves and should reject the efforts of straight, white patriarchs, however "liberal" and gay-friendly, to speak for us—I think Bishop Spong's construction also rests upon a projection of twentieth-century American homophobia onto first-century Rome. As John Boswell and other historians have pointed out, the phenomenon of

[18]Galatians 4:14.
[19]Wallace K. Tomlinson, M.D., is professor of psychiatry at Tulane University Medical Center in New Orleans. The letter, dated February 5, 1991, was printed in *The New York Times,* Tuesday, February 12, 1991, p. A18.

homophobia as we know it was largely unknown until it was introduced by the Christian Church. You might even say Christians *invented* homophobia. The systematic persecution of queers and the widespread societal disapproval of homosexuality didn't exist until around the twelfth century, when the church had become fundamentally sex-negative. Paul's writings may well have planted the seeds of that homophobia, but it would be several centuries before the Church had developed enough political clout to impose and enforce its views. So for us to assume, even if Paul was queer, that he was "self-hating" is a major assumption. The sort of self-loathing created by society's compulsory heterosexuality is a much more recent phenomenon. Paul, in fact, would have had plenty of positive role models of homosexuality, including those in the Roman army and in the emperor's court. It is perhaps true that the Jews were not enthusiastic about homosexuality; but they did not have the political power to create the social structures that could cause intense self-hatred. Besides, Paul's upbringing and lifestyle were as much Greek and Roman as they were Jewish. Finally, given the fact that I believe Jesus himself was *at the very least* nonjudgmental about homosexuality, Paul, who never met Jesus, would surely have heard this from eyewitnesses to Jesus' teachings, and he could then have rejected the Jewish distaste for homosexuality just as he rejected other, much more fundamental, Jewish ideas.

The fact that the roots of Christian homophobia and heterosexism are in Paul's writings also makes the idea that he was queer seem less likely. Of course, we've all known closet cases who were publicly homophobic, but if what Paul was describing as his "thorn in the flesh" was in fact a penchant for sex with men, and he was doing it often enough to congratulate the Galatians on not "despising" him for it, then the Galatians were fools. If Paul, after preaching that "men who lie with other men" will not enter the kingdom of heaven, was then found to be "lying with other men" himself, I would hope the Galatian Christians would have thrown him out on his ear.

What is especially troublesome to me about Bishop Spong's speculation about Paul, particularly since in the same breath in which he claims Paul was homosexual he refers to Paul's homosexuality as his "dark side," is that he thinks we would be *happy* to learn Paul was queer. Personally, I'd be more than a little embarrassed; wouldn't you? Bishop Spong expects queer Christians to hold up Paul as some sort of role model; but that would be rather like celebrating Terry Dolan or Malcolm Forbes as role models. Who needs a "self-loathing" closet case for a role model?

Besides, I have a much more positive role model in mind—but we'll save that for Chapter 8.

Devotional Reading

Once you've developed enough of a "hermeneutic of suspicion" that you can dismiss the parts of the Bible that seem to be negative and antiqueer, you are in a much better position to undertake some sort of regular, devotional reading of the Bible—and regular reading of the Bible is an important component of living the Christian life. Because it is devotional literature, the Bible does not lend itself to reading through from cover to cover, as you would read another book. It is much more rewarding to read relatively short passages on some sort of daily schedule, taking the time to reflect on their meaning to you. You might, for instance, use the technique described in Chapter 2 to enter into biblical texts. A number of manuals and listings are available that suggest passages for daily reading. The lectionary, a listing of what is called "the propers," passages to be used in worship services for particular days, is used by Roman Catholics, Episcopalians, Lutherans, and several other churches and is usually found in their prayer books. With a few minor exceptions, all these churches use the same cycle of readings, so when you read and reflect on the Bible passages in the lectionary, you know you are concentrating on the same passages as thousands of other Christians around the world. My own Bible-reading discipline is to say the liturgy of the Daily Office (Morning Prayer) each morning, using the propers for the day.

Expanding the Canon of Scripture

Our current idea of which books are to be considered part of the canon, which books are contained in the official Christian scriptures, is the result of an arbitrary decision made by early church bishops. Their list of which books to include was partly traditional, partly political. The motivation for identifying a canon of scripture was to defend the doctrines of the Catholic party against those of other Christian parties, especially the Gnostics, Marcionites, and Monatists. Each of these groups chose scriptures that supported its own beliefs, and the list we now think of as "canonical" was simply the list that supported the beliefs of the Catholics, the party that won the struggle. Several other books that the Catholic bishops rejected had been used by Christian communities as scripture for years, and many of the books they did include were fiercely disputed. There was a strong sentiment, for instance, against including the Gospel of John, since it was so different from the other three gospels. The reason there are four gospels, and not three or five, is that Irenaeus, the bishop of Lyons in the late second century C.E., thought four was an appropriate number, citing reasons we would classify as an appeal to "numerology."[20] It was Irenaeus, in fact, who erroneously attributed the authorship of the fourth gospel to the Apostle John, in order to strengthen his argument that it should be included in the Catholic Bible.

One of the other gospels that was popular at the time but eventually rejected was known as "The Gospel of Thomas." Irenaeus and his colleagues rejected "The Gospel of Thomas" because it supported the Gnostic doctrines more than the Catholic doctrines. As a child in Sunday school, I first heard about this rejected gospel, and the teacher gave us an example of why it was rejected. It contained "silly stories" about Jesus as a boy doing frivolous things, she said, such as turning clay pigeons into real ones. While that example might have persuaded Sunday school kids, I was shocked when one of my seminary professors cited the same clay pigeon story as reason for the rejection of "The Gospel of Thomas." By that time, I was armed with enough biblical knowledge of my own to counter that the clay pigeon story is no more frivolous than the

---

[20]Irenaeus wished to link the four gospels to the four winds or four directions, as well as the four creatures guarding the throne of God in Ezekiel's vision (Ezekiel 1:10) and in the Apocalypse, or "Revelation to St. John" (Revelation 4:7). (See Henry Chadwick, *The Early Church* [Vol. 1 in *The Pelican History of the Church*] [New York: Penguin Books, 1967], 43.)

canonical account of Jesus' turning water into wine at Cana. In fact, another story of Jesus in the canonical gospels is considerably more silly and frivolous:

> *In the morning, as* [Jesus] *was returning to the city, he was hungry. And seeing a fig tree by the wayside he went to it, and found nothing on it but leaves only. And he said to it, "May no fruit ever come from you again!" And the fig tree withered at once.*[21]

Why is an account of Jesus, as a child, turning clay pigeons into live ones any more "frivolous" or out of character than an account of Jesus, as an adult, destroying a fig tree because it didn't have a fig when he wanted one? (And it wasn't even the season for figs!) In fact, the fig tree story presents a rather fascinating image of Jesus being quite human and getting *very* annoyed—even bitchy.

Since Christians affirm as a matter of faith that the Holy Spirit still moves among the Christian community, there is no reason to assume the decision of the early church about which books are to be included in the scripture is final. Just as some passages in the officially canonical books must be rejected as being destructive, some passages in noncanonical literature embody truth and life. The books the early bishops rejected included many useful passages, such as several of the so-called "Gnostic Gospels."[22] In fact, the scholarship currently being done on the Dead Sea Scrolls and at the Nag Hammadi library is making it more and more clear that many of the words we attribute to Jesus (such as the famous "sermon on the mount") were in fact taken from earlier books, books Jesus probably read and studied as scripture, such as the Book of Enoch. Why shouldn't these recently recovered books, then, be a part of our scriptures today?

Nor does a text have to be ancient in order to be sacred. Reversing Farley's test of canonicity mentioned earlier, a text is sacred when it "rings true to our deepest capacity for truth and

[21]Matthew 21:18–20. The same story appears in Mark 11:12–14, 20–25.
[22]See Elaine Pagels, *The Gnostic Gospels* (New York: Random House, 1979).

goodness." Some texts by contemporary authors meet this criterion. Perhaps for you, some of the essays of Audre Lorde or the poetry of Adrienne Rich or Walt Whitman are scripture. My own canon of scripture includes the myth of "the Other Half" from Plato's *Symposium,* and passages by Judy Grahn, Morris West, Audre Lorde, Walt Whitman, Elie Wiesel, Chaim Potok, Taylor Caldwell, Nikos Kazantzakis, and Tennessee Williams—passages that speak the truth to me. Most recently, I have added to my personal canon of scripture the three-volume work about gay spirituality channeled by Andrew Ramer, *Two Flutes Playing, Spiritual Love/Sacred Sex,* and *Priests of Father Earth and Mother Sky.*[23]

At my ordination, I included among the readings in the liturgy of the word a long passage from Audre Lorde's essay "The Transformation of Silence into Language and Action," a letter my fellow gay Episcopal priest Zal Sherwood wrote to his friend the night before his ordination, and a monologue from the play *Inherit the Wind.*

During Holy Week 1990, the Metropolitan Community Church of San Francisco held a service of Tenebrae, an ancient liturgy of readings and meditations. The lessons they used for this liturgy ranged from a passage from James Baldwin's *Giovanni's Room* to poems by Judy Grahn, Walt Whitman, Adrienne Rich, and Audre Lorde, to the closing words of Harvey Milk's will—all of them scripture, none of them biblical.

A special liturgy at Episcopal Divinity School recently featured a student's reading, as part of the scripture of the day, a letter she had received from the woman she had recently learned was her grandmother's lover, a letter speaking of what it meant to live as a lesbian two generations ago.

Christian worship could be greatly enhanced by expanding the canon of scripture, and using some of these contemporary scriptures in the liturgy. Some churches do occasionally branch out to nonbiblical literature for readings in the Sunday liturgy, but they invariably treat these passages as being of less importance than the biblical passages. Why? If these passages embody the truth, they are

---

[23]Available in one volume from Body Electric Publishing, 6527A Telegraph Avenue, Oakland, CA 94609. (415) 653-1594. As of 1991, the price was $15.95 plus tax and shipping.

sacred, they are scripture. When we hear the conclusion of Lorde's essay, "there are so many silences to be broken," why shouldn't we proclaim it as "the Word of God"? As a queer Christian, you can draw from other sources, particularly from the sacred writings of your own people, past and present, as well as from the "rather grossly overrated" Bible.

5

HOLY MOTHER CHURCH VS. THE QUEER NATION

The Authority of Community

When it comes to affiliating with a congregation, you will probably find yourself caught in a dilemma. Christianity is not a matter of "me and Jesus." Authentic Christianity is not an individual path, but a community path. The Christian understanding is that God is most present when a *group* of believers are gathered (it need not be a large group; the scripture suggests "two or three"[1]); and while God's revelation may come to an individual, it must be verified by the authority of a community of faith. The other side of the dilemma, however, is that it is almost impossible to find a parish of any Christian denomination that has truly exorcised its homophobia to the extent that a radically self-affirming queer Christian can participate in it with integrity. The church down the street from your house may offer beautiful architecture, a glorious organ, and a professional choir—along with a stifling dose of homophobia.

Larry is one of those incredibly beautiful young men—so physically attractive he literally makes me nervous. He's been a

[1]Matthew 18:20.

71

fashion model, and he's an avid wind surfer. He's also extremely bright and deeply spiritual. He was baptized Roman Catholic, but like the vast majority of queer Catholics, he left the church behind long ago. As he was becoming more and more deeply involved in the exploration of spiritual issues, he consulted with a psychic adviser who told him, among other things, he should adopt a religious tradition and become involved in a church. He went back to his childhood Roman Catholic Church . . . once. He tried the Unitarian Universalist Meeting House, but it left him cold—there was no feeling of transcendence there. He knew that the local Episcopal church was rather homophobic. He asked me for advice. "How do you find a Christian church that isn't homophobic?" he asked. I told him you don't—at least not in Provincetown, where he lives.

"One thing you need to know," I told him, "is that finding the perfect parish is like finding the perfect lover. It just doesn't exist." He was shocked to hear me say that—not about the parish, but about the lover. "I'm still idealistic enough to believe I *can* find the perfect lover," he said. Well, he's only thirty. I wish him luck. With his looks, charm, brains, and inner depth, maybe he *can* find the perfect lover. But I would be willing to bet he will never find a parish of any established institutional church that offers him (or any other truly self-affirming queer) absolute, unconditional acceptance.

Click your heels together three times and repeat, *There's no such thing as a perfect parish.* If you begin with that understanding, you are much less likely to be disappointed. And if you should actually stumble across a truly inclusive Christian parish, you will be pleasantly surprised. (And drop me a note, would you?—because I don't believe such a place exists.)

Who Says?

You will recall from Chapter 2 that the trick in meditation is always to step aside, to get yourself out of the way and listen to the Spirit. How do you know when you have done that? We all have dozens of voices in our heads—you could be hearing the voice of your mother, the voice of your childhood minister, or the voice of the Evil One (who is alive and well). If you receive a message in meditation, how do you know who the messenger is?

At the Southern Baptist college I attended it became popular for some of the more pious students to approach a member of the opposite sex (approaching a member of the same sex would get you expelled!) and say, "The Lord has laid it on my heart that you and I should be dating." Well, fine, except what if the Lord laid it on *my* heart that you're a creep?

What happens if the Holy Spirit tells you the carpet for the new church building should be green, but tells someone else the carpet should be blue? Precisely for this reason, the church developed the concept of *the authority of the community*. You need a community of faith, a community of accountability, against which to check out what you feel are your personal revelations.

Ideally, that community of faith and accountability is a parish, a small, intimate group of Christians who meet together for worship, prayer, and communion at least once a week. Unfortunately for you, it is often difficult to find a parish where you can be yourself and be truly accepted as a part of that community.

Until very recently, I would have recommended the primarily lesbian and gay Metropolitan Community Church, without reservation, to those whose background and preference is an evangelical style of Christianity. However, in July 1991, the Rev. Elder Troy Perry, founder of the denomination, spoke out against the dangers of "goddess worship" at the MCC General Conference in Phoenix.[2] It is truly unfortunate that Perry has taken such a stance. The mostly queer MCC could be the one church capable of doing truly creative work in developing and articulating queer theology, but Perry's arbitrary dismissal of "goddess worship" cuts off that possibility. As a lesbian friend of mine commented, "It just confirms for me that there is no Christian church for women." Besides being offensive to a host of Christian women, Perry's diatribe is detrimental to the

---

[2]Reported in *Bay Windows* (Boston), August 1, 1991, 4. What Perry is quoted as saying is "This church has nothing to do with goddess worship as I understand it. . . . I do not believe goddess worship is consistent with the Christian church. We did not remove God's penis to replace it with a vagina."

spiritual health of gay men, too, for we especially *need* the images of the divine feminine. Perry's unfortunate speech places him, on this issue, far to the right of many mainstream Christian clergy and theologians. Today, I would be much more hesitant in recommending the MCC to radically self-respecting queers.

The problem is further compounded if you prefer, as many queers do, the sacramental approach to worship (sometimes called "smells and bells"). I happen to believe that not only is small-c catholic, sacramental worship the most authentic expression of Christianity, it is also the style of spirituality with which queers have the most natural affinity. (There's more on this in Chapter 9 on sacrament. In a nutshell, I believe that sacramental worship is a holistic experience—involving your body, mind, and spirit—while most protestant and New Age worship is strictly a head trip.) There are some notable exceptions, but as a general rule, whether Roman, Anglican, or Lutheran, the more sacramental and ceremonial the worship of a parish, the more homophobic, sexist, and fascist its social policy. Show me a parish that offers the liturgy called the Benediction of the Blessed Sacrament (a beautiful and deeply moving ceremony, by the way), and I'll show you a parish that oppresses women and queers. What's a liturgy queen to do?

Nothing inherent in catholic worship itself promotes sexism and homophobia. For one thing, there are rare catholic worship communities deeply committed to sexual justice (up to a point). The Church of St. John the Evangelist in Boston and its parent organization, the Society of St. John the Evangelist in Cambridge, are shining examples, as is Trinity Episcopal Church in San Francisco.

But such communities are few and far between. If you don't happen to live within comfortable driving distance of one of these rare places, what are your options?

Well, you've got to get creative. You may, for instance, have to have two faith communities. You might go to an anglo-catholic church on Sunday morning and the MCC on Sunday night—but don't join or give money to either. Or find a weekday Quaker meeting (your body will be totally ignored, but Quakers are the

most politically correct religious group on the face of the earth!).
You could try a New Age church such as Unity or the Church of
Religious Science—again, your body's not likely to get any attention, but neither are you likely to be told you're going to hell. You
might visit a meeting of one of the denominational lesbian/gay
caucuses (Dignity, Integrity, Lutherans Concerned, etc.)—but most
of these groups are so conservative and assimilationist that they're
out of touch with the out-and-proud queer community. They have a
strong tendency to be the gay equivalent of Uncle Toms. For instance, Dignity just officially adopted an "anti-outing" policy, and the
members of Integrity issued positive statements about the decision
of the 1991 Episcopal General Convention to continue the status
quo on the issues of same-sex marriage and gay ordinations—a
decision that outraged more radical queer activists.

In fact, even those parishes I have mentioned as being unusually committed to social justice are not *totally* committed. They
can't be as long as they remain affiliated with national hierarchical
structures. You can't create justice within the confines of an inherently unjust organization. This is a particular problem for Episcopal parishes, because of their form of church government. There
are several parishes with a large percentage of queer members,
many of whom are on the vestry; and the day-to-day life of these
places is generally very gay positive. But in every case, when their
commitment to justice and inclusiveness leads them to a conflict
with the church hierarchy (which it inevitably does, sooner or
later), all of these parishes ultimately opt to obey the hierarchy
rather than to follow the call of justice. In a sense, it shouldn't be
surprising—they are, after all, *Episcopal* churches, and what "episcopal" *means* is "governed by bishops." However strong the conviction of the parish and the local clergy about justice for queers, when
the bishop tells them to stop what they are doing, they stop. Always,
without exception.

Ironically, the less aware you are of the issues, the more
comfortable you can be in such a parish. You can sail along happily
for months thinking this is the most welcoming, inclusive, gay-
positive church you've ever encountered. Then *blam!* suddenly you

are rudely reminded this is, after all, a hierarchically structured church, and what Daddy says goes.

For instance, my friend Robert Warren Cromey, the rector of Trinity San Francisco, is a brave, outspoken proponent of social justice. Since he estimates his parish to be about 65 percent queer, he has quite naturally been called on often to perform queer weddings or blessings of same-sex couples, or whatever is the currently fashionable term. He says he has done over fifty such ceremonies. Yet in 1988, when circumstances brought the upcoming blessing of a male couple to the attention of the media, Bishop William Swing of California (who just *swears* he's not homophobic!) stepped in and told Father Cromey he could not allow the ceremony. Cromey fussed and fumed, but ultimately gave in. Very similar stories could be told about St. John's Bowdoin Street and St. Mary's Provincetown.

My fantasy is that when a queer-positive parish with a commitment to total inclusiveness has made a decision based on prayer, study, and careful thought that is supported by the vestry, the clergy, and the parish as a whole, and yet that decision is opposed by the bishop, the parish would have the guts to tell the bishop to go to hell. I would like to see such a parish truly and totally stand for justice, even if it means dissolving the bishop's power over them by declaring themselves to be independent, no longer affiliated with the Episcopal Church or any such national structure. Then the parish would be free to go on doing what they believe the Spirit calls them to do.

I am absolutely convinced that the congregational structure of church government, which provides for *all* decisions affecting the parish to be made within the local parish itself, is the *only* form of church government that is appropriate for queers—or women or racial minorities or, for that matter, sympathetic straight, white men. In fact, I believe the congregational structure is the only form of church government that can embody the original intention of Jesus Christ—because hierarchy is inherently anti-Christian. Self-respecting queer Christians have absolutely no business being in a church that has any kind of hierarchical decision-making structure beyond the local parish itself—whether the hierarchs are called bishops, elders, or district supervisors. Unfortunately, even the Metropolitan Community Church has replicated this mistake, creating a large, multinational hierarchy with several levels of authority figures (elders) who exercise power over local congregations.

My friend is right: There *is* no Christian church for women, or for queers—if by "church" you mean an existing denominational structure. The best option might be to form your own worship community. Band together with a group of like-minded queer Christians and begin celebrating Mass on Sunday in your living room. You could call it St. Aelred's Community Church or St. Joan of Arc Queer Catholic Church—or if you're feeling especially heretical, St. Origen's Gnostic Catholic Church. Maybe you can't pull off a solemn High Mass in a city apartment, but your church could grow large enough to at least rent a building. The MCC, now a large international organization, began in Troy Perry's living room. My prayer is that such communities would spring up all over the country. Don't have a priest handy? Not to worry. Even the most orthodox Christians admit ordination is conveyed not by the power of the reigning hierarchy, but by the Holy Spirit through the prayers of the community. Ordain your own priest. By doing so, you will be closer to the practice of the earliest form of the Christian church. And forget bishops—they're absolutely unnecessary. Queers need bishops, to borrow a feminist slogan, like a fish needs a bicycle. Or to use my grandfather's more colorful West Texas expression, bishops are, for us, about as useful as "tits on a bull." Let me say it one more time: *Any form of hierarchy that takes precedence over the parish community itself is not politically correct for self-affirming queers,* not to mention a direct affront to the cherished Christian ideal of "the priesthood of all believers." We should know better than to replicate patriarchal, hierarchical structures.

The sad truth is, however, not many of these independent queer catholic parishes are likely to spring up. I know. It takes a tremendous investment of time and energy. I should have founded such a parish myself, but I haven't felt up to making the commitment it would require . . . thus far, anyway.

In the meantime, the best solution may be to stretch your definition of what constitutes a "community of faith and account-ability." Your community may be much more loosely structured—just a group of close friends. You may, for instance, be more likely to find your Christian community at an ACT UP meeting than in church on Sunday. Besides, I think the queer community is a community of accountability in its own right, one that we must acknowledge and honor.

The Rev. Dr. Carter Heyward, radical lesbian priest and theologian, my mentor, and as impeccable a human being as I have met, defines her community of accountability as being considerably broader than "the church":

> My people hold me accountable—responsible for what I say. And there is nothing abstract about "my people": They are my students and my teachers, my friends and my lovers, my *compañeras* and colleagues. They have names, faces, commitments, values, problems, questions, feelings, and ideas. With me and with one another, these people are healers, teachers, priests, pastors, counselors, therapists, organizers, politicians, poets, artists, mothers, fathers, daughters, and sons.[3]

I came to the painful realization that "my people" are not geographically concentrated—they are scattered all over the country and in other countries. If they all lived in the same place, these people could make up one hell of a parish (though God knows, we'd never be able to agree on so much as the selection of one hymn!). However, we will probably never have a chance to break bread together as a community.

Your people have faces and names, too. You just may not be used to thinking of them as a community of accountability. If you are somewhat of a pioneer or a prophet, if you are comfortable with the "radical" label—and I hope you are, for that is your double

---

[3]Carter Heyward, *Touching Our Strength: The Erotic as Power and the Love of God* (San Francisco: Harper & Row, 1989), 7–8.

vocation as a queer and a Christian—then you might never find a ready-made community of accountability. You will have to put it together yourself, piece by piece, like a jigsaw puzzle. Being accountable to a group that is so diverse and that does not gather as a group requires being very intentional about your relationship with that group. The first step is being very clear with yourself about exactly who makes up your community. (I find it helpful to list their names from time to time.) If you are dealing with a spiritual dilemma, since you can't take it before them as a group, you will have to poll them individually.

I'll give you an example from my personal experience. Recently, I began to feel that God was calling me into a ministry of healing. I had done some exploration of Christian healing in the past, but had more recently neglected it. This call was so strong I eventually decided I should drop out of the Ph.D. program I was in, in order to devote full time to the study of spiritual healing, and that I should move from New York to Provincetown, both so I could be apprenticed to a particular healer whose work I admired, and so I could surround myself with a support community that believed in healing.

All this came to me as an intensive spiritual experience, so intensive that I was more than a little embarrassed to try to articulate it. I felt self-conscious to say, "I believe God is calling me to be a healer." Yet I also felt it was extremely important that I talk about it, check it out with other people, to try to determine whether I was truly responding to God's call or to self-delusion. So I began to share my experience with my community of accountability. Those who lived nearby I took out to lunch. Others I wrote to or spoke to on the phone. I told them what I had experienced, what I felt God was calling me to do, and what I thought I should do about it. Although I expected some sarcasm and ridicule, every one of these people responded positively. One by one, they told me they thought I was right—that I should drop out of my doctoral program, that I should move, that I should pursue training in the healing arts.

Sharing this kind of experience with your community, telling them what you *think* God is saying to you, and getting their confirmation that it sounds true to them is an important step. Otherwise, you would always have a nagging voice in the back of your head saying, "But what if this is all bullshit? What if I'm fooling myself?"

Who Called You?

Perhaps you have a special calling, a vocation to the ordained ministry or to what evangelicals would call "full-time Christian service." Now you've got real trouble on your hands! The Christian tradition has long held that an individual vocation, a sense of being called by God into a particular form of ministry, must always be *confirmed* by the community of faith. If you confuse the institutional church with the community of faith, however, you are setting yourself up for disappointment. If a parish, a diocese, a bishop, or a committee has preconceived notions about whom God can call into ministry, especially the ordained ministry, then they have precluded any possibility of truly helping anyone discern and confirm a vocation. Within the institutional church, most of the groups that have the authority to pass judgment about whether or not an individual has a vocation to ministry do not believe that God can call a "practicing homosexual." Others might feel that God can occasionally call a polite, articulate, well-dressed lesbian or gay man who is in a "long-term, committed relationship" to the ministry; but never a single, radical queer. You must reject the authority of such groups. Their prejudice has rendered them incapable of discerning what God may or may not be calling you to do. Besides, if your vocation is to be a *pastor,* the institutional church might be able to accommodate you. If, however, your vocation is to be a *prophet,* you will probably scare the hell out of the institutional church because a major part of the prophetic vocation is to critique and criticize the institution. You'll probably find the more invested people are in the church as institution, the more frightening they will find your prophetic vocation.

There is a powerful story about vocation in the First Book of Samuel.[4] Samuel, who had been "dedicated to the Lord" as an infant by his mother, was living in the temple and working as a sort of

[4] 1 Samuel 3:1–10

apprentice to Eli, the priest. According to the text, prophecy was in short supply: "the word of the Lord was rare in those days; there was no frequent vision." Young Samuel, however, was called by God to be a prophet. When Samuel was sleeping in the vicinity of the ark, the most concentrated presence of God (not unlike the Christian understanding of the tabernacle containing the Blessed Sacrament), he heard a voice calling his name. Samuel assumed Eli was calling him, so he went to him, saying, "Here I am, for you called me." Eli said no, he did not call, and told Samuel to go back to bed. This happened three times, and the third time, Eli was wise enough to suggest to Samuel that it was God who was calling him—calling him to be a prophet.

Hundreds of queer Christians are being called by God to be prophets and priests, shamans and healers—in fact, it seems that queers are called into ministry in much greater proportions than the straight population. But most of us do not fare as well as Samuel because those with the established authority are seldom as wise as Eli. Every day, dozens of our people hear the voice of God calling us. We go to our Elis, usually church officials, and say, "Here I am, for you called me"; and they say, "I didn't call you. Go back to sleep. Go back to your closet." Don't give them the chance. If you feel a vocation to ministry you need to realize it is not Eli who is calling you, it is God. There is no point in going to a homophobic hierarch for the confirmation of your vocation.

If you think God might be calling you, it is important that you get some confirmation of that call—but if you go to any existing denomination, they'll probably tell you to go back to sleep. Find your own intentional community of accountability, and ask *them* to confirm your vocation. If you feel you have a vocation to the ordained ministry, and are fighting the lonely and costly battle of trying to get any mainstream denomination to take you seriously, consider that maybe your call is not to the ministry of any mainstream denomination. Maybe God is calling you to be a priest in the Queer Catholic Church!

PART TWO

I Believe:
Basic
Christian
Doctrines

6
GOD

Healing Our Images

Timmy's mother came to pick him up from Sunday school. "What did you learn today?" she asked.

"We learned God's first name," Timmy said proudly.

His mother raised her eyebrows. "Oh? And what is God's first name?"

"Howard," Timmy answered.

"Timmy, who told you God is named Howard?"

"It was a prayer we learned: 'Our Father, who art in heaven, Howard be thy name.'"

The biggest obstacle to your adult faith may well be that you are still operating with a God image you acquired when you were about Timmy's age. You may not think God is named Howard, but if you haven't done any serious study or discussion or thinking about God since you were in Sunday school or catechism class, you have outgrown your God. You are operating with a theology, a set of beliefs about God, that is as inappropriate for your adult needs as the shoes you wore when you were five years old. You might bronze them and put them on your mantel, but you can't walk in them.

Or even worse, if you're like the majority of queers, you have an image of God that's not only inadequate, but downright destructive. Around the time you were being taught about God, you also began to discover that you were queer. Long before puberty, even before there was a sexual element at all, you knew you were somehow *different*. For the vast majority of us, this difference was manifest in our reluctance or refusal to conform to gender-role expectations.

Whatever early form your queerness took, you knew you were different, and you quickly learned different was not good. Since God, in our culture, is portrayed as a sort of straight, white gentleman farmer, he, like the average country club member, is clearly opposed to anything that is disturbingly different. So you probably got it wired up that God disapproved of you. When you reached puberty and began to discover sexual urges, it became even worse. Then you were sure God hated you—you were taught God frowns on "touching yourself" down there—whether it's boys or girls you think about while you do it.

If you're a parent, stop and think for a moment about what an awesome responsibility you have in helping to shape your child's image of God and adult spirituality. Be very, very careful about using God as a threat or an incentive. Anytime you say anything like "God doesn't like it when you do that," which someone probably told you as a child, you are helping to create a negative relationship with God for your child. Imagine how it could be if you made an effort never to speak to your child about God except in the context of God's unconditional love and acceptance, like "That's okay. Sometimes people just don't like you, but you know God always loves you." Imagine how it must feel to grow up with such a totally positive God image.

Even if you were one of the lucky ones and were taught you are a "child of God," to grow up queer in our culture is to grow up feeling like an illegitimate child. It has not always been this way, everywhere. Other cultures (such as many Native American tribes) have affirmed not only that queers are children of God, but that we are *special* children of God, especially gifted, especially close to and loved by God. But not our culture, and not the mainstream Christian church.

So chances are you grew up believing in a God who did not truly love you. A God who—like your human parents, perhaps—was disappointed in you, ashamed of you. In that secret place, down deep in your soul, you may have a demanding, angry, impossible God, a God who tells you that you are no good—not as good as the other children of God—not good enough to be treated as a full member of the family. No matter what you do, you cannot please this God. No matter what you accomplish, how you overachieve, this demanding Father is never satisfied. In fact, if you grew up in either the Roman Catholic Church or a Fundamentalist tradition, you may well have endured virulently antiqueer sermons and teachings. Just remember the advice of John Irving's character Owen Meany: "IF SOME PREACHER'S AN ASSHOLE, THAT'S NOT PROOF THAT GOD DOESN'T EXIST!"[1]

Firing the God of Your Childhood

It may be that an important and necessary next step in your spiritual journey is to *fire the god of your childhood*. Regardless of what you say you believe or don't believe at the conscious level, what sort of "god" lives deep down inside you? Unless you've done some very intentional work on developing a more appropriate adult theology, you probably still have that childhood god, that angry, judgmental god, controlling much of what you do at the unconscious level. You need to go down to that secret chamber where *he* (and it almost always *is* a *he*) hides, to walk right up to him and say, "You're not God. You are a cheat and a liar. You do not have my best interests at heart; you are abusive and destructive. You are a false idol, a demon, a satanic image, and I renounce you. I want no more to do with you. You are fired. Get out of my heart."

That, of course, is a very frightening thing to do. Counselors and psychologists who work with severely abused children know that an abused child will fight fiercely to protect the abusing parent.

[1] John Irving, *A Prayer for Owen Meany* (New York: Ballantine Books, 1989), 309–10.

Even when the parent beats and humiliates and rapes the child, the child will cling to the parent, defend the parent: because a *bad* father is better than no father at all. Living with an evil parent is better than feeling like an orphan.

But you can't just flip a switch and replace one God image with another. It is a process of healing, and like healing a wound, it takes time. You have lived with this negative image, probably built it up over the course of your life. You have, at best, fleeting glimpses of alternative images. You have to take a very frightening *leap of faith*. You have to be willing to renounce the false god image, to exorcise that demonic being that lurks deep within your soul, and the terrible fear is that *nothing* will replace it.

It is rather like coming out. You see glimpses of a whole new world, an exciting world, a world where you truly belong, a world where you may really be able to live and love. But to get there, you must acknowledge who you are, and that means renouncing who you are *not* but may have pretended to be over the years—especially your early years, when your god image was formed. It means leaving behind everything that is familiar and comfortable.

It is a scary thing to do. The risk *is* great, but the reward is even greater. You just might find a God you can truly believe in.

Trying on Some New Images of God

It is impossible to think about God at all without images. Whatever the objective reality of God may be, we must resort to inadequate metaphors to describe God. Even if you have had a mystical experience, a direct apprehension of God, you have to turn to metaphors to describe it. The writings of the mystics are filled with their frustration at trying to put what is essentially a nonverbal understanding into words. Let's preface this section, then, with a caveat: We are talking about *images* of God, and none of these images can exhaust the *reality* of God. It is not an "anything goes" proposition. It is certainly legitimate to determine whether your images are true or false—and you need to remember that each image you come up with, however true it is, is only a *part* of the reality of the Living God.

God as Female

We'll discuss this in much more detail in the next chapter, but let's take a moment to think about it here. What happened with the metaphor of God as Father is that the church forgot it was a metaphor and began taking it too literally. As we saw in the discussion of the Lord's Prayer, when Jesus used the image of God as *Abba* or Daddy, he was conveying God's intimacy and tenderness, not God's *maleness*. The early church adopted that image, of God as a loving, intimate parent. But in later centuries, the image became frozen into an idol, and Christians began to think that God was literally Father, which of course meant God was male. But there have always been images of God as female in the Judeo-Christian tradition. For instance, the Book of Deuteronomy uses for God a metaphor of a mother eagle teaching her young to fly. Ironically, in the 1611 "King James" Version, the feminine pronouns were used in this passage, but the contemporary Revised Standard Version rendered the pronouns neuter—although it retained the male pronouns for God in other references. In the King James translation, the passage read:

> *As an eagle stirreth up her nest, fluttereth over her young, spreadeth abroad her wings, taketh them, beareth them on her wings: so the Lord alone did lead Jacob. . . .* [2]

Jesus spoke of Wisdom, one aspect of God, as feminine and referred to himself as feeling like a mother hen. The Apostle Paul wrote of God's groaning in labor to give birth to the creation. Virginia Ramey Mollenkott's *The Divine Feminine* lists more than fifteen such feminine images from the pages of the canonical scriptures, from God as Mother Bear to Bakerwoman God. [3]

Just try, for a while, substituting feminine pronouns for the usual masculine ones when you talk about God. You don't have to say "Goddess"; "God" *is* a gender-neutral word. The next time

[2]Deuteronomy 32:11.
[3]Virginia Ramey Mollenkott, *The Divine Feminine: The Biblical Imagery of God as Female* (New York: Crossroad, 1983).

someone mentions God, saying something like "The Lord moves in mysterious ways," try responding with "Yes, she certainly does." Or use the familiar table blessing with a pronoun switch: For these and all her mercies, God's holy name be blessed and praised . . . When I preside at a Eucharist, I like to alter the familiar offertory sentence, the invitation to Communion, softening the image of God as "Lord" by changing the pronouns: Ascribe to the Lord the honor due her Name; bring offerings and come into her courts.

Get a hymnal and go through all the hymns you know, changing the male language to female:

Crown Her with many crowns . . .
My Shepherdess will supply my need, Jehovah is Her name . . .
Almighty Mother, strong to save . . .
God is working Her purpose out, as year succeeds to year . . .
Because She lives, I can face tomorrow . . .
Praise God, from whom all blessings flow; praise Her all creatures here below . . .

Re-visioning God as female can be especially life-giving for women. Given the astronomical incidence of sexual abuse in our society—the fact that one in four women has been sexually abused by her father or another male relative—learning to think of God as female may be the only way some women can have any sort of relationship with her. I think gay men can benefit from the experience, too. A gay priest I know often refers to God as "the Old Girl," implying an image of God as a tough, crusty old lesbian. I first started using feminine pronouns in my God-talk for their shock value, occasionally dropping them into sermons and liturgies just to hear the conservatives gasp. But very quickly, I found changing the language changes the image. I began to think of God as female—not exclusively; I still use male images of God, too—but the occasional use of female images has changed who God is for me and how I relate to her. (My favorite female God image, by the way, is modeled closely on Oprah Winfrey. Whoopi Goldberg suggests a good God image, too—especially since I heard her *preach* once—no kidding—in the Cathedral of St. John the Divine.)

God as Grandmother

Everyone's life experience is different, of course, but if you're like the majority of us, you probably had a more loving, less ambiguous relationship with your grandmother than with either your mother or your father.

My conversion to female God images came about, as conversions usually do, reluctantly. I was visiting Union Seminary in New York as a prospective student. The whole idea of using gender-inclusive language in worship was still very new, and I was from Dallas, where it wasn't even seriously discussed. Our tour of the seminary ended with the chapel. It happened to be women's history week, so the chapel service was planned and directed by the women's caucus. "Oh, no," I thought. "This is going to be one of those weird pagan goddess-worship things."

But in place of a sermon, a woman led us through a guided meditation, in which she asked us to remember and honor those women who had been important in our lives. I instantly thought of my grandmother, and it suddenly struck me: The person in my life who has consistently offered me the closest thing I have ever experienced to truly unconditional love is not my father or mother or lover, but my grandmother. I have warm childhood memories of Grannie cooking in the kitchen, sewing clothes for me, singing Baptist hymns and honky-tonk songs as she worked. But the warmest memories are of her always loving, always caring, always positive. No matter what she was doing, Grannie never seemed too busy to spend time with me. While my father seemed to be always working, and my mother was often too busy with her own work, I can't remember Grannie ever telling me not to bother her.

One characteristic of God's nature you should affirm as an article of faith is that God's love for you is absolutely unconditional. God loves you, period. That is a given. You can do, or did do, absolutely nothing to *earn* God's love; you can do nothing to make God love you *more;* and you can do nothing to make God *stop* loving you. God, the Relentless Lover, never gives up on you. Affirm that as creed; believe in it as strongly as you believe the sun will rise in the east tomorrow.

If God is unconditional love, then for some of us, God the Grandmother is a much more viable image than God the Father. The gospels tell us that at Jesus' baptism, which marked the beginning of his mission, the heavens opened and God's voice said, "This is my beloved son, with whom I am well pleased." For many of us, it is difficult if not impossible to imagine our fathers ever saying to us, "You are my beloved child. I am proud of you."

When I came out, it was Grannie who accepted it first. It didn't take her long to begin asking about my lover when she called on the phone. When I took my lover to my family's lake property, my parents got in the car and drove back home. My grandmother shrugged her shoulders and said, "Well, it's their loss. We'll have a nice weekend," and then acted as a gracious hostess to us. The only time my parents ever came to visit me in my own city after I came out, they stayed in a hotel room in another part of town—away from the gay ghetto. My grandparents, on the other hand, were honored to stay with my lover and me, as they were honored to have us in their home. My grandmother keeps in touch with both of my ex-lovers, and when I have been with a lover at Christmas, she has always sent him a gift.

So it was a major spiritual breakthrough for me when, thanks to participating in a feminist liturgy, I allowed myself to be open to the image of God the Grandmother. It is God the Grandmother, warm, wise, loving, and fat, who holds me and strokes my hair and soothes me in my darkest hours. Whenever I am engaged in an important or difficult project, it is God the Grandmother, my biggest fan, who is sitting in the front row applauding enthusiastically, and waiting for me afterward, beaming, "I knew you could do it! You are my beloved grandchild. I'm proud of you!"

I hope you have a loving grandmother in your past. Maybe you experienced unconditional love from a grandfather or an aunt or even a teacher. Whoever in your life came closest to offering you unconditional love can be a model for one very useful, healing new God image.

God the Lover

Theologian Dorothee Solle has urged us to dispense with *all* parental images of God—Mother as well as Father—because they imply an unhealthy dependence.[4] After all, we see an important part of the psychological maturing process to be breaking away from one's parents and becoming emotionally independent. Isn't it a form of psychological reversion to go to church week after week to pray for and sing of total dependence on God? And simply changing the gender of the pronouns won't change that.

By imaging God as Lover, you can dare to leave the parental imagery behind altogether, risking a new maturity of faith that is not dependent upon a God who takes care of you. To image God as Lover is to dare to recover that revolutionary *intimacy* with the divine that Jesus evoked with *Abba,* but which, in our society, could never be done with a parental image. Also, to speak of God as the Divine Lover is to do something no inclusive-language liturgy I have yet seen can do: It can simultaneously evoke in the worshipers images of God that are male and female—depending on their sexual orientation.

There is quite a bit of precedent in Christian history for imaging God as Lover, but it tends to be swept under the ecclesiastical rug. Almost invariably, it is the Christian mystics who turn to the erotic language of lovers to describe their relationship with God—and, more often than not, mystics whose contributions to spirituality and theology are considered somewhat marginal by the church. You are probably familiar with the famous Bernini statue *The Ecstasy of St. Teresa,* portraying Teresa slumped across a couch, clutching her chest, and looking exactly as if she's in the throes of an orgasm. The diarist Boswell is reported to have sniffed upon viewing the statue, "If that's the beatific vision, I've seen it before!"

[4]Solle, *Beyond Mere Obedience,* 17, 37.

The Song of Songs, a long poem celebrating the love and eroticism between two people who are identified as a bride and a bridegroom, is a part of both Jewish and Christian canons of scripture. However, it is so overwhelmingly erotic that it has embarrassed and perplexed both rabbinic and Christian commentators, who have for centuries found inventive ways of explaining it away. The lectionary in the Book of Common Prayer, setting out scripture readings for two cycles of Morning and Evening Prayer and three cycles of Sunday and feast-day Eucharists, does not include even one selection from the Song of Songs (but the most violent Psalms about bashing the heads of your enemies are, of course, included).

About the only way the church has tolerated erotic language for spiritual experience has been when those using such language have taken vows of celibacy. It's okay for monks and nuns to speak of God as the Divine Lover because it tends to sound like some sort of spiritual sublimation—the ecclesiastical equivalent of playing volleyball to keep your mind off your raging hormones.

One of the greatest gifts queers can give the church is a graceful blending of sexuality and spirituality—to have the courage, as people who are *not* celibate but actively "practicing" our sexuality (as they call it), to point out the erotic dimension to the spiritual journey. While society has chosen to define us by "what we do in bed," we have turned that around and claimed it by celebrating our bodies and our sexuality in ways that often frighten heterosexuals. *God's Fierce Whimsy,* a book by a group of feminist theologians, speaks of the church's amusing fascination with "the terrible, titillating lesbian."[5] We are a frankly sexual people, *and* we are a deeply spiritual people. We can model for straight Christians how these two realms can come together.

In order to do so, we must dare to image God as the Divine Lover. You can dare to know and to proclaim that the yearning you feel for a human lover is a gleaming icon of the yearning you feel for God; that the curious interplay between the opposite urges of wanting to lose yourself totally in another and wanting to more

---

[5]The Mud Flower Collective, *God's Fierce Whimsy: Christian Feminism and Theological Education* (New York: Pilgrim Press, 1985), 180.

The NORTHSHIRE BOOKSTORE
is dedicated to the art of browsing.
We want your visit to be pleasant
and comfortable. We are always
ready to help with your selection
and will gladly special order any
title in print. We also search for
out-of-print titles and we ship
anywhere in the world.

Our CHILDREN'S DEPARTMENT
is a complete store within a store,
highly acclaimed throughout
New England and beyond for its
breadth, friendly atmosphere and
knowledgeable staff.

NORTHSHIRE BUSINESS BOOKS
offers a wide variety of business-
related titles and the expertise to
help you choose among them.

Our MUSIC DEPARTMENT is
known for its outstanding selection
in classical, jazz and contemporary
tapes and CDs.

We also carry a complete line of fine
stationery and cards.

HOURS

Sunday-Thursday	10:00-5:30
Friday	10:00-9:00
Saturday	10:00-7:00

Address correspondence to:

NORTHSHIRE BOOKSTORE
P.O. Box 2200
Manchester Center, VT 05255

clearly define yourself in the context of your love is the same interplay you feel in prayer and meditation. You must take the risk of finding in your human experiences of love and sex new images of God—whether they be male images of filling, penetrating, thrusting, and finally spilling out your very life into the other; or more feminine images of exploring the dark, secret, and safe places of the other.

As the Divine Lover, it is God who seeks you out, God who *cruises* you, if you will, who seduces you. And this Divine Lover is absolutely *relentless* in her pursuit of you. No matter how often you are unfaithful to him, he always returns. No matter how indifferent or insensitive you may be to her love, she never quits loving you. No matter how you ignore and insult him, he never gives up. Whether or not you have a human lover, you are constantly being pursued by God, the Relentless Lover, whose desire for you is so strong it is, in the words of the Bible, "as strong as death."

The Relentless Lover never turns her back on you, but you often turn away from him. One of the ways the church has tried to soften the erotic impact of the Song of Songs is to see it as "a metaphor of God's love for the church." According to this interpretation, we are to see God as the bridegroom and the church as the bride in the drama. It was the ever-prophetic Julian of Norwich who suggested that that interpretation should be turned on end: You can read the Song of Songs by seeing God as the bride, and yourself as the bridegroom. Hear, then, with Julian's ears, this passage of the Word of God from the Song of Songs, a passage that is brimming with female erotic imagery:

> *My beloved put his hand to the latch, and my heart was thrilled within me . . .*

You see, Julian is saying something fascinating about God—that God is "thrilled" when you seek out relationship.

> *My beloved put his hand to the latch, and my heart was thrilled within me. I arose to open to my beloved, and my hands*

dripped with myrrh, my fingers with liquid myrrh, upon the handles of the bolt. I opened to my beloved, but my beloved had turned and gone.[6]

In other words, in Julian's view, you tease God. You flirt and arouse, then turn your back and go, leaving the Divine Lover broken-hearted. But the Relentless Lover always gives you another chance, always seeks you out. The choice is yours.

The God Who Suffers

If you were taught anything at all about God by any sort of religious institution, you were probably taught that God is omnipotent. *Omnipotent* is a funny, archaic word, one of those words that aren't used much except in a religious context—although Lily Tomlin, in her persona of Ernestine, the telephone operator, did tell a customer (Gore Vidal) that the phone company is omnipotent. ("That's *potent,* with an *omni* in front of it," she explained.) God, in classical theology, is a being of unlimited power and might. Because this God has all the power, he calls all the shots and makes all the rules, and you'd better like them or else. A Christian hymn sums up this feeling:

> *Take what he gives*
> *and praise him still,*
> *through good or ill,*
> *whoever lives!*[7]

As Dorothee Solle has pointed out, this view of God constitutes a "sadomasochistic" spirituality.[8] In this view, sometimes God gives us incredible gifts and showers us with love; other times God kicks us in the teeth—but we are to love and praise God in either case. God, according to this classical view, sounds rather like an abusive parent.

[6]Song of Songs 5:4–6, rendered inclusive.
[7]See the Hymnal 1982 (according to the use of the Episcopal Church), no. 625. The hymn is known as "Ye Holy Angels Bright."
[8]Solle, *Beyond Mere Obedience,* 17, 37. Believe me, I am not opposed to S/M sex play; but an S/M spirituality strikes me as extremely unhealthy!

Because the God of classical theology sat alone at the very top of the power pyramid, he was also viewed as being absolutely self-sufficient and independent, a tough guy who needs nothing and no one. Traditional theology affirms that God is personal, but then typically goes on to construct a concept of God that is anything but personal. One of the "attributes of God" catalogued by Thomas Aquinas (who derived it from Augustine, who, in turn, derived it from Aristotle) is what is known as *aseity*. God is the First Cause who has no other cause, who *needs* no other cause, and is therefore the "Prime Mover Unmoved." The bulk of Christian theology has continued to affirm this doctrine. Søren Kierkegaard, for instance, the nineteenth-century Lutheran theologian, calls the notion that God needs us "absurd":

> This is stupidity, for God needs no man. It would otherwise be a highly embarrassing thing to be a creator, if the result was that the creator came to depend upon the creature.[9]

Feminist theologian Catherine Keller has criticized this stance as symptomatic of the distortions of a male-dominated theology:

> But why should this be? Why is it so stupid, so embarrassing, to imagine a creator interdependent with the creation? Quite clearly because this God is to stay absolutely self-sufficient, independent of the world. He has created and so reigns in utter omnipotence. . . . Our love is absolute dependence; his love an infinite transcendence. In our culture this God could only take the pronoun *he*.[10]

For myself, I have completely rejected the notion of God's omnipotence, and I hope to convince you to do the same. There is a compelling theological reason and even more compelling personal reason to do so. The school of thought known as process theology is an outgrowth of the philosophy of Alfred North Whitehead,

[9]Søren Kierkegaard, *Concluding Unscientific Postscript* (Princeton: Princeton University Press, for the American-Scandinavian Foundation, 1941/1944), 122.
[10]Catherine Keller, *From a Broken Web: Separation, Sexism, and Self* (Boston: Beacon Press, 1986), 35.

known more broadly as "process thought." In contrast to the static, fixed view of the world of traditional theology that sees God's laws as being immutable, process theology sees the entire universe as evolving. Human beings, nature, and even God herself are constantly changing, constantly in process. In the process view, God does not "rule" or coerce the creation, but relates to you and to the world through love and persuasion. God coaxes, coaches, even *seduces* you to move in a particular direction, but never forces you to do so. Although God has a particular plan for the universe and for you, you and all creatures are always free to accept or reject that plan. The God envisioned by process theology is a far cry from the traditional view of God as an omnipotent, absolute, and often whimsical king of the universe.

The personal reason for rejecting an omnipotent God is AIDS. AIDS has been a great teacher for all of us. We are not, of course, the first generation to experience widespread human suffering and death. There have been other plagues—but this one is ours, our special challenge, our particular lesson; and it teaches us something important about God. Nearly everyone except a few Fundamentalist crazies (both Protestant and Catholic) rejects the idea that God "sent" AIDS into the world. However, if you really see God as "omnipotent," as a sort of cosmic puppeteer pulling the strings of all the universe, then the idea that God created AIDS is an inevitable conclusion. At the very least, even if you don't think God *created* AIDS, but you believe God is all-powerful, then you have to ask why God continues to allow AIDS to exist. Why doesn't a divine thunderclap simply blow the virus out of existence? Sometimes people try to hold on to a view of a God who is "almighty" and still loving by saying, "God has a purpose in all this. We just can't see it." But the very act of allowing sickness and death for some inscrutable "hidden purpose" would constitute unspeakable cruelty on God's part.

The only answer to the question of why God doesn't wipe out AIDS is that God just doesn't work that way. The solution is to affirm that God is *not* in fact omnipotent—at least, not in the way the word is usually meant. God so values the free will of the universe that she refuses to force or coerce any of her creatures into any choice. This awesome free will, process theology affirms, extends to all of creation, not just humans. It extends to the molecular level and certainly to the level of viruses. A virus, too, has the freedom to choose—and HIV is choosing to assert itself and live, at the expense of its human hosts. You can affirm that God is *disappointed* and *hurt* by the current animosity between HIV and the human race, and that God is constantly coaxing and urging a different direction. But it is not in the nature of God to "wipe out" a virus or a human tyrant or a natural process. God never coerces any of her creatures.

The corollary of this alternate view of God is that while it is not in the nature of God to "fix" things for us, to make AIDS or any of our other troubles "go away," it is very much in the nature of God to suffer with us. This is a reversal of the classical theological position. Thomas Aquinas wrote, "To sorrow, therefore, over the misery of others belongs not to God, but it does most properly belong to him to dispel that misery."[11] I am claiming just the opposite: *To dispel the misery of others belongs not to God, but it does most properly belong to God to sorrow over that misery.*

Jewish theologian and storyteller Elie Wiesel is not a process thinker as such, but a story he tells beautifully illustrates the concept of a creative-responsive God. Wiesel writes of his experience in a concentration camp. After an apparent insurrection attempt, three prisoners are hanged, one of them a young boy. As they are dying, the other prisoners are forced to march past them. As the march begins, a prisoner behind Wiesel asks, "Where is God? Where is He?"

> Then the march past began. The two adults are no longer alive. Their tongues hung swollen, blue-tinged. But the third rope was still moving; being so light, the child was still alive. . . .
>
> For more than half an hour he stayed there, struggling between life and death, dying in slow agony under our eyes. And we had to look him full in the face. He was still alive when I passed in front of him. His tongue was still red, his eyes not yet glazed.

[11]*Summa* I, Q. 21, art. 3, answer.

Behind me, I heard the same man asking:
"Where is God now?"
And I heard a voice within me answer him:
"Where is He? Here He is—He is hanging here on this
gallows. . . ."[12]

For the Christian, the cruel execution of another Jewish prisoner by crucifixion is the ultimate icon of God's compassion, God's
suffering with the world.

Two of my favorite hymns affirm this theme of God's suffering
with us. One, which begins, "There's a wideness in God's mercy,"
states:

> *There is no place where earth's sorrows*
> *are more felt than up in heaven.*[13]

The other, "God is love," asserts:

> *And when human hearts are breaking*
> *under sorrow's iron rod,*
> *then we find that self-same aching*
> *deep within the heart of God.*[14]

Officially, holding the belief that God suffers with you is a
heresy—but hey, as a queer Christian, heresy is where you live. In
the third century, the catholic bishops said that Patripassianism, the
belief that God the Father is capable of suffering and passion, is
heretical. But why would you want to be in any sort of relationship
with a "passionless" being? Expressing devoted love to a God (or
anyone) who doesn't need you, and isn't moved by your sorrows
and joys, should strike you as psychologically and spiritually unhealthy. So confess it: You're a heretic. Remember that the root
meaning of heresy is *choice;* so you might even take pride in being
theologically prochoice!

[12]Elie Wiesel, *Night* (New York: Bantam, 1982), 76.
[13]Episcopal Church hymnal, nos. 469, 470.
[14]Episcopal Church hymnal, no. 379.

7
MARY

The Divine Feminine

When I eschewed my Fundamentalist background and became a (very) High Church Episcopalian, one of my first pious acts was to acquire a statue of Mary for my apartment. I admit it was at least partly to pique my Fundamentalist friends and family, but I also think there was a deeper (although at the time unconscious) reason. I have always been drawn to what Mary represents: the feminine aspect of God.

As a child, I had a recurring dream that was so vivid at first I didn't know it was a dream. I was with my parents at a fair. Across the aisle from us was a fortune-teller's booth. I wanted very badly to go to the fortune-teller, and I asked my parents to take me there. Suddenly, the aisles were roped off for a fencing demonstration, which prevented our crossing over. When the fencing match was finished, the fortune-teller had gone. I have a vivid image of the fortune-teller, sitting in her booth of purple and deep blue velvet drapes decorated with a crescent moon and stars, holding her crystal ball. Years later, when I learned to read tarot cards, I was shocked to find the image of the High Priestess was so similar to my fortune-teller—the blue drapes, the crescent moon, the crystal orb. I now know my childhood dream was a classical image of the

Goddess. It was also rich in traditional imagery of Mary—the color blue, the orb of the world she is often depicted holding, and the moon and stars. Catholics take a verse of the Book of Revelation to be an image of Mary, in her cosmic manifestation as the Queen of Heaven: "a woman clothed with the sun, with the moon under her feet, and on her head a crown of twelve stars."[1]

My dream of this woman who so obviously symbolized Mary and/or the Mother Goddess is all the more remarkable because growing up in a Fundamentalist home in an overwhelmingly Fundamentalist culture where displays of catholic piety were suppressed by strong social taboos, I would never have encountered these traditional symbols. I believe the dream was a direct revelation of God herself; and a warning not to let strife (the sword fight) keep me from reaching her.

Protestants, for the most part, are terrified of Mary. Protestant churches may be named after the most obscure saints, such as Matthias, a minor character in scripture, about whom we know almost nothing; but they will never call their parish "St. Mary's." Among Episcopalians, Mary is a sort of rallying point, a dividing line. If you see an Episcopal church with a statue of Mary in it, you can bet it's a "high" catholic parish. Low Church Episcopalians tell a joke about this:

Father Edgar Wells, the rector of the Church of St. Mary the Virgin in New York, died and arrived at the pearly gates. St. Peter was busy with paperwork and didn't notice him. Father Wells cleared his throat. St. Peter looked up. "Yes?"

"I'm Father Edgar Wells, rector of St. Mary's. I expect to be admitted."

St. Peter looked at his appointment book. "We're not expecting you."

"What do you mean you're not expecting me? Do you know who I am? I am Father Edgar Wells, the rector of the Church of St. Mary the Virgin."

[1] Revelation 12:1.

St. Peter checked again. "I'm sorry, I don't have your name here."

"Then there is obviously some mistake," Father Wells said. "Please check with your superiors."

St. Peter shrugged, picked up the phone, and called Jesus. "There's a guy here named Edgar Wells, says he's a priest from New York. He wants to come in, but I don't have him on my list. Do you know him?"

Jesus thinks for a moment. "Edgar Wells . . . New York . . . ?" He snaps his fingers. "Oh, yes, let him in—he's a friend of Mother's."

Among the Southern Baptists with whom I grew up, a favorite proof that Catholics are evil was "They worship Mary, you know."

Well, of course, if you went to Catholic school, or attended catechism classes in an anglo-catholic parish, you know that is not accurate. Catholic children learned the answer to give when their protestant peers charged them with Mary-worship: "We *venerate* the Virgin Mary; we *worship* only God." And actually, this distinction between *veneration* and *worship,* as legalistic and contrived as it may sound, was originally suggested in the eighth century by the theologian John of Damascus. During the iconoclast controversy, John distinguished between the *respect* or *veneration* shown to created objects that point us toward God (such as icons, crosses, the gospel book, and the altar) and the true *worship,* which is reserved for God alone. John was refuting the Manichaeistic heresy, which held that matter was essentially evil, by affirming the sacramental principle—that material objects can lead us to God.

But the truth is, it's largely a semantic argument. In fact, it is really impossible to worship God at all without directing your worship through some intermediary-created object—even if it's only your own mental construct of God. And in popular religion, in the "operational theology," the theology that really lives and works in the hearts of the people, there's not much distinction between veneration and worship. People have worshiped Mary for centuries, and will continue to for centuries to come, because the worship of Mary meets a deep psychic need.

Fertility, Not Virginity

In southern New Jersey, for example, there is a large Roman Catholic population that is also largely poor and uneducated, and therefore not exposed to current theological thought. About half the families on any given street have statues of Mary in their gardens (often in an upended old bathtub!). The idea that Mary can bless your garden has almost nothing to do with her mundane role as the mother of Jesus, and nothing at all to do with anything we know about Mary from the scriptures. But it has everything to do with her cosmic role as the Holy Birthgiver, as Gaia, goddess of the earth and the source of all fertility. Just as Jesus has both a mundane and a cosmic role, as the carpenter from Nazareth and as the cosmic Christ, so does Mary have a dual role. In her mundane aspect, she is the mother of Jesus. In her cosmic aspect, she is the Mother of us all.

The frank worship of Mary would bring a tremendous spiritual healing for us because Mary is much more than just the mother of Jesus, she is the Goddess herself—or given the Christian commitment to monotheism, it is more precise to say she is the feminine manifestation of the one God/dess. It is the legacy of centuries of the Mary cult, kept alive mostly because the people demanded it, that can rescue Christianity from its hypermasculinity.

The Protestant Reformers tried to obliterate Mary's popularity, and the Catholic Church itself tried to keep the strong folk tradition of "mariolatry" in check by making that belabored "worship/venerate" distinction. But the people kept right on worshiping Mary because they instinctively knew they needed the Goddess. Now that you don't risk being burned at the stake as a witch, you can bring out of the closet your frank veneration (or worship) of Mary.

But not, Goddess forbid, the *virgin* Mary!

The original Mother Goddess was never thought of as a virgin—that was a typically sex-negative Christian invention. The Goddess was venerated for her fertility and her motherhood—in fact, her worship often involved sexual rituals. The scriptural reference that has been used to justify all this virginity business about Mary is probably a mistranslation, anyway. Isaiah 7:14, the prophecy of the Messiah, is no doubt familiar to you in the King James Version. It is the text that opens Handel's *Messiah:*

> *Behold, a virgin shall conceive, and bear a son, and call his name Emmanuel, God with us.*

But in the Revised Standard Version, which is actually a very conservative, literal translation, that verse reads:

> *Behold, a young woman shall conceive and bear a son, and call his name Immanuel.*

If Christian orthodoxy states that Jesus Christ was fully human—and to be a human being means to have forty-six chromosomes, twenty-three inherited from each of your parents—then how could Jesus be fully human without the twenty-three chromosomes from Joseph? The opening of the Gospel of Matthew, concerned to show that Jesus is a direct descendant of both Abraham and David, does it by tracing *Joseph's* genealogy, asserting that because he is *Joseph's* son, Jesus is in the royal lineage.

The Mother of God

The emphasis on Mary's virginity was a twelfth-century development, a part of a general sex-negative trend in the church that happened around the same time priests were first required to be celibate and the church began to persecute queers. That is a part of the tradition surrounding Mary we need not celebrate. At any rate, whatever you believe about how the Incarnation of Jesus was accomplished, Mary is clearly not venerated because of her virginity, she is venerated because of her *motherhood.* An early ecumenical council officially decided to call Mary the *Theotokos,* which is Greek for "the God-bearer." In English, *Theotokos* is usually translated "Mother of God."

But beware: Even the aspect of Marian devotion that celebrates

Mary as an archetypal symbol of the feminine has both its positive and negative sides. The negative side is that Mary as the great symbol of the Perfect Woman has suffered much the same fate women in general have suffered throughout history. She is sentimentalized, put on a high pedestal, thought of as sweet and gentle and loving—but also as remote and protected, like a princess secure in her castle. An entirely male (and as some scholars have noted, often largely *gay* male) clergy and church hierarchy used the symbol of Mary for the cathexis of their unfinished emotional business with all the women in their lives. It is then that we get some of the most cloyingly sentimental prayers addressed to Mary:

> *Mother undefiled*
> *Mother most amiable*
> *Mother most admirable*
> *Virgin most faithful*
> *Vessel of honor*
> *Mystical rose*
> *Tower of ivory*
> *House of gold*
> *Morning Star*
> *Queen of the Angels*
> *Harbor of the shipwrecked*
> *Treasure of the faithful*

Can't you just see all that on a Hallmark Mother's Day card?

But the *positive* aspect of seeing Mary as the symbol of universal femininity is that regardless of what the church taught about Mary through the centuries, what really went on with the people in their practice of religion was that through the worship of Mary, they kept alive their devotion to the Goddess, which had been officially banished by our male-dominated religion. When so-called Christian "missionaries" thundered into a new territory and violently suppressed the folk religion, they were almost always suppressing the worship of a central Mother Goddess. And so the people kept right on worshiping the Mother Goddess, but just began referring to her as the Blessed Virgin Mary, and everyone was happy. Sometimes the church even encouraged this substitution, by building shrines to Mary in places that had been shrines to the Goddess, or by celebrating major Christian festivals on the days that were sacred to the Goddess. The primary feast of Mary, celebrated as The Assumption by Roman Catholics and The Feast of St. Mary the Virgin by Episcopalians, falls within a few days of the ancient feast of the birthday of Isis. Much of the liturgy associated with Mary, including her lists of titles such as "Queen of Heaven" and "Morning Star," was lifted directly from the liturgy of the Goddess worship. Some of the elements of Marian iconography that seem strange and foreign to us are vestiges of the symbolism of the Mother Goddess—the most notable being the snake and the crescent moon that are often under her feet. The temple of Gaia was guarded by a python, and the moon, ruler of the night, is associated with the Mother Goddess in almost all of her various cultural manifestations.

From the beginning of the modern period of religious scholarship, up until very recently, liturgical scholars, both Catholic and Protestant, tended to see all this as a very bad thing—at best superstitious, and at worst idolatrous. But then feminist Christian scholars began to write and speak about this phenomenon, and they began to point out that the reason people have been so tenacious about Marian devotion is that it speaks to our deep psychic needs, our profound religious needs. We *need* a feminine image of the deity. The symbol of Mary or of the Mother Goddess strikes a resounding chord in our souls because it says something important and true about God. Intellectually, people may assent to an all-male Trinity, but in our hearts, we know better.

Holy Wisdom

As we saw in the last chapter, there have always been feminine images of God in both the Hebrew and Christian scriptures, but an all-male hierarchy fixated upon the masculine images and suppressed the feminine. There is, for instance, the Wisdom tradition.

The Book of Wisdom, one of the "apocryphal" or intertestamental books, speaks of Wisdom, always identified as feminine, as though she is a part of the godhead:

> *With thee* [God] *is wisdom, who knows thy works and was present when thou didst make the world. . . .*[2]

The affirmation that Wisdom was present at the creation of the world is in the same sort of language that is used of both Christ and the Holy Spirit. So you might well wonder why those two, together with the Creator, get to be the Trinity. Wisdom might just as well be included as an essential part of God, giving us what Carl Jung said Christianity needs to make it more holistic: an androgynous *quaternity* rather than an all-male *trinity*.[3]

Wisdom is also celebrated in an ancient hymn as the liberator of the oppressed:

> *A holy people and a blameless race Wisdom delivered from a nation of oppressors. . . .*
> *She brought them over the Red Sea, and led them through deep waters;*
> *but she drowned their enemies, and cast them up from the depth of the sea.*[4]

But the early church *fathers* (which is a quite accurate description of them) decided upon a trinity, not a quaternity, and Christianity ended up with a totally male godhead—"the three men I admire the most, the Father, Son, and Holy Ghost." And so the veneration of Mary, the Mother of Jesus, kept us in touch with the divine feminine during a period of male hierarchical domination that tried to suppress it. Mary paved the way for our current understanding that it is restrictive to address and image God as only male; that we need to recover feminine pronouns and images for God as well.

[2]Wisdom 9:9.
[3]See Wallace B. Clift, *Jung and Christianity: The Challenge of Reconciliation* (New York: Crossroad, 1983), 132–33.
[4]Wisdom 9:15, 18–19.

Priests and Priestesses of Gaia

Queers need the Goddess more than anyone. We have, in dozens of cultures, been closely associated with her worship and devotion. The very word *gay* is probably derived from the Greek name of the earth goddess Gaia. As Judy Grahn writes, "Western homosexual people truly deserve to consider themselves the children of Gaia, having kept her name alive for thirty or forty centuries after her fall from grace, mostly by word of mouth."[5] Gay Roman Catholic priest and theologian John McNeill arrives at roughly the same conclusion from a very different perspective. "I have always had a strong intuition that there is a special relationship between Mary and those of us who are lesbian and gay," he wrote.[6] Perhaps, as the joke suggests, we have a special vocation to be "friends of the Mother." As Christian queers, we can recover our ancient office as the votaries of the Goddess (and do penance for the church's attempt to repress her worship) by celebrating the place of Mary in the Christian tradition. I have a collection of ear studs to wear in my pierced right ear, and my favorite is a silver crescent moon. It has astrological significance as my ruling planet (I am a Cancer), but I also see it as a symbol of Mary/Gaia, the Goddess whose priest I aspire to be.

Sadly, the Rev. Elder Troy Perry, founder of the Metropolitan Community Church, recently betrayed his Fundamentalist roots by declaring, at the General Conference of the MCC in July 1991 in Phoenix, "I do not believe goddess worship is consistent with the Christian church."[7] Perry's statement, I believe, constitutes a sort of prior restraint on the Holy Spirit, who I believe is calling many Christians, and especially queer Christians, to the task of integrating the goddess worship with Christianity.

It is not simply the worship of Mary that is empowering for us, however, but the worship of Mary *and* our conscious understanding that whom we are actually worshiping is Gaia, the goddess, the divine feminine. Buying into the official party line and venerating

[5] Judy Grahn, *Another Mother Tongue: Gay Words, Gay Worlds* (Boston: Beacon Press, 1984), 105.
[6] McNeill, *Taking a Chance on God,* 137.
[7] Reported in *Bay Windows* (Boston), August 1, 1991, 4.

Mary the virgin, "Mary most lowly," helps promote Christian sex-negativity and helps keep the marginalized on the margins. A recent book by a group of feminist theologians, exploring images of the feminine in Christian art, makes a reference to these two views of Mary in its title, *Immaculate and Powerful.*[8] While I commend to you the worship of Mary as an important part of your queer spirituality, it is with the caveat that you not worship the docile, quiet, weak, perpetual virgin, but the awesome, powerful, beautiful, and fertile Queen of Heaven.

---

[8]Clarissa W. Atkinson, Constance H. Buchanan, and Margaret R. Miles, *Immaculate and Powerful: The Female in Sacred Image and Social Reality* (Boston: Beacon Press, 1985).

8

JESUS THE CHRIST

Our Elder Brother

It may sound rather obvious to say, but you can't practice Christian spirituality without dealing with Jesus Christ. Christianity is the only world religion so absolutely built around one person. He is not simply a prophet of the religion, like Muhammad; or a teacher of the religion, like the Buddha; or an ancestor, like Moses. For Christianity, Jesus, the Christ, *is* the religion. We had a slogan when I was a peripheral member of the early seventies' "Jesus Movement": *Christianity is a relationship, not a religion.* It is a relationship with Jesus—both in the cosmic sense of the risen Christ and in the mundane sense of the Galilean rabbi.

Much of Christian thought and speculation over the past twenty centuries has wrestled with this tension between the Cosmic Christ and the man from Galilee. In theological language, this debate is called christology, "discourse about Christ." Christologies are classified as "low" or "high," depending on which of these two concepts of Jesus Christ is emphasized. A "high" christology, also called a christology "from above," emphasizes the Cosmic Christ, whom the Bible calls "the Alpha and the Omega," the beginning and end of all things. A "low" christology, on the other hand, done "from below," places its emphasis on the humanity of Jesus of Nazareth, focusing on the thirty-three years of his life on earth.

Some christologies emphasize one of these concepts to the exclusion of the other. Some Christians think of Jesus as only human, a great teacher; others think of him as divine, as a part of the godhead, and tend to deny the fact he was truly human. The Christian orthodoxy, actually, is supposed to hold the two "natures" of Christ in tension, in absolutely equal balance. According to the classic doctrine, Jesus the Christ is 100 percent human *and* 100 percent divine.

It's meaningless to talk about having a relationship with someone who died two thousand years ago if you think of him as only a human being. The only way you can pull off being what Paul calls "in Christ" is with the Cosmic, Risen Christ, whom you encounter through prayer and meditation.

On the other hand, I want to make a case for doing a christology "from below." Actually, and ironically enough, I am making a case here for retaining the orthodox position, for keeping an equal balance between the humanity and divinity of Jesus. (Not everything that's orthodox has to be rejected. They got some things right!) Actually, those who claim to hold the orthodox position seldom do. In fact, most practicing Christians today believe in the *divinity* of Jesus, but tend to deny his actual *humanity*. To truly keep the balance, to say Jesus was fully human, and yet was God, is a radical act that most contemporary religious people find frightening. Over the centuries, the implications of the doctrine have so disconcerted Christians that they have gradually tilted the balance—and the vast majority of Christians see Jesus as divine to the point of being less than human. They are uncomfortable with being reminded that he was a first-century Jewish rabbi who lived and laughed and loved and probably had dirty toenails.

Consequently, we have lost the startling power of the doctrine of the Incarnation—that God became flesh.

To believe that Jesus is "the son of God," literally that Jesus *is* God, and yet also to believe that he lived thirty-three years on earth as a normal human being—that's a wonderful affirmation of humanity and of the human body. We tend to use *Christ* as though it were Jesus' last name, but in fact it is his *title*. The phrase *Jesus Christ* is an equation; it is a simple creed. *Jesus* is the carpenter-turned-rabbi from Nazareth; *Christ* (from the Greek *christos*) means the Messiah, the anointed one of God. To say *Jesus Christ* is to proclaim that the carpenter from Nazareth with dirty toenails *is* the Messiah, the anointed one, God's chosen instrument. And that was, to the neighbors of the early Christians, a scandalous statement. The next time you find yourself using *Jesus Christ* as a swearword, stop and think that hundreds of first-century Christians were awestruck by the sheer power of the phrase, even died rather than give up the right to proclaim it. I'm not a prude about language—shit, no!—but it seems to me that to use *Jesus Christ* so casually is to dishonor not only Christ, but a host of Christian martyrs. Just as it is the custom in catholic worship to genuflect at the *Incarnatus,* it is also a catholic custom to bow your head slightly whenever you say the words *Jesus Christ,* as a way of honoring the mystery of the divine made human.

Jesus the Sissy

As with our images of God, most of us have been fed such distorted and incorrect information about Jesus that a relationship with him may be difficult to achieve. I couldn't *stand* Jesus when I was a kid! First of all, the pictures of the adolescent Jesus we were shown in Sunday school presented him as what could only be called a sissy. He always wore a dress, and he had longish, curly hair. My internalized (and as yet unidentified) homophobia was such that these traits pushed all my buttons. Then to top it all off, he behaved as a sort of teacher's pet—he always did exactly what adults wanted him to, usually without being told. Who would want this smug, self-righteous little sissy for a friend?

A hymn popular at Christmastime, "Away in a Manger," suggests that this inhuman perfection was exhibited by Jesus from the time he was an infant:

The cattle are lowing,
the baby awakes,
but little Lord Jesus
no crying he makes.[1]

As a child in Sunday school, did you ever wonder why, if Jesus had this halo glowing around his head, anyone ever doubted who he was? It's the same principle—either Jesus was a human being, or he wasn't. If he was, then he certainly didn't have a visible halo,[2] and he certainly did cry as a baby (and as an adult). At first glance, Jesus' ability to work miracles may give you a little trouble, but Jesus himself is recorded as having told his disciples, essentially, "Anything I can do, you can do better." That leaves you with two choices—either you must reject the idea that Jesus did in fact heal the sick, raise the dead, and walk on water; or you must believe *you* are capable of doing the same things (and ask yourself why you aren't!). Personally, I choose the latter option. (More on this in Chapter 19 on healing.)

Casting Jesus

Except for a few works by contemporary artists like Dalí, most of the art depicting the adult Jesus is just as bad as if not worse than that showing of the adolescent Jesus. It's difficult to look at those paintings that portray Jesus as skinny and pale, with long, curly hair and a pained expression on his face, without feeling a sense of revulsion. No life-of-Christ film yet has cast Jesus appropriately.

Whom would I cast? How about Mandy Patinkin? Or better yet, I think, Kevin Kline (aside from being extremely sexy, Kline has a spark of humor that I believe Jesus had). Here is a good exercise: Ask yourself, if you were producing a movie, whom would you want to play Jesus? It helps you get a handle on your current image of him.

---

[1]Episcopal Church hymnal, no. 101.
[2]Actually, the halo, although it became conventionalized in art, was probably an attempt to capture the aura, the energy field that surrounds all human bodies, which in spiritually developed people is strongest around the head. So in a sense, Jesus *did* have a "halo," just as we all do, but his halo, like ours, would be visible only to those who are especially gifted clairvoyants. Still, the point is, clairvoyants who could see an energy field around Jesus could also see one around Judas, or any other human being.

Giving detailed physical descriptions of the people whose actions are described was not customary in the literary style of the gospels. However, a physical description of Jesus is in the Vatican archives. It is a report written by a non-Christian Roman, Publius Lentulus, to the Roman emperor Tiberius, so it is presumably relatively objective. Publius Lentulus' description of Jesus doesn't sound much like Kevin Kline, but it doesn't sound much like those awful paintings, either. He is described as a "tall, well-proportioned man," with hair "the color of new wine" (I assume this means what we might call strawberry blond) and eyes that are gray and "extremely lively." Publius Lentulus even goes so far as to say "his arms are very beautiful" and concludes the description with "He is the handsomest man in the world."[3]

Jesus Had a Penis

It doesn't matter that much what Jesus looked like, except to point out he probably didn't look much like either the Hollywood versions or the Renaissance paintings. Jesus wasn't an effete and otherworldly hermit, but an earthy, lusty, passionate radical. He lived and loved and laughed in Palestine almost two thousand years ago, and he sweated, farted, and urinated.

Father Malcolm Boyd once unintentionally stirred up a hornet's nest when, in response to badgering from an interviewer on national television, he said, "What do I *mean* that Jesus became fully human? Well, I *mean* that Jesus had a head, shoulders, chest, stomach, a penis, legs and feet." Dozens of angry phone calls reached the media and the church hierarchy, and shortly afterward, Father Boyd was fired from his church position. One woman called her bishop and exclaimed wrathfully, "Jesus did *not* have a penis!"[4]

Most Christians don't want to be reminded that Jesus had a penis because most Christians are profoundly sex-negative, and they'd rather not think of Jesus as a sexual being. Okay, pop quiz on Bible knowledge: *Where in the New Testament does it say Jesus was*

---

[3]The document is quoted in full in Jeffrey Furst, ed., *Edgar Cayce's Story of Jesus* (New York: Berkley Books, 1976/1984), 238–39.

[4]Boyd's account of this story can be found in Malcolm Boyd and Nancy L. Wilson, ed., *Amazing Grace: Stories of Lesbian and Gay Faith* (Trumansburg, New York: Crossing Press, 1991).

celibate? Answer: *It doesn't.* The Christian tradition of the celibacy of Jesus grew out of the medieval church's profound discomfort with accepting that Jesus was truly human. Since sexual desire (and experience) is a major part of being human for all but a handful of people, to image Jesus as asexual is a way to keep our distance from him, to deny that he was a real, embodied human being. If you believe Jesus never even had an erection, or never thought about sex, wouldn't you have some trouble using him as a guide for patterning your life? I certainly would!

Jesus Was Gay

In truth, Jesus is a very good guide on whom to pattern your life because you have some major things in common. *I believe that Jesus was gay.* I presented this idea in a sermon once, on Palm Sunday, at the Church of St. John the Evangelist in Boston. I think the rafters are still shaking! Sorry, but I truly believe this with all my heart. Here's why.

First of all, it is remarkable that the Bible does *not* tell us Jesus was married. Sometimes, the folk tradition has paired him up with Mary Magdalene, in the same way your aunt is always trying to pair you up heterosexually with someone—just because straight people can't bear to think of a nice young woman without a man to take care of her, or a handsome young man who doesn't have a girl-friend. William Phipps has even written a book attempting to prove that Jesus was married to Mary Magdalene, arguing that being married was a requirement for a rabbi in those days.[5] I don't think his evidence is convincing—unless you start with his assumption that Jesus was heterosexual, and that is a major assumption. Phipps's point, though, is well-taken: The very fact that the Bible *doesn't* tell us Jesus had a wife is unusual.

Second, there is a mysterious and compelling character in the gospels who is usually referred to as "the disciple Jesus loved." Traditionally, this disciple has been thought of as the Apostle John, the presumed author of the gospel by that name and of the Book of

[5]William E. Phipps, *Was Jesus Married?* (New York: Harper & Row, 1973).

Revelation, because the end of the Gospel of John has a reference to the beloved disciple, and the note, "This is the disciple who is bearing witness to these things, and who has written these things."[6] Yet today, we know that just because the gospel is called John doesn't necessarily mean a man named John wrote it, any more than *Poor Richard's Almanack* was written by someone named Richard. Actually, the Gospel of John takes care *not* to name this disciple, always referring to him as "the disciple Jesus loved."

You may be objecting: *But Jesus loved all his disciples!* Yes, and that is precisely the point. Given the fact that Jesus loved all his disciples, and expected them to love him, it is all the more striking that this one disciple is singled out, identified, as though by title, as the beloved of Jesus. In fact, the scriptures make a point of describing the uniqueness of Jesus' relationship with this particular disciple. It even seems to have caused some jealousy among the others.

For instance, at the Last Supper, this unnamed disciple is "lying close to the breast of Jesus."[7] Removing the religious language, this translates as, he was snuggled up against Jesus' chest. If you have John Boswell's *Christianity, Social Tolerance, and Homosexuality* in your library—and if you don't, you should—get it out right now and turn to the last of the photographs between pages 202 and 203. This fourteenth-century German sculpture of Christ and St. John depicts Jesus, looking thirty-something, with the beloved disciple, looking about twenty, resting his head on Jesus' chest. The sculptor (who I'd be willing to bet was gay) understood perfectly. An even more striking artistic representation of this special relationship is the icon of Jesus and the beloved disciple produced by Bridge Building Icons, a group that specializes in unusual and contemporary subjects painted in the traditional iconographic style. This icon was reproduced in the summer 1991 issue of the gay and lesbian quarterly journal *Out/Look*.[8] (If you live near a "liberal" religious bookstore, such as one run by the Paulist community or by a liberal

[6]John 21:24.
[7]John 13:23.
[8]Issue 13, p. 101. The icon was painted by Robert Lentz for Bridge Building Icons.

seminary, you might be able to find this icon on an inexpensive greeting card.)

And there's more. During the meal, Jesus made the startling announcement to his closest followers, "One of you will betray me." They want to know more, of course, so Peter gets the attention of the beloved disciple and says, "Tell us who it is of whom he speaks."[9] Isn't that interesting? Peter, whom Christian tradition has made the first among the disciples—the holder of the Keys of the Kingdom of God, even the first pope—seems to have less intimate information from Jesus than the beloved disciple has. Peter, in fact, seems to assume the beloved disciple *knows* whom Jesus is talking about. He doesn't, though. He turns to Jesus and whispers, "Lord, who is it?"

There's an even more compelling passage at the end of the Gospel of John. Evidently, the uniqueness of the relationship between Jesus and the beloved disciple had given rise to some jealousy among the other disciples. A rumor had arisen that the beloved disciple would never die. In one of the post-Resurrection appearances of Jesus, Peter glances at the beloved disciple and asks, "Lord, what about this man?" Jesus seems to be a little angry, and he snaps, "If it is my will that he remain until I come, what is that to you?"[10]

So far, we have dealt only with the information available in the Bible, the canonical scriptures. Another source, however, provides a new wealth of evidence. A biblical scholar named Morton Smith, doing research in a remote mountain monastery on Mt. Sinai in 1958, ran across a fragment of an ancient manuscript, a letter that he and dozens of other biblical scholars believe contains a lost fragment of our existing Gospel of Mark. This passage, which was probably not "lost" but purposely weeded out of the Gospel manuscripts by church hierarchs who felt it was too dangerous for the laity to deal with, would originally have been between verses 34 and 35 in chapter 10 of the existing Gospel of Mark. It is, essentially, the story of Jesus' raising Lazarus from the dead (which is interest-

[9]John 13:24.
[10]John 21:21–23.

ing, because in our current Gospel of Mark, that story is omitted entirely).

In the secret gospel, after Lazarus (who is described as "a youth") is restored to health, the text says:

> *But the youth, looking upon him, loved him, and began to beseech him that he might be with him. And going out of the tomb, they came into the house of the youth, for he was rich.*[11]

The fragment of the text goes on to say:

> *In the evening the youth comes to him, wearing a linen cloth over his naked body. And he remained with him that night, for Jesus taught him the mystery of the Kingdom of God. . . . And the sister of the youth whom Jesus loved and his mother and Salome were there, and Jesus did not receive them.*[12]

You may think I am being fanciful in hearing a sexual connotation in this passage, but the fact that it seems so sexual is evidently why it was edited out of the Gospel. The manuscript that Smith discovered was a letter from Clement, a late-first-century bishop of Rome (or pope, if you believe they had popes that early—I don't). Clement was writing to a priest named Theodore, who had heard some rumors about this edited-out portion of the Gospel, and wrote to ask his bishop whether they were true. The reason we now have the passage restored is that Clement quotes it at length in his letter to Theodore. He evidently feels that Theodore, a priest, can be trusted with information that is too radical for lay people. But he is also careful to give Theodore the "true explanation." In one sentence, after quoting the suppressed passage, Clement adds:

---

[11]Morton Smith, *The Secret Gospel: The Discovery and Interpretation of the Secret Gospel According to Mark* (Clearlake, California: Dawn Horse Press, 1982), 52. Originally published by Harvard University Press, 1973.

[12]Ibid., 17. If you want to venture onto really controversial ground, Smith believes that the reference to "the mystery of the Kingdom of God" is a specific ritualistic initiation, probably sexual in nature. He writes about this concept in more detail in his earlier book, *Jesus the Magician* (New York: Harper & Row, 1977).

But "naked man with naked man" and the other things which you wrote about are not found.[13]

Theodore evidently thought it sounded sexual. So did Clement. In fact, I believe Clement and his brother bishops conspired to remove the passage from the Gospel text for just that reason.

Now, if we put all these pieces of evidence together like a jigsaw puzzle, we begin to get a composite picture of Jesus and the beloved disciple. My theory is that "the beloved disciple" was not John, but Lazarus. The canonical scriptures do tell us that whenever Jesus was in Bethany, he stayed in the home of Lazarus and his sisters, Mary and Martha. Evidence also connects Lazarus, a wealthy and powerful young man, with the unnamed young man we usually call "the rich young ruler," whom Jesus told to sell all his possessions. In that story in the Gospel of Mark, we are told, "Jesus looked at the young man and loved him."[14] When Lazarus' sister reports his death to Jesus, she says, "He whom you love is ill,"[15] using the same language as that used for the unnamed "beloved disciple." It is also significant that the death of Lazarus is the occasion for the only record in the four gospels of Jesus crying, the celebrated shortest verse of the bible, John 11:35: "Jesus wept." Seeing Jesus crying, the bystanders exclaimed, "See how he loved him!"[16]

Another powerful image of the special relationship between Jesus and this disciple, whom I believe to be Lazarus, is the moment when Jesus is dying on the cross, and according to the gospel, "his mother and the disciple Jesus loved" are standing at the foot of the cross. As his last act, Jesus turns to his mother and says, "Woman, behold your son." To the beloved disciple, he says, "Behold your mother." And after his death, the two of them, mother and lover, remain together as a family.[17]

[13]Ibid.
[14]Mark 10:21.
[15]John 11:3.
[16]John 11:36.
[17]John 19:26–27.

My own revisionist interpretation of this data is that these three references, to "the disciple Jesus loved," to Lazarus, whom Jesus raised from the dead, and to the wealthy young man who asked Jesus, "What must I do to inherit eternal life?" are all references to the same disciple: Lazarus, the beloved of Jesus.

There are other intriguing references to this beloved disciple. St. Aelred of Rievaulx, the patron saint of queers, saw great significance in the image of the beloved disciple reclining on Jesus' chest at the Last Supper:

> Some are joined to us more intimately and passionately than others in the lovely bond of spiritual friendship. And lest this sort of sacred love should seem improper to anyone, Jesus himself, in everything like us, patient and compassionate with us in every matter, transfigured it through the expression of his own love: for he allowed one, not all, to recline on his breast as a sign of his special love. . . .[18]

I am not by any means the first to suggest that Jesus might have been gay. In 1968, Canon Hugh Montefiore published an essay (in a collection, by the way, edited by gay theologian Norman Pittenger) that explored the idea.[19] Bishop John A. T. Robinson, in his book of christology, *The Human Face of Jesus,* refers to Montefiore's essay, along with other speculations about the sexuality of Jesus, pointing out that to think of Jesus as sexless "for most people today is about the most effective way of saying that he was not fully human."[20] Bishop Robinson also acknowledges the fact that we will never have a conclusive answer, in the scientific/historical sense, to this question, but he writes:

---

[18]Aelred of Rievaulx, *On Spiritual Friendship,* 3:109–10. This translation from the original Latin is John Boswell's. The only available English translation, by Walker and Webb, omits the passage—which, by the way, points up the need for more of us queers to undertake such research for ourselves.

[19]Hugh W. Montefiore, "Jesus, the Revelation of God," in W. Norman Pittenger, ed., *Christ for Us Today* (London: SCM Press, 1968), 91–116.

[20]John A. T. Robinson, *The Human Face of God* (Philadelphia: Westminster Press, 1973), 64.

Of course there is no answer. The gospels are not there to answer such questions. It is, however, a good question to ask *ourselves,* to test our reaction.[21]

As Canon Montefiore points out, the vision of a queer Jesus would be consistent with the theological affirmation that God and Christ are particularly identified with the outcast.[22]

When we put all these puzzle pieces together, and add a healthy dose of intuition, faith, and the wisdom of the heart, this is what we get:

Jesus was the passionate lover of Lazarus, a young man who became his disciple. When the two of them met, there was that electricity we have learned to call limerence, or "love at first sight."

Lazarus was powerful and established—a yuppie, if you will—and at first the radical demands of Jesus' marginal lifestyle were too much for him, so he went away—and both hearts broke. But he came back and came to be known as "the disciple Jesus loved."

Once, while Jesus was away, Lazarus became seriously ill. His sister sent word to Jesus, saying, "Lord, he whom you love is ill." When Jesus arrived and found him dead, he cried. And the passion between them was strong enough to overcome death.

At the last meal Jesus and his followers had together, Lazarus, his beloved, leaned against him at the table, his head snuggled against Jesus' chest. The other disciples realized the unique significance of Jesus' relationship with this particular disciple, and sometimes expressed some jealousy about it—as when the rumor spread that somehow Jesus would see to it that the beloved disciple would never die.

[21]Ibid.
[22]Montefiore, "Jesus, the Revelation of God," 91–116.

And as Jesus was dying, his mother and Lazarus were standing at the foot of the cross. Jesus, who was being suffocated to death, used some of his last breath to encourage the two of them to care for each other. Perhaps this moment even marked the reconciliation of a long-standing tension between them. "Woman, behold your son." "Behold your mother." And after his death, the two of them, mother and lover, remained together as a family—a family made by choice, not chance.

Under the canons of traditional (i.e., patriarchal) biblical scholarship, if we cannot conclusively prove something, we are not allowed to suggest it is true (especially not in print!). But the canons of traditional biblical scholarship do not serve queer Christians well; in fact, they help oppress us. We cannot "prove" or "disprove" the above reconstruction. Is it speculation? In a sense, yes. But all theology is speculation—the quantity of data that can actually be verified, in the scientific sense, is tiny. But it is not *just* speculation. It is, rather, employing the technique you learned in Chapter 2 on prayer and meditation. It is gathering together all the "hard data" you can find, then adding the insights of faith, of prayer and meditation, and of the wisdom of the heart. And if it is speculation, it is holy speculation, because it helps you keep the faith in a homophobic world and in spite of an even more homophobic church. It makes it possible for you to be out and proud and still be a passionate follower of Jesus the Christ.

9
THE WORD MADE FLESH

Incarnation and Sacrament

The Incarnation, the assertion that "God became flesh," is *the* central doctrine of Christianity. When we recite the Creed, which is a distillation of the most basic teachings of our religion, it is customary to kneel or make a profound bow at the *Incarnatus,* the phrase that declares:

> *by the power of the Holy Spirit,*
> *he became incarnate from the Virgin Mary*
> *and was made human.*

We make a special act of reverence at those words because they are absolutely central to our faith. If, when Christians assemble together on Sunday, we didn't say anything else but this one phrase, we would have proclaimed the gospel.

When Christians speak of the doctrine of the Incarnation, they usually say it means "God became flesh," but *flesh* is one of those religious words that has lost its power. It's not even in our normal vocabulary anymore. My friend Katherine Black, an Episcopal priest and Latin scholar, once pointed out that a more faithful and more powerful translation would be "God became *meat*." (*Meat,* here, has roughly the same connotation as when the very cruisy park benches in front of Provincetown's Town Hall are referred to as the "meat rack.")

The fact that *flesh* and *meat* were once thought of as interchangeable words was brought home to me when a group of us were trying to decipher a menu in a restaurant in Sweden. We asked the waitress to translate *pit i panna,* the name of a popular Swedish dish that is basically a potato-and-ham hash. She told us, "It's potatoes and flesh." Does that make you cringe? If so, you have an idea how first-century people reacted when Christians spoke of "God becoming flesh." They were absolutely horrified. "Scandalized," as Paul said. The human body was not much esteemed in that society. The body was seen as a prison of the soul, something to be transcended. The very idea that God would use such a vile object as a human body as the vehicle of self-revelation was not only absurd, it was shocking, vulgar. Imagine how it must have felt to be a Christian in those days. Today, if you describe yourself as a Christian, most people assume you are a sort of goody-two-shoes. In the first century, to be a Christian was to practice a religion based on a central belief your neighbors considered obscene!

Yet Christians proclaimed the Incarnation, the in-meat-ment of God, as a central tenet of their faith. Early on they realized the doctrine had profound implications for the way we think about our own bodies. If God chose to be revealed to us through a human body, then human bodies must be pretty special, even sacred. The respect the early Christians felt for bodies led to the Christian belief that healing the sick, feeding the hungry, and clothing the naked are religious responsibilities as important as the more obviously "spiritual" ones such as prayer and worship. These became known as "acts of corporeal mercy," or acts of caring for the body. While their neighbors avoided touching dead bodies, for fear of being contaminated (if the body is the prison of the soul, what can be more vile than a body without a soul?), Christians took care to bury bodies reverently, even those of strangers. Historical theologian Margaret R. Miles has asserted the early Christians "cared for living bodies and dead bodies because they understood that the Incarnation of Christ had once and for all settled the issue of the value of the human body."[1]

Radical Incarnationalism

Urban T. Holmes wrote of the doctrine of the Incarnation and its powerful implications as "radical incarnationalism."[2] Even Christians have found this notion frightening, and over the centuries the church has tended to shy away from it. Every now and then, the doctrine reasserts itself, almost in spite of the church hierarchy. One such instance of the truth of the Incarnation shining through is the Book of Common Prayer of 1662. The marriage liturgy from that prayer book (the liturgy used at the marriage of Prince Charles and Lady Diana) has the groom say these deliciously incarnational, frankly sexual words to the bride:

> *With my Body I worship you, with my worldly Goods I thee endow, and with all that I am and all that I have, I honor you, in the Name of the Father, and the Son, and the Holy Ghost.*[3]

My other favorite incarnational passage is a relatively new liturgy, the prayer for—no kidding—the blessing of a bathroom in the form for the blessing of a home in the 1979 *Book of Occasional Services:*

> *O holy God, in the incarnation of your Son our Lord you made our flesh the instrument of your self-revelation: Give us a proper respect and reverence for our mortal bodies, keeping them clean and fair, whole and sound; that, glorifying you in them, we may confidently await our being clothed upon with spiritual bodies, when that which is mortal is transformed by life; through Jesus Christ our Lord. Amen.*[4]

[1]Margaret R. Miles, "The Incarnation and Its Meaning for Human Embodiment," Matriculation Address, September 1985, Episcopal Divinity School, Cambridge, Massachusetts. (Unpublished manuscript.)
[2]Urban T. Holmes, *What Is Anglicanism?* (Wilton, Connecticut: Morehouse-Barlow, 1982), 31.
[3]Book of Common Prayer according to the use of the Church of England (1662), 293.
[4]Church Pension Fund, *The Book of Occasional Services* (New York: Church Hymnal Corporation, 1979), 136.

Occasionally an inspired theologian or preacher comes along to remind us that the doctrine of the Incarnation of God is the heart of the Christian faith. Richard Hooker, the Reformation theologian, wrote, "The honour which our flesh hath by being the flesh of the Son of God is in many respects great."[5] Recently, theologian James B. Nelson, who developed what he calls "sexual theology," has suggested replacing the impoverished word *incarnation* with the more inescapable *embodiment*.[6] Christianity is an *embodied* religion. The Christian path is not to "rise above" our bodies, or to free our spirits from "the prison house of the body," but to celebrate our bodies, to *use* our bodies as a pathway to God.

Sacrament

If you ever attended catechism classes, you may remember the official definition of sacrament: *The outward and visible sign of an inward and spiritual grace*. In dechurchified language, we might say sacrament is *the spiritual made physical*.

The concept of sacrament is a natural outgrowth of the doctrine of the Incarnation of God. If God's chosen method of self-revelation is through the material realm, and specifically through the human body, then the way you can know God is through your body, and through embodied, *sensual* experiences. Sacraments make use of sensuality and sensuous objects to bring us into the presence of God. Good catholic liturgy is embodied and overwhelmingly sensual. You don't just sit still; you stand and kneel and bow and make the sign of the cross. You taste bread and wine. You smell incense. You are bombarded with visual images—stained glass, sculpture, colorful vestments, candles. You listen to and participate in the making of music.

In a baptism, you hear the splashing of water poured into the font, and those being baptized feel water poured over their heads. (In some churches, the candidate for baptism has the profoundly

---

[5]Richard Hooker, *Laws of Ecclesiastical Polity* V.LIV. 5. (New York: E. P. Dutton, 1960), 215.
[6]James B. Nelson, *Embodiment: An Approach to Sexuality and Christian Theology* (Minneapolis: Augsburg, 1978).

embodied experience of having his entire body submerged in warm water.) In a healing service, you smell the subtle scent of the holy oil, and feel it applied to your forehead by the healer. At an ordination, the candidate kneels and feels the weight of dozens of hands pressing on her head. At a wedding, the couple's hands are bound together in the fabric of the priest's stole.

The more catholic-leaning parishes offer an even wider array of sensual experiences. The interplay of darkness and light, one of the most powerfully evocative sensations of our collective unconscious, is celebrated in such liturgies as Compline, Tenebrae, Candlemas, and the Great Vigil of Easter. On Good Friday, you are invited to kiss the wood of the cross. On St. Francis's day, at the blessing of the animals, you can worship God amid barking and mewing and growling and whining and purring pets. On St. Blaise's day, a priest crosses lighted candles under your chin to bless your throat. On Maundy Thursday, you can have the overtly sexual experience of having your bare feet washed, or washing someone else's feet. All these experiences are an affirmation of the basic doctrine of the Incarnation. They remind us that you do not need to "rise above" your body in order to know God; rather you *use* your body to worship God.

My quarrel with most New Age religious services, as well as most mainstream Protestant worship, is that it is all mental. You might as well check your body at the church door. You sit and listen, have your head filled with ideas, maybe meditate and pray a little—but your body is not involved. Once I was seriously considering becoming a member of the Unity Church, a Christian-based New Age approach. I lost interest during the inquirer's class when we discussed sacraments. "We feel the spiritual meaning of the sacraments is more important than the material forms," the minister said. "Receiving Christ in your heart is much better than receiving bread and wine." Mary Baker Eddy, the founder of Christian Science, said roughly the same thing about sacraments.

The problem is that human nature itself, as well as centuries of Christian tradition, testifies that the best way to "receive Christ in your heart" is to do something concrete and material and sensuous with your body. It's like the line in Maxwell Anderson's *Mary of Scotland*: "I need a religion palpable to the touch."

You have probably noticed by now I am quite biased in favor of a small-c catholic, sacramental approach. I make no apology for this bias. I would certainly not recommend that any self-affirming queer join the Roman Catholic Church, and these days my feelings about the Episcopal Church are just as negative. Yet I believe that the catholic tradition within Christianity, when it is separated from the institutional abuses, is not only the most authentic expression of Christianity, but the form best suited for queer Christians.

Straight society stereotypes us as being overly sexual, projecting its own frustrated and unfulfilled sexuality onto us. Yet to some extent, straights are right—we are by nature a deeply sensual people. We seem instinctively to resist the body-denigrating, sex-negative philosophy of our dominant culture, and to insist on celebrating the inherent goodness of our bodies, sensual experience, and sex itself. I don't care if a New Age church has a sign on its front lawn that says, "Lesbian and gay people welcome." If the philosophy it teaches and practices is fundamentally anti-body, yet another version of the old body-versus-spirit dualism, some form of minimizing the importance of the body and the material world in order to be more "spiritual," it is no place for self-affirming queers. We belong in world-affirming, body-positive, sex-positive religions. And that's exactly what *authentic* catholic Christianity is.

In fact, the largest concentration of queers (or at least of gay men) to be found in any given city (outside the largest gay bar) is in the "spikiest," most anglo-catholic parish in town. My parish in Dallas, the Church of the Holy Cross, was once referred to in the gay press as being, after the MCC, "the second-largest gay church in Dallas." The rector and vestry were not pleased, but it was *true*. Well over 50 percent of that congregation, on any given Sunday, was queer.

To some extent, the location of the Church of the Holy Cross explains its queer attraction. It sits in the center of Oak Lawn, Dallas's gay neighborhood. But the high gay-to-straight parishioner ratio is found in dozens of other "high" anglo-catholic parishes throughout the country, regardless of their neighborhoods. St. John the Evangelist (aka Bowdoin Street) in Boston; the Church of the Advent, also in Boston; St. Paul's K Street or St. Agnes and St. Anne's in Washington; St. Mary the Virgin in New York; the Church of the Ascension in Chicago—the list could go on for several pages.

But although the number of gay parishioners may be quite high, a certain closeted mentality, a sort of discreet gentlemen's club atmosphere, often pervades such parishes. Although the rector, the assistant to the rector, the organist, three-fourths of the choir, and well over half the congregation may be gay, the "g" word is never heard from the pulpit. Suggest the parish carry a banner in the local gay pride parade and watch the vestry members, one by one, go into cardiac arrest.

About the best advice I can offer you, unless you are fortunate enough to live near one of the truly exceptional parishes, is to choose the one with the sacramental worship and take a cue from the children—read, squirm, color, or otherwise entertain yourself in order to ignore the sermon. Of course, you could help raise the political consciousness of such a parish in dozens of ways once you become involved with it.

John Irving's memorable character Owen Meany is as decidedly anticatholic as I am procatholic. He expresses his disapproval of the biblical-epic film *The Robe* by sniffing, "WHAT'S A BIG FUSS ABOUT A BLANKET! THAT'S SO CATHOLIC—TO GET VERY RELIGIOUS ABOUT OBJECTS."[7] Owen Meany is quite right, but I would argue that in Christianity, the religion of the Incarnation of God, the religion that has its roots in the Hebrew scriptures that affirm God created everything on earth and "saw that it was good," it makes a lot of sense to "get very religious about objects." Sacrament helps us restore the balance between the spiritual and the physical.

If you attended catechism classes in either the Roman Catholic or Episcopal Church, you learned there are seven sacraments, sometimes broken down into the "two great sacraments," in which all Christians are expected to participate (baptism and communion), and "five lesser sacraments" of confirmation, marriage, ordina-

[7]Irving, *A Prayer for Owen Meany*, 270.

tion, the sacrament of the sick, and penance. Other instances in which physical objects or actions take on a spiritual significance are technically not called sacraments, but *sacramentals*. Who cares? The sacramental principle, making use of "an outward and visible sign" to both signify *and convey* "an inward and spiritual grace," is the same whether it is blessing bread and wine at the Eucharist or blessing our pets on the Feast of St. Francis. Let's look at some specific sacraments in the light of their meaning to queer Christians.

Baptism

Thanks to convenience and laziness, the contemporary Christian church has lost much of the original power of the sacrament of baptism. Today, an adult candidate simply bows her head over something that resembles a birdbath, and a little bit of water is poured over her. Chances are, in fact, you were baptized as an infant and have no memory of the experience at all.

In the early church, baptism was a sensual, total body experience. The candidate, who had prepared for the ceremony by a period of intense prayer and fasting, stripped off all his clothes (including any jewelry—the nudity was to be complete) and was then completely submerged in a pool of water. Upon stepping out of the pool, the candidate was anointed with oil, which also probably covered his entire body, then was dressed in a new, white robe, symbolic of his new life, and presented to the waiting congregation and the bishop. Baptisms originally took place at the Great Vigil of Easter and so were held around midnight by the light of candles. The muted sound of the chanting of the congregation in the next room, the candlelight, the incense and the fragrance of the anointing oil, the warm water and the nudity, together assaulted the senses of the candidate, almost surely bringing him into an altered state of consciousness. An early church bishop, Theodore of Mopsuestia, wrote of these ceremonies as "the spine-tingling rites of Christian initiation."

Today a few churches—but only a few—are beginning to recover the power of the ancient rites, starting with replacing birdbath fonts with real baptismal pools, providing what one liturgist has called "enough water to die in." In contrast to today, the candidates for baptism in the early church were usually adults, adults who were fully aware they were making a commitment that, given the persecution of Christians by the government, might well cost them their lives. But since the year 312, when the Emperor Constantine made it respectable to be a Christian, most candidates for baptism have been babies. My critics might suggest it's a hold-over from my evangelical days, but I believe the rite of Christian baptism should be reserved for adults. The birth of a child is certainly an important rite of passage, but we can mark it with a ceremony of thanksgiving for the child, saving baptism for those who have made a mature decision to follow Christ. We would probably have fewer "Christians," but those who called themselves Christian would be more committed.

Two powerful metaphors are at work in the ceremonies of baptism—one of death and rebirth, and one of cleansing. The death and rebirth symbolism is totally lost in the modern form of pouring a few drops of water over the head. But when the person being baptized is completely submerged in water, it is a powerful symbol of being buried and raised to a new life.

The other obvious symbol of baptism is that of cleansing. Ceremonial baths, representing a washing away of sins, were already familiar to the Jews before John the Baptizer, and later the Christians gave them a new interpretation. In fact, since the early church met in buildings that were originally built as homes, the baptismal room was most likely the actual bath. (But Roman baths were more like communal hot tubs than our current tiny bathtubs.)

What is significant about the cleansing symbolism is that the new Christian is having her sins washed away now, at the *beginning* of her new life. Christianity is not a lifelong striving for perfection; rather, the Christian path *begins* with our being forgiven, renewed, washed clean. Any confession of sin that takes place afterward is simply a way of reminding yourself you are *already* forgiven and made perfect in God's sight. For those of us who have grown up queer in a homophobic culture that has eroded the very founda-tions of our self-esteem, it can be tremendously healing to stop and remember, *I'm baptized. I'm washed clean. I'm forgiven. I'm perfect in the sight of God, right now.*

John Westerhoff III, a Christian educator, says we should tell people being baptized that from now on, wherever they go, all the angels and saints go before them, shouting, "Make way for the image of God." I heard him say that in a seminar one Saturday, and when I left the seminar and went to a gay disco, I was still imaging all the angels and saints clearing a path before me and shouting, "Make way for the image of God." The extra boost of self-esteem I projected made me *very* popular in the disco that night!

In some of the more sacramental churches, the Mass begins with what is called the *asperges.* The priest walks down the center aisle with a bucket of holy water, literally slinging it onto the congregation as she passes by. The people are supposed to make the sign of the cross as the blessed water strikes them. This is a symbolic cleansing to prepare us for the Mass; but it is, above all, a *reminder* of our baptism. In some churches, after a baptism, the water from the baptismal font is used to asperse the entire congregation. The act of sprinkling the casket and the open grave with holy water at a funeral is similarly a reminder that the person being buried was washed in baptism. This is also the meaning of the catholic custom of dipping your hand into a holy water stoop and making the sign of the cross upon entering or leaving a church. It is to remind you that you are baptized; that you have a new identity; that your last name has been changed to *Christian.* In fact, some liturgically creative parishes have removed the small holy water stoops, keeping the actual baptismal font, constantly filled with water, by the entrance of the church instead. Upon entering the church, you literally "rebaptize" yourself.

Being reminded of baptism is useful for any Christian. For us queers, still recovering from the insidious effects of systemic homophobia, it can be a profoundly healing act.

The Holy Eucharist

The Eucharist is variously referred to as the Mass, Communion, the Holy Mysteries (by Eastern Orthodox Christians), or the

Lord's Supper (by Evangelicals). The Eucharist is the central act of worship in the Christian tradition. It is what Christians do, or should do, whenever they gather. For centuries, the Christian tradition has taught that at least once a week (on "the Lord's Day," the first day of the week) the Christian community gathers to celebrate this sacrament.

The heart of the ceremony is a three-part action of the priest. She receives the offerings of bread and wine, usually from members of the congregation; gives thanks to God for them (which is what "blessing" means); and then distributes them to the people. These three steps parallel the biblical account that Jesus, at the Last Supper, *took* the bread (and later the wine), *blessed* and broke it, and *gave* it to the disciples.[8]

Reflecting upon the meaning of the Eucharist can be astonishing. We call the consecrated bread and wine "the body and blood of Christ" because Jesus himself set up that metaphor at the Last Supper, which was, remember, a dinner party Jesus had with his disciples—and not just any dinner party, but a sort of going-away party. Jesus had told them, and tells them again during the meal, that he is about to be arrested and executed—so the meal takes on the overtones of "eat, drink, and be merry, for tomorrow you die."

Jesus picks up the bread, says the traditional Hebrew blessing over it, breaks it, and passes it out to his friends, saying:

> *Take, eat: This is my Body, which is given for you. Do this for the remembrance of me.*[9]

At the conclusion of the meal, Jesus picks up a cup of wine, says the blessing for wine, and hands it to them, saying:

> *This is my Blood of the new Covenant, which is shed for you and for many for the forgiveness of sins.*[10]

[8]See Mark 14:22–23.
[9]Luke 22:19.
[10]Matthew 26:27–28.

I imagine the disciples were blown away by this. Can't you hear them whisper, " 'This is my body'! What the hell does he mean by that?" It would only be later, when they thought back to this moment, that it would begin to make sense to them.

The primary metaphor, of course, is one of sacrificial death. But we should claim and celebrate another metaphor in the Eucharist, a profoundly sexual one. Think of it: In this age of avoiding the exchange of body fluids, you may well get a little shiver at the thought of the entire congregation sharing in the Blood of Christ. If you take the words too literally, you can be repulsed by the connotations of cannibalism (the early Christians were accused of cannibalism by those who overheard the words of the liturgy). But going one step deeper, we find overtly sexual connotations. In fact, Morton Smith, the scholar who discovered the "Secret Gospel of Mark," described at length in Chapter 8, suggests that the very origins of the eucharistic ritual may be in the specifically erotic rituals of the older mystery religions.[11] And what a mind-boggling sort of intercourse is implied here! Jesus the Christ, whom we affirm to be the Incarnation of God, allows you the most awesome intimacy: to take his body into your body.

To further strengthen the sexual metaphor, you would do well to remember that Jesus said these words and performed this ritual while a young man, known as "the disciple Jesus loved," snuggled up against his chest.[12]

Marriage

I am a crusader for the right of same-sex couples to have marriage ceremonies—not civil ceremonies, which carry too much of a heterosexist society's baggage about property rights and the ownership of one person by another; but religious ceremonies that sacramentalize the love and commitment a couple feel for each other. I also insist on calling these ceremonies *marriages,* not some

---

[11]Smith, *The Secret Gospel,* 140.
[12]See John 13:23; also the more extensive discussion of the beloved disciple in Chapter 8.

euphemistic term such as *covenant ceremonies, blessings of union,* or *blessings of relationship,* because I believe they are exactly the same whether the couple consists of two women, a man and a woman, or two men.

In Chapter 15, we will discuss the theology of same-sex relationships; here, let's just focus on the ceremony itself. Gay weddings are, to say the least, quite controversial. Most mainstream ministers will not (cannot) perform them openly (although closeted gay marriages officiated by ordained clergy take place with astounding frequency). Even when the word *marriage* is carefully avoided, the very mention of such ceremonies causes heated and angry debate at church conventions of even the most liberal denominations. They are also controversial among the queer community itself. The more radical among us feel marriage is such an inherently sexist and heterosexist institution that no self-respecting queer would want to get mixed up with it. In general, I agree with this sentiment, which is why I make the distinction between the legal contract and the religious ceremony.

Regardless of the unfortunate associations in the past, a specifically *Christian* marriage today is understood to be a covenant between two equals, two consenting adults who are making very intentional promises to each other in order to live together in a common life. It should be obvious such a covenant is equally valid for queer or straight couples.

Since queer marriages are not recognized by the government of any state or municipality in our country (they are recognized, with certain limitations, in Denmark and Sweden; and more and more American cities are enacting "domestic partnership" laws that offer a degree of legal protection, at least for municipal employees), and since no Christian church except the MCC officially recognizes such unions, many people have trouble understanding why a same-sex couple would want to have a marriage ceremony. Those who don't understand probably don't understand the concept of sacrament. When a Christian couple (or a couple in which one of the parties is Christian) wants to have a Christian blessing bestowed upon their union, what they are doing is sacramentalizing the covenant of love they already have.

In a wedding ceremony the way I officiate it, several sacramental actions are used to celebrate and sanctify the covenant. First, the couple exchange promises. These promises are spoken in the presence of witnesses—their friends and family—and then I ask those witnesses to vow to help the couple keep their promises. I require the couple to exchange gifts. Each person is to give the other some item of value, though not necessarily monetary value. It might be a poem or a work of art, for instance; but each partner gives the other some valuable gift to sacramentalize the fact that they are now sharing their possessions and resources. Most often, couples choose rings as these gifts, and the sacramentality of the covenant is strengthened every day as they wear these rings in public. Next, the couple join their right hands, which I symbolically bind together with my stole, the symbol of my priestly office. I then pronounce God's blessing upon them and upon their intentional covenant, and they celebrate by kissing each other. The kissing, an unmistakably bodily, physical action, reminds us of the other important sacrament the couple share—sex. The ceremony is then concluded with a celebration of the Eucharist, reminding the couple and their witnesses that the covenant they make is not only between them and their friends, but also with God in Christ.

John Westerhoff III defines sacrament by saying "a sacrament doesn't make true what wasn't true before; it makes *real* what was already true." Two people do not *become* a couple at the moment of their wedding ceremony; rather the ceremony makes *real,* tangible, obvious, the covenant they had previously made with each other. The ceremony, then, is "the outward and visible sign" of the "invisible and spiritual grace" of their mutual love and commitment.

The Blessing of a Home

I'm sure John Irving's Owen Meany would condemn them as being "SO CATHOLIC," and he would be right. The ceremony of the blessing of a home is one of the most incarnational, most sacramental rituals in Christianity. It sends an important message to the guests who are invited to witness the event: that God is not confined to Sundays or to the four walls of the church, but is concerned with our daily lives, too.

Most sacramental churches (Roman Catholic, Eastern Orthodox, Anglican, and Lutheran) have some form, usually short, of blessing the homes of parishioners. Both Roman and Orthodox Catholics, for instance, have a custom of the parish priest's visiting the home of each parishioner during the season of Epiphany and saying a prayer for the members of the household. The fullest form of the Episcopalian ceremony, though, is anything but short—and it's something to behold. The priest, the members of the household, and their friends gather in the living room of the home, then process to each room with some combination of white candles, incense, and holy water. A special prayer is said to bless each room, and then the party returns to the dining table for a celebration of the Eucharist.

House blessings are not reserved for freestanding houses that are owned outright. It is quite appropriate to bless your apartment. Although the more rational and protestant-minded are uncomfortable being reminded of such, the original purpose of a house blessing was to exorcise any forces of evil from the space and to ask for angelic protection—a request that is just as valid today as it ever was. If you believe quite literally in both angels and demons, such a blessing of your living space makes great sense. Having a house blessing is also a wonderful way for a Christian, or a Christian couple, to proclaim to their nonchurch friends the centrality of Christ in their lives (we call that "witnessing"). Same-sex couples, in fact, often use the ceremony to affirm their relationship when the church will not allow them a marriage ceremony. Even the most homophobic priest is unlikely to turn down a request to bless a couple's home. (Although I will never forget the priest who blessed an apartment I shared with a lover and literally trembled with nervousness when he blessed our *one* bedroom!)

If you are single, you can use a house blessing as a way of affirming the wholeness and completeness of your life and your household without a partner. And what, pray tell, is more incarnational and body affirming than asking God's blessing on your bathroom?

Grace Before Meals

The simple act of pausing before a meal to give thanks to God can be one of the most powerful ways of sanctifying your daily life. If you believe in the power and efficacy of blessing, the act of asking God to bless your food "to the nourishment of your body" is in the best interest of your health. To use the New Age vocabulary, such a prayer attunes the vibrations of the food to the vibrations of your body. It literally infuses the food you are about to eat with holy energy.

I think all of us, especially those of us with AIDS who are taking powerful and potentially toxic drugs, would be greatly served by "saying grace" over our medications, too. Dr. Bernie Siegel has written that studies have shown a patient's attitude and expectations have much to do with whether or not a particular drug has side effects. Asking God to bless a pill "to the nourishment and health of your body," then, is a powerful way to maximize its positive effects and minimize the negative. Healing circles and public healing groups might want to do a ritual blessing of medications—placing all the bottles of pills in the center of the circle and praying over them. (Personally, being hopelessly sacramental, I would want to sprinkle them with holy water!)

Like a house blessing, a short and sweet grace before meals is also a "witness" to your dinner guests of the central importance of God in your life. It echoes the biblical affirmation "As for me and my house, we will serve the Lord." It is a simple but meaningful sacramental act you can begin at any time.

What is the ceremonial for a grace before meals? Because you are actually channeling energy, it is good to extend your hands, palms down, over the food. You may want to begin by rubbing your hands together for a few seconds, to "awaken" the energy. Bowing your head is more common, but unless you're alone, that loses the communal aspect. I've been in many households where the custom was to hold hands for the grace, and in one home where we stood behind our chairs and *sang* the grace before being seated. An old catholic custom is to make the sign of the cross on yourself at the conclusion of the prayer, to personalize and receive the blessing. And it is so much nicer when *everyone* says the "Amen."

You can, of course, say just about anything you want as a grace. For those of you who prefer a prepared text (as I do), here are some sample prayers:

> *For these and all Her mercies, God's holy name be blessed and praised, through Jesus Christ our Savior. Amen.*

> *Bless, O God, this food to our use and us to your service. Make us ever mindful of the needs of others, and bring us closer to those we love. Amen.*

> *Bless, O God, this food to our use and us to your service. Make us ever mindful of the needs of others, and give us the courage to do something about it. Amen.*

> *Blessed are you, O God, Ruler of the Universe. Through your goodness we have this food to share. Fruit of the earth and work of human hands, may it become our spiritual food and drink. Amen.*

> *Food does not make its way to the table without someone's labor. There are hands deserving of rest and thanks. May God bless this food and bless the cook. Amen.*

> *Some have food, some have none. God bless the revolution! Amen.*

You get the idea. I can't end this list without telling you one of our favorite jokes when I was a student in a Baptist college. Saying a blessing before a meal was expected in the cafeteria there. If you didn't actually pray, you at least bowed your head for a second and *pretended* to. Forgetting the grace was serious business, so we decided if you did forget, then you could say the first verse of Psalm 103:

> *Bless the Lord, O my soul; and all that is within me, bless his holy name!*

So much for that old-time Baptist humor!

10
KEEPING THE FEAST

Celebrating God's Gifts

If Jesus were on earth today, would you invite him to your next dinner party? And if so, which of your friends would you *not* invite, for fear they would say something embarrassingly inappropriate? What do you think would be the general tone of a dinner party with Jesus as the honored guest? Subdued? Serious?

When I was in "Beginners" (preschool) Sunday school, one of our teachers used to keep an empty chair in our room, which she told us was for Jesus—the firm implication being that if we thought Jesus was sitting in the class, we'd behave ourselves. Jesus, in the Sunday school teacher's view, was a sort of wet blanket who would squelch any fun kids might want to have.

I hope you reject that concept of Jesus and see that the Sunday school teacher's twisting of the image of Jesus into that of a stuffy disciplinarian borders on blasphemy. Again, if you have children, please don't use Jesus to threaten them.

If I had a chance to have a dinner party for the Jesus whose passionate follower I am today, I'd invite as many of my friends as could fit into my apartment. I'd cook something hearty and simple, such as chili or spaghetti or fajitas. I'd stock up on lots of beer or cheap champagne (only because I can't afford expensive champagne in sufficient quantity!). And I'd not make plans to have to be anywhere the next morning—because I'd fully intend to tie one on with Jesus.

Sound shocking? While he was on earth, Jesus' critics called him "a glutton and a drunkard."[1] We do have some evidence in the scripture of Jesus fasting and going on lonely retreats and spending time in quiet prayer and meditation, but he did these things as part of a rhythm, balanced with other periods of eating and drinking and making merry—to an extent religious people found excessive. There is biblical evidence to suggest Jesus was a sort of first-century party animal.

Actually, partying is great theology for Christians. In the Gospel of John, Jesus says to his followers, "I came that they might have life, and have it abundantly."[2] Unfortunately, *abundantly* is one of those religious words that has been robbed of its original power by pious overuse. But think about it, what does *abundantly* mean? I'll bet Jesus would have been in total agreement with the philosophy of the old beer commercial: You're only going to go round once in life, so grab all the gusto you can. According to the religious tradition in which Jesus grew up, the world was created *for* us, for our use and enjoyment. To celebrate life, to "grab the gusto," is simply to echo God's assessment of the creation: And God saw that it was good; *very* good.

God Likes to Party

I've always thought it significant that the very first miracle the canonical scriptures accord to Jesus was perfectly frivolous: turning water into wine. Jesus did this miracle at a wedding reception in Cana, not for any grave or important reason, but just so his relative, the host, wouldn't be embarrassed by running out of wine. And this was not just *any* wine, but *the best* wine—not André, but Dom Pérignon. According to the biblical account, the caterer was so impressed with the quality of the wine Jesus made he commented to the host that he had done it backward—serving the best wine

[1]See Matthew 11:18–19.
[2]John 10:10.

after the guests were too drunk to know the difference. And Jesus made somewhere between 120 to 180 *gallons* of this fine wine![3]

You may also have been told in Sunday school that Jesus never performed a miracle that didn't have a higher purpose. Whenever he did something we might call supernatural, it was always "for the greater glory of God." Yet here he is making large quantities of good wine—and what lofty purpose is served? No one's life is saved, no healing occurs, no real disaster is averted. The only purpose is to prevent the party from being ruined. So if we buy my Sunday school teacher's assertion that all Jesus' miracles were in accord with the higher purposes of God, then the inescapable implication is that God *likes* parties! After describing this extraordinary wine making, the Gospel of John comments, "This, the first of his signs, Jesus did at Cana in Galilee, and manifested his glory, and his disciples believed in him."[4]

What a concept: The glory of God is manifest in good wine. In contrast to many of his religious contemporaries, Jesus taught and practiced a religion of the celebration of life.

Episcopalians are sometimes called "whiskeypalians," or Matthew 18:20 is paraphrased, "Where three or four Episcopalians are gathered, you'll find a fifth." I must confess that after spending years in the teetotal Baptist Church, the relaxed attitude toward drinking was *one* of the things that attracted me to the Episcopal Church. "Why, those Episcopalians," my grandmother once said, "they even drink *in church*!"

In Brownwood, Texas, part of the Bible Belt where Fundamentalism is so strong, the Episcopalians I knew used to load ice chests of beer in their car trunks when they went to church on Sunday morning. Since their service began at ten, and the Baptists' at eleven, the Episcopalians would be standing in the parking lot chugging beers by the time the Baptists drove by. And in Fundamentalist-dominated West Texas, that, I submit, was "evangelism."

When I was considering joining the Episcopal Church, I met

[3]John 2:1–11.
[4]John 2:11.

with the local rector. I was trying to explain my dissatisfaction with the Baptist approach. "They're just so, so *negative,*" I complained, "about—"

He finished my sentence for me: "About drinking, dancing, and sex?"

Yes, I told him, exactly that.

"Our approach is that nothing is good or evil in itself," he said. "It depends on how it is used."

So I became convinced the Episcopal Church was the church that celebrates "drinking, dancing, and sex." Later, I found out that's not usually true—but it was a nice idea while it lasted.

It is no accident that the person who presides at the Eucharist, the central act of Christian worship, is referred to as the celebrant. The Mass is not merely *performed* or *said,* it is *celebrated.* It is, after all, a liturgical re-creation of a dinner party Jesus had with his disciples, a living out of "eat, drink, and be merry, for tomorrow you may die." I have in my kitchen a framed poster showing a glass of wine and a loaf of bread that says, "Jesus of Nazareth requests the honor of your presence at a dinner to be given in his honor." That's what the Mass is—a dinner party to remember Jesus. *Therefore let us keep the feast.*

Jesus didn't invent the idea that celebration is the proper response to God's gifts. He simply recovered a tradition of celebration in Judaism that had been lost over the centuries. When David, the new king of Israel, brought the Ark of the Covenant to Jerusalem, he led the people in "making merry before the Lord with all their might,"[5] accompanied by tambourines, castanets, and cymbals. David himself was "leaping and dancing before the Lord,"[6] and he was apparently naked or nearly so, for his wife accused him of being "vulgar" and dancing in the manner of the pagans.[7]

Psalm 23, a poetic vision of heaven, describes being in the presence of God as being the honored guest at a festive meal, the Messianic Banquet:

[5] 2 Samuel 6:5.
[6] 2 Samuel 6:16.
[7] 2 Samuel 6:20.

You prepare a table before me
in the presence of my enemies;
you anoint my head with oil,
my cup overflows.[8]

Do you realize Christianity is the only major world religion that has no dietary restrictions, no lists of prohibited foods or drinks? Some Fundamentalists want to find prohibitions against alcohol in the Bible, but they're just not there. Quite the contrary. The Psalmist praises God for creating wine that "gladdens our hearts."[9] If you want to find scriptures prohibiting the use of alcohol, you'll have to go to the Koran, not the Bible. Fasting is a part of the Christian tradition, but only as a part of a rhythm, balanced with joyous feasting. When Christians fast, it is never because we believe the things we are temporarily giving up are *bad*. Rather, we are temporarily giving up *good* things, as a matter of discipline, at least in part to make sure we have not become enslaved (addicted) to them. When we end the fast and take up those things again, we can enjoy and appreciate them all the more. We fast on Fridays and feast on Sundays. (Which is why the queer traditions of Sunday brunch and Sunday-afternoon tea dances and "beer busts" are so liturgically correct!) We fast for the forty days of Lent, then party for the fifty days of Easter (and it is not insignificant that the feast period is longer than the fast). Personal discipline for a Christian is not a matter of a life of self-denial, or even "moderation," but of keeping a balance, a rhythm, between feasting and fasting.

Unfortunately, a growing tendency within the queer nation is to equate "spirituality" with a self-denying, body-denying ascetic lifestyle. Some people measure how "spiritual" they are by how many things they refrain from eating or drinking—and most recently, by how many times they resist the desire to have sex. Isn't that just dreadful?

Just as an aside, did you know that Jeff Smith, the "Frugal Gourmet," is *The Reverend* Jeff Smith, an ordained Methodist minis-

[8]Psalms 23:5.
[9]Psalms 104:15.

ter? *He* gets the connection. So does Robert Farrar Capon, a priest and gourmet cook who has written several books that are combination cookbooks and devotional manuals.[10] Alfred North Whitehead, the founder of process thought, once said, "Cooking is one of those arts that most require to be done by persons of a religious nature."[11]

It is easy to understand how we got into this denial business. Since we are a deeply spiritual people by nature, when we reject Christianity (or rather when Christians reject us), we look elsewhere for a spiritual discipline. Many of us have turned to so-called New Age movements because they often seem, on the surface, to be more gay-positive. Please hear this: I am not categorically trashing New Age thought. Much of what goes under this heading is compelling and useful. The problems come when these philosophies are swallowed whole without any sort of critical analysis. Much of the New Age movement has borrowed heavily from earlier movements such as Theosophy, which in turn borrowed heavily from Hinduism—especially the Hindu tendency to see absolutely everything as "illusion," and therefore to deny the importance of flesh-and-blood, material reality. *A Course in Miracles,* for instance, is almost pure Hindu philosophy, expressed in a sugarcoated pseudo-Christian vocabulary.[12]

The goal of Christian spirituality is not to "rise above" your body, but rather to *use* your body and the material world as a path to God. Christianity is, in the famous words of Archbishop William Temple, "the most avowedly materialistic of all the great religions."[13]

---

[10]The books are *The Supper of the Lamb: A Culinary Reflection* (Garden City, New York: Doubleday, 1969); *Food for Thought: Resurrecting the Art of Eating* (New York: Harcourt Brace Jovanovich, 1978); and *Capon on Cooking* (Boston: Houghton Mifflin, 1983).

[11]*Dialogues of Alfred North Whitehead* as recorded by Lucien Price (Boston: Little, Brown & Co., 1954), 203.

[12]*A Course in Miracles* is a three-volume set of supposedly channeled books that have become very popular recently. Countless other books, including those of Louise Hay, draw from the *Course in Miracles* material, and several study groups are based on the books. It is no secret I am not fond of *A Course in Miracles.* A longer discussion about its apparent disregard of the reality of evil is in Chapter 11. *A Course in Miracles* is published by the Foundation for Inner Peace, Farmingdale, NY.

[13]William Temple, *Nature, Man and God* (Gifford Lectures, 1932–1934) (London: Macmillan, 1951), 478. A similar statement is made in the introduction to Temple's *Readings in St. John's Gospel* (London: Macmillan & Co., 1952), xx.

It would be irresponsible of me not to say something about substance abuse and addiction at this point, since it is such a pervasive problem in our community. Nothing that I am saying here about the importance of feasting, and particularly about alcohol, is meant to diminish the seriousness of the widespread epidemic of substance abuse in our community. But by the same token, the possibility of alcoholism and substance abuse should not negate a basic affirmation of the goodness of the material creation, and of the nonabusive use of alcohol. In fact, most recovering alcoholics who are in a relatively advanced stage of their Twelve Step program are quite gracious about other people's drinking. They do not project their illness onto others. If I am allergic to shellfish, does it make any sense for me to go on a crusade to get you to stop eating shellfish?

As the Psalmist knew,[14] alcohol is a gift of God that can be celebrated as heartily as good food and good sex. I believe the need for a nonhomophobic spiritual discipline contributes, in part, to the astounding numbers of our people who sometimes express an almost frantic tendency to climb on the Twelve Step bandwagon. Yes, many of us are addicted, but many of us are not.

The Holy Feast of Carnival

Over the centuries, the Christian church tended to forget that Jesus' own way had been this cycle of feasting and fasting. A one-sided emphasis on fasting, self-denial, and monastic asceticism began to be held up as *the* Christian life. The folk religion of the people, however, kept the rhythm in place. Our own cultural traditions of having a big Christmas dinner, a feast of lamb on Easter, or even the tradition of my natal family of having a big fried-chicken meal on Sunday are remnants, hints, of the Christian concept of feasting. The most striking example, however, is the festival called Carnival, or Mardi Gras.

Carnival was originally a Christian institution and only later became secularized. It was part of the cycle, part of the balance of the Christian year. Before undertaking a period of austerity in Lent,

[14]Psalms 104:14–15.

it was thought appropriate to have a celebration—a *carne valle,* "farewell to meat," or probably more correctly, a *carnem levare,* "putting away meat." To be cavorting and carousing in the streets of New Orleans on Mardi Gras, then to drag yourself to Ash Wednesday Mass the next morning at the Cathedral of St. Louis—that's excellent theology. There is a time to feast and a time to fast, and if it is true that some Christians are called to the ascetic life, to a particular emphasis on prayer and fasting and self-denial, then maybe there is also a Christian vocation to the sensuous life—and it is probably queer Christians who most often have this vocation. Since the church has gotten out of the act, the celebration of Carnival—at least in North America—is primarily in the hands of queers. In those countries where Carnival is a broader cultural celebration, such as Brazil, we take a significant leadership role in the festivities. (Perhaps, since Easter is called the Queen of Feasts, Carnival should be called the Feast of Queens?)

One of the characteristic traits of our people is that we know how to play—we understand the importance of celebrating. The enthusiasm with which we celebrate our embodiment—eating and drinking and dancing, celebrating our bodies, our sexuality, and *sex* itself—is just one of the things we have to teach other Christians. It will be one of the major elements of the emerging queer spirituality. Many other Christians have forgotten how to celebrate life. They have bought into the one-sided approach that says to be a Christian is to say no to life. When we so desperately want the approval of straight people that we begin denying our inner voices and trying to act in ways that straight society finds acceptable, we, too, begin to say no to life. When we are true to our deepest instincts, I think we know better. We, as a people, instinctively say yes to life.

Every Mardi Gras (and every Halloween) thousands of our queer sisters and brothers, and even a handful of liberated straight people, keep the feast of Carnival. To some extent we do so on behalf of those who don't know how to party and those who haven't learned to celebrate their bodies. And God sees it. And it is good.

11
RIGHTING THE WRONGS

Queer Ethics, Sin, Evil, and Reconciliation

In one of his early routines, the comedian Richard Pryor said he was always taught, growing up, that oral sex was especially dirty and to be avoided at all costs. He says he *couldn't wait* to try oral sex: "They'd been wrong about everything else!"

We as a people have been told by the straight church for so many centuries that our very being is sinful that traditional Christian ethics and moral teachings are absolutely bankrupt—they have little or nothing to say to us. They've been wrong about everything else, so what can they possibly have to say to us about morality? We can, however, turn to the insights of the various theologies of liberation, especially black theology and feminist theology, for help in understanding what "sin" might mean to an oppressed minority.

The basic insight of all theologies of liberation, which straight, white, "liberal" Christians find so hard to accept, is that *God is not neutral.* God takes sides; and God *always* takes the side of the oppressed against the oppressor. God is on the side of blacks against white superiority; on the side of women against sexism; on the side of the poor against the rich; and on the side of queers against heterosexist privilege.

Theologies of liberation understand God's primary work in the world to be the liberation of the oppressed. Thus, "sin" is primarily defined as oppression in its many forms. Racism is sin; sexism is sin; homophobia and heterosexism are sin. So far so good. That defines *their* sin; but what about *our* sin? What is God's message to those of us who are oppressed minorities?

God's message to us is to resist the oppression, to stop participating in our own subjugation. In a specifically queer context, it is to come out. We'll explore this in much more detail in Chapters 12 and 13, but in a nutshell, pride, far from being a sin for queers, is the remedy against sin. Our greatest sin is self-hatred, self-denigration, or what Susan Nelson Dunfee, in the context of women's theology, calls "the sin of hiding."[1]

We can learn much from the insights of black theologians. James Cone, the formative thinker for black theology, defined sin, for black people, as being a rejection of the impulse toward liberation and a rejection of black community values in favor of white values:

> To be in sin has nothing to do with laws that are alien to the community's existence. Quite the contrary, failure to destroy the powers that seek to enforce alien laws on the community is to be in a state of sin. It is incumbent on all members of the community to define their existence according to the community's essence and to defend the community against that which seeks to destroy it. To be in sin, then, is to deny the values that make the community what it is.[2]

Even more strongly and succinctly, Cone defines sin for black people as a rejection of black pride:

[1]"The Sin of Hiding: A Feminist Critique of Reinhold Niebuhr's Account of the Sin of Pride," *Soundings* (Fall 1982): 316–27.
[2]James Cone, *A Black Theology of Liberation,* Second Edition (Maryknoll, New York: Orbis Books, 1987), 104.

Because sin represents the condition of estrangement from the source of one's being, for blacks this means a desire to be white. It is the refusal to be what we are. Sin, then, for blacks is loss of identity.[3]

In our own context, it is a sin to want to be straight, to "pass for straight." Every personals ad that describes the advertiser as "straight acting and appearing" is a sin. Every attempt to be assimilated into the mainstream, to be "respectable" on the terms of the dominant society, to be "just like you, except what we do in bed," is grievous sin—sin against your very identity. Such actions say to God, "I hate who you created me to be."

The Need for Queer Ethics

Of course, lack of pride in ourselves is not our *only* sin. We are as capable of hurting and destroying other people (including our own people) as anyone else. But liberation theology proclaims to oppressed minorities that we, and we alone, are qualified to define what constitutes "sin" within the context of our own community.

I was once participating as a panelist in a discussion of sexuality and spirituality at a presentation hosted by my seminary. We were all calling for a radical redefining of sexual ethics. After a break, we took anonymous questions from the audience, written on index cards. The first question demanded, "Are there then to be *no* standards, *no* morality?"

Lesbian theologian Carter Heyward took the microphone to respond: "Of course there are to be standards, but the question is who decides, and for whom." Cone and other liberation theologians would say we decide for our own community. What constitutes sin for the queer community can only be determined by queers. What constitutes queer Christian morality can only be determined by queer Christians. Although this concept is so basic it might be called Liberation Theology 101, it is still the hardest lesson for straight Christians—especially "liberal" straight Christians—to learn.

[3]Ibid., 108.

Cone asserts whites "are not permitted" to speak of what constitutes sin for the black community. "For whites, to do so is not merely insensitivity, it is blasphemy!"[4] We should adopt Cone's concept and label *any* straight cleric's attempt to define the ethics by which our community should live as blasphemy. Only queers can know what constitutes ethical behavior for the queer community. Only queer Christians can know what constitutes acceptable behavior for queer Christians. Any attempt by nonqueers to define these things for us is patriarchal and condescending and, as Cone would say, blasphemous.

For instance, an organization within the Episcopal Church called the Commission on Health and Human Affairs, which presumes to make pronouncements about sexual and reproductive ethics, including homosexuality, repeatedly refused to appoint even one openly queer member to its ranks. Whenever that commission speaks of sexual ethics, queer Episcopalians, who, unfortunately, are for the most part far too docile to do so, should be staging ACT UP–style actions, drowning out whatever the commission is saying with screams of "Blasphemy!" The so-called "Ratzinger letter" issued by the Roman Catholic Church, with the perversely inappropriate title "On the Pastoral Care of Homosexual Persons," which identifies the state of being homosexual as "an intrinsic moral evil" and "an objective disorder,"[5] is blasphemous. We should go into the Catholic bookstores where copies of the document are sold and write the word *blasphemy* across them in chicken blood! It is high time queer Christians put an end to letting others tell us how we should behave, to letting others who have no knowledge or experience of our community tell us what is moral for us and what is sin. We need to tell the straight church to keep their doctrines off our bodies.

No doubt all of us in the queer nation face dozens of ethical dilemmas every day—sexual and otherwise. The straight church not only has been no help in the past, it has no business getting in-

[4]Ibid.
[5]Sacred Congregation for the Doctrine of the Faith, *Letter to the Bishops of the Catholic Church on the Pastoral Care of Homosexual Persons* (Washington, D.C.: Office of Publishing and Promotion Services, United States Catholic Conference, October 1, 1986), 4.

volved in the process in the future. It is our responsibility to articulate our own ethical systems for our community. No one else is qualified to do so. Since there are no *openly* queer bishops, there is not a bishop or similar church leader in any church in the world (except the MCC, which doesn't exactly have bishops) who is qualified—who has the right—to speak about queer ethics. It is as monstrously inappropriate for any straight man—however "liberal"—to presume to talk about morality to the queer community as it is for a man—any man—to presume to make pronouncements about the morality of abortion. The old joke from the early seventies about the pope and birth control is actually quite pertinent: *If he don't play the game, he don't make the rules.*

Beyond Fundamentalism: The Law of Love

Usually, when we use the word *Fundamentalist,* we are referring to evangelical protestant Fundamentalists—and they are certainly the people who perfected the concept. But Fundamentalism is not limited to evangelical protestants. There are Catholic Fundamentalists—more and more of them among the bishops, these days. I've met more than my share of Episcopalian Fundamentalists—although I still insist that very phrase is a contradiction in terms. Nor is Fundamentalism limited to Christianity. Today on the streets of New York, you can encounter Jewish Fundamentalists, driving their "mitzvah vans" and buttonholing those they assume to be lapsed Jews. Islam, an ancient and venerable religion, has such a bad reputation among us today because of the antics of the highly visible Islamic Fundamentalists, ranging from the Ayatollah to Cat Stevens (who said in a public interview he supports the Ayatollah's "death sentence" for Salman Rushdie).

Fundamentalism is, at heart, the desire for easy answers. A Fundamentalist wants rules—clearly defined and articulated rules that tell you in advance what to do in any situation that might arise. I believe Fundamentalism is the antithesis of Christianity, which is why I capitalize the word—this is not a type of Christianity, it is a religion in itself.

Fundamentalism seems to be a strong, almost universal, human tendency. Even the totally nonreligious have a penchant for Fundamentalist rule systems. Radical AIDS activists speak of those who uncritically accept the medical establishment's information about AIDS as "HIV Fundamentalists." Macrobiotics is classic Fundamentalism. The organizers of the women's music festival who wanted to exclude women who are into leather and S/M were exhibiting Fundamentalist behavior. Even ACT UP meetings, in spite of the (sometimes excessive) commitment to democratic process, can degenerate into Fundamentalism, as the "politically correct" agenda becomes more and more predetermined and inflexible.

Whenever you hear yourself saying such words as *always, never, absolutely,* and *all,* there's a good chance you are acting like a Fundamentalist—and whenever you're acting like a Fundamentalist, you're not acting like a Christian. At the very least, these words are warning signals to check yourself for the tendency.

Jesus opposed the Fundamentalists of his day, and his ethical teachings are a direct contradiction of Fundamentalism. In the fifth chapter of the Gospel of Matthew, Jesus runs through several of the most basic ethical teachings of the law, putting his own stamp upon them, saying over and over, in effect, "The Law says . . . but I say . . ." In each case, Jesus shifts the ethical emphasis from the specific behavior to the inner motivation. For instance, he reinterprets the ancient prohibition against murder by saying that if you insult and verbally abuse another person, you are as guilty as if you had killed someone.[6]

St. Augustine, God knows, lapsed into Fundamentalism often enough, but he also had his moments when he broke loose from it. In those rare moments, he developed a teaching about sin that is wonderfully radical: *Anything* can be used for good, and *anything* can be sinful, depending upon your inner motivations and intentions. For example, he suggested that even something as seemingly innocent as church music could be sinful if the worshipers focused on the music rather than letting it lead them to God.

A contemporary Christian ethicist, Joseph Fletcher, popularized what came to be known as situation ethics, which is es-

[6]Matthew 5:21–24.

sentially a restatement of what Augustine (and Jesus) taught. The ethical action for a Christian to take, Fletcher said, is to do whatever is the most loving thing within the context of the situation: to do *whatever love requires.* Situation ethics recognizes only one law, the law of love.

Conservatives (and Fundamentalists) get upset with situation ethics because they think it promotes libertinism and selfish, irresponsible behavior. But in fact, if you truly follow the principle of *whatever love requires,* you will be acting in an unselfish, highly responsible manner. Situation ethics (which we could see as being an interchangeable term with *Christian* ethics) requires intensive self-examination. In order to know whether the actions you choose are truly the most loving, you must constantly analyze your motivations and intentions. You cannot simply turn to the correct page in the Bible (or any other rule book) to be told what to do.

For instance, pacifism is clearly a Christian principle. War is almost always immoral—because it is difficult to imagine war as being the most loving course of action. I have no qualms about saying that George Bush and James Baker (both practicing Episcopalians) were in a state of sin due to their role in the Gulf War. The prohibition against taking human life is so clearly and consistently stated in scripture that it is certainly one of the most basic Christian teachings. The early church wouldn't even baptize a soldier unless he left the army. Yet Dietrich Bonhoeffer, a German theologian, was executed because he was discovered participating in a plot to assassinate Hitler. He had become convinced that killing Hitler was the most loving, most Christian thing he could do under the circumstances. You can be a pacifist, opposing war and opposing the taking of human life, and still kill, if you have to, to save your own life, or the life of someone you love. Late-term abortion, suicide, and euthanasia are all the taking of human lives, and yet in some cases they are clearly the most loving action. (In other cases, they all could be sinful.)

The only rule is, *there are no rules.* Christian ethics cannot be determined in advance. What love requires of you today may be the direct opposite of what love requires of you tomorrow—and either day, it may be the opposite of what love requires of someone else.

Adopting this sort of ethical system means taking on tremendous responsibility. It means growing up. It means giving up the idea that you can turn to any other person or any book of rules or any outside system to know what you should do in the situation facing you. You can consult the various rule books, you can solicit the opinions of the various authority figures, and you can examine different ethical systems, but the buck stops, finally, with you. The ultimate decision about which course to follow is yours and yours alone. Professional ethicists speak of the concept of *moral agency.* The moral agent is the person (or institution) making the decisions about right and wrong. In Roman Catholicism, the moral agent is the church hierarchy. In evangelical Fundamentalism, the moral agent is usually the preacher, following a certain carefully defined interpretation of the Bible. In situation ethics, which are simply authentic *Christian* ethics, YOU are the moral agent. You're a big girl now, you get to decide for yourself!

The vast majority of people don't *want* to decide for themselves. That's why Fundamentalist churches, and some of the more bizarre religious sects, are growing so rapidly. People want someone else to make their decisions for them. Most people are willing to give up a significant amount of freedom in order not to have to face uncertainty.

You, however, are hardly like the vast majority of people. You've been different all your life. You're a queer, after all, and that difference is what queer *means.* So taking responsibility for your own decisions, adopting the paradoxically simple and yet demanding ethic of *whatever love requires,* should be right down your alley.

The next few pages of this book are about some specific ethical applications. Please read them with the understanding that I am talking about *principles,* not absolutes. There are no absolutes. I can no more be your ethical authority than Cardinal O'Connor or Jerry Falwell can, because no one can be your ethical authority, except you—and what the New Testament calls "Christ within you," what you might be used to calling your "Higher Power." The Christian doctrine called "the priesthood of all believers" means you do not need (nor do you get, even if you *want*), anyone to be your mediator between you and God. As a Christian, *you* and you alone are the moral agent.

Sexual Ethics

Episcopal priest and theologian Norman Pittenger is a process theologian, a situation ethicist, and a queer Christian, so he is eminently qualified to speak to us about sexual ethics. Over ten years ago, he published an essay titled "Some Notes Towards an Ethic for Homosexuals,"[7] in which he outlined a queer Christian sexual ethic. Essentially, Pittenger said to ask yourself, when you leave a sexual encounter: Am I leaving a body that has given me some pleasure for a few moments, or am I leaving another human being with whom I have shared joy and life? If the former, it was a sinful encounter, even if it was someone with whom you've been in a monogamous relationship for ten years; if the latter, it is good and holy, even if you don't know your partner's name.

Like most examples of situation ethics, Pittenger's scheme is simultaneously simple and incredibly complex. It remains, for me, the best statement of sexual ethics I have ever encountered, and the one by which I live. I commend it to you as the basic outline for a queer sexual ethic.

S/M Sex

Pittenger's system is broad enough to include S/M sex, of course, but since S/M tends to push some people's buttons so easily, it may not be obvious. S/M sex that is "safe, sane, consensual," the motto of a number of gay and lesbian S/M organizations, can be just as good and holy as more conventional sex. In fact since it is so very important in an S/M scene to pay close attention to your partner, and to communicate, often nonverbally, how it is working for each of you at any given moment, S/M sex quite often exhibits *more* caring and concern than many vanilla sex encounters.

[7]*Integrity Forum* 5, no. 1 (November/December 1978), 1, 6–8.

Safer Sex and the Transmission of Disease

As Christians, we are told our bodies are the temples of God's Holy Spirit. You have a particular responsibility, then, to care for your body. Certainly the practice of "safer sex" falls into this category. Knowingly and willfully doing anything that exposes you or others to an otherwise avoidable threat of sickness or death is sinful. Of course, exactly what does and does not constitute "safer sex" is highly debatable—and the lists of acceptable behaviors, which are usually drawn up with the consultation of our highly conservative and homophobic medical establishment, inevitably bear the stamp of our sex-negative culture. They usually err on the side of caution—which is understandable if you don't start from a position that sex is a good thing in and of itself.

The responsibility of a Christian in regard to safer sex, it seems to me, is to be as informed as possible. This would include reading the various lists of safe and unsafe behaviors, and then asking the people responsible for the lists *why*. More often than not, you'll find a behavior listed as "possibly unsafe" when in fact there is *no* data to suggest it is. In other cases, the various experts disagree on whether specific actions are safe—oral sex, for instance. Some classify oral sex as unsafe or at least "possibly unsafe," while others believe oral sex that stops short of swallowing ejaculate is safe. If you think it is unsafe, don't do it. The point is, know *why* you think a particular action is relatively safe or unsafe, and don't take someone else's word for it.

I don't necessarily think that those who are HIV-positive (including those who have been diagnosed with AIDS) have a strong moral imperative to "warn" their potential sexual partners. You should not, after all, be participating in unsafe behaviors with *anyone,* regardless of HIV status—it takes two to transmit. Think in terms of safe *behaviors* rather than safe *individuals.* Safe sex is just as safe with a person with AIDS as it is with a person who's HIV-negative. For the person who's positive, the moral imperative, the most loving course of action, is to take precautions to make sure you don't do anything that might transmit the virus, not necessarily to tell your partner your status. In my own case, I usually do tell my partner in advance that I am positive—not to "warn" him, but to protect myself. If he's going to freak out because some doctor said I have a disease, he strikes me as more than a little shallow, and I wouldn't want to get involved with him, anyway. If I get into a situation where the subject has not yet come up, and my partner begins a sexual activity that would be on the "unsafe" list, I stop him and say, "Hey, you need to know that I'm positive." Then we can negotiate what is and is not mutually acceptable behavior.

I have to say, by the way, that I have had very good experiences with telling potential sexual partners about my HIV status. Most of them say something like "So what?" (If not "Me, too.") The first time I dealt with the problem, I waited until what seemed like the right moment. After I blurted it out, my partner said, "Why are you telling me this? We haven't done anything unsafe, and I don't intend to." The few men I've met who have been upset by the knowledge of my HIV status have, as I have predicted, generally been men whose value systems are incompatible with my own, anyway.

About the issue of AIDS "confidentiality" in general: As a person who has AIDS, I am, frankly, tired of it. It's just as important to me to be out of the AIDS closet as it is to be out of the queer closet. The rigmarole I have to go through for the most mundane procedures (such as signing dozens of consent forms) strikes me as contributing to the very problem it was designed to prevent. I found it empowering to come out of the AIDS closet, and to refuse to treat my HIV status and AIDS diagnosis as dirty little secrets. If you have AIDS, or are HIV-positive, I urge you to consider going public about it. The technique of coming out, which helps remove the stigma of being queer, can work equally well to remove the stigma of having AIDS.

Outing

What I believed for years was that, while everyone *should* come out, and while I would encourage and goad every closeted queer to do so, the final decision about how and when to come out should be left up to the individual. What I am certain is wrong is to use the closet as a vantage point from which to take potshots at those of us who are attempting to live honest lives. In such cases, I have no qualms about "outing" that person.

My friend, queer priest Zal Sherwood, recently wrote to me:

> Robert, I have slept with so many closeted clergy, including three bishops. Plus, I have a very good memory for detail. Do you have any thoughts on outing in the Church? Is it too violent an act? Is it time for retaliation and fighting back? I believe it is.

I wrote him my usual line—if they are doing something to actively harm us, then yes, I think outing them is in order. If they are simply living their lives quietly, it is not. In Zal's next letter, he asked, pointedly, how can *anyone* who's in the closet be seen as not causing the community any harm? The very fact of being closeted, rather than out and proud, *is* harmful. And you know, I believe he is right. Everyone who remains in the closet helps sustain the atmosphere of homophobia in which you must live your life. It is particularly offensive when someone who is in a position of privilege, and thus in a position to create some real change (such as a bishop, a politician, or a celebrity) doesn't have the guts to come out.

Besides, those who remain in the closet have the leisure to do so, to live their comfortable lives, only because of the efforts of those who have been more courageous in the past. We all owe our current relatively easy lifestyle to the drag queens and bulldykes who dared to confront the police at Stonewall, and to a host of others who have suffered and even died for our freedom. David Goodstein, the late publisher of *The Advocate* and creator of the Experience Weekend, was fond of saying, "The difference between helping create a world that works for everyone from outside the closet, and remaining inside the closet, enjoying the fruit of other people's labor, is the difference between chicken salad and chicken shit."

And my patience is growing shorter and shorter in response to that line about "I am choosing to work quietly from within the system." First of all, I question whether such an approach can create any significant change (remember Audre Lorde's warning that *the master's house will never be dismantled using the master's tools*). Secondly, most of those who hide behind this excuse actually do little or nothing. The next time a closet case says something about "working quietly from within," ask, "Okay. What have you done, quietly and from within the system, for the queer community today?"

Is outing morally defensible? In general, yes. It should be used carefully, cautiously, even prayerfully, because you can wreak havoc in someone's life. Again, it is simultaneously simple and complex, for you must ask yourself, "What would be the most loving action in this case?"

Giving the Devil Its Due

A few years ago, Karl Menninger wrote a book titled *Whatever Became of Sin?*[8] Since sin is basically defined as choosing evil over good, we can't understand sin without understanding evil. Perhaps it's time someone wrote a book titled *Whatever Became of Evil?* It has become unfashionable to believe in evil at all—particularly among certain New Age groups. The immensely popular *A Course in Miracles,* and all the books, workshops, and groups that are based on it, are examples of those who deny the very existence of evil. *A Course in Miracles,* which is basically Hindu philosophy written in Christian language, teaches that absolutely everything in the universe is illusion anyway. If something appears to be evil to you, you are just not seeing it right.

That's nonsense—and *dangerous* nonsense, at that. Have you ever noticed that the people who are the most adamant that there is no evil are those who, by virtue of their socioeconomic status, are the most isolated from its effects? Have you ever met a poor black woman from the ghetto, for instance, who goes to a Course in Miracles group? Walk into an inner-city crack house, or an AIDS ward in a public city hospital, and then tell me it's only my misperception that makes it seem evil. In fact, it's not only socioeco-

---

[8]Karl A. Menninger, *Whatever Became of Sin?* (New York: Hawthorn, 1973).

nomic status, but also a great deal of *luck* that allows one to entertain this notion. Try telling a mother who just saw her ten-year-old child run over by a Mack truck that there is no evil in the world.

For centuries, "the problem of evil" has plagued theologians, philosophers, and everyone else. Perhaps the most universal religious quest is the struggle with the question of why there is suffering and evil in the world. For a person of faith, the question is often framed as "If God is all-good and all-powerful, why does God allow suffering and evil?"

Only five answers are really possible:

1. God creates evil and sends it to us for some inscrutable "higher purpose."
2. God somehow allows or uses evil or is in collusion with it—which still does not explain its very existence.
3. We create our own life situations that we may *perceive* as evil, though they are really only "lessons to be learned," as various New Age thinkers teach.
4. The question itself is meaningless because the universe is simply random and without a plan or purpose. So "good" and "evil" are mere chance.
5. The existence of evil in the world is the work of the Evil One, the enemy of God and humanity.

The explanation that works for me is a combination of numbers two and five. Concurring with process theologians, I believe that God has endowed the universe, at all levels, with a tremendous capacity for freedom. God doesn't "do something" about evil because it is not in the nature of God to interfere with the awesome freedom of the creation. The answer to why there is evil in the world, then, is that God allows us, and all creatures, the freedom to make our own choices, and we often choose to create evil for each other.

The question that remains unanswered, however, is *why* we so often choose evil. What is it that causes us to choose to do harm to ourselves, to each other, and to the world itself? Is something wrong with us, that we choose evil over good? Is it true, as Reformation theologian John Calvin taught, that human beings by nature are "totally depraved," or, as the 1928 Book of Common Prayer phrased it, "there is no health in us"?[9]

Do you believe human beings are "totally depraved"? I don't. AIDS activist Michael Callen likes to say he thinks the contest between human evil and human goodness is a "dead heat." I believe we have at least as much capacity for goodness, love, and unselfish choices as we do for evil and sin. In fact, I think queer Christians, women, and racial minorities should be very suspicious of any form of the Calvinist doctrine of "total depravity," for it can be (and has been historically) a powerful tool for keeping the marginalized on the margins. Besides, the Christian teaching is that we are all "sinners," yes, but we are *redeemed* sinners—we have experienced God's forgiveness. I used to belong to a parish where the custom, just before receiving Communion, was to bow your head and mutter, "Lord, I am not worthy to receive you." We had already said a confession of sin and received absolution; why not accept the forgiveness? As long as I retained a significant degree of self-hatred and internalized homophobia, it seemed appropriate to say, "I am not worthy," but the more out and proud I became, the more that phrase stuck in my throat, until finally I refused to say it. I *am* worthy of the blessings and gifts of God, because Christ has made me worthy. I am redeemed.

The more satisfying explanation for why we often choose the path of evil is that we are being constantly seduced into evil by Satan, "the tempter."

Among other things, process theology teaches that God never coerces us into anything, never forces divine "will" upon us. God does have a will, a plan for us, but we are not forced to accept it. Rather, God relates to us by coaxing, inviting, encouraging, even *seducing* us to follow the path God has designed for us. The theologian Pierre Teilhard de Chardin, whose writings are often seen as a sort of forerunner to the process school, saw in the force of evolution the hand of God, the will of God. The very urge toward growth and life, toward reproduction and survival, toward ever

[9]General Confession in Morning Prayer, Book of Common Prayer (1928), 6.

evolving into more and more complex forms of life, is in fact God's call to us and to all of the creation. The urge toward life and health and wholeness is precisely what is meant by "the will of God."

The corollary of this doctrine is that there is also a pull, a call, a seduction, in the opposite direction, calling us away from God's will and plan for us. That pull is none other than what has traditionally been called Satan, the Evil One, God's enemy and ours. Since God always calls us to life, health, wholeness, Satan always calls us to death, sickness, brokenness.

Satan's favored dwelling place is in your mind. That constant negative "mind talk," the constant chatter that says, *You can't do it, you're not good enough, you don't deserve good things, you are not worthy of God's blessings*—that is none other than the voice of Satan. Any manifestation of internalized homophobia is the voice of Satan, the tempter.

One of the best arguments for affirming the reality of Satan comes from those who are involved in the ministry of Christian healing. When we examine the scriptural accounts of healing, especially the healings performed by Jesus in the four gospels, it becomes quite evident that Jesus saw sickness and disease as being caused by Satan. It is sometimes difficult to separate the healing stories in the gospels from the exorcism stories because Jesus didn't seem to make a distinction between physical healing and exorcism—if you are physically ill, Jesus believed, a demonic force is at cause.

For instance, in the Gospel of Luke, Jesus heals a woman who had been crippled for eighteen years, who was "bent over and could not fully straighten herself." That sounds like a spinal problem, doesn't it? And yet Jesus described the woman as "a daughter of Abraham whom Satan bound for eighteen years."[10] In another account, in the Gospel of Matthew, Jesus heals a man who had not been able to speak, and he does it by commanding a demon to leave the man's body. "And when the demon had been cast out," the Gospel says, "the dumb man spoke."[11]

[10]Luke 13:10–17.
[11]Matthew 9:32–33.

You can believe in the demonic origin of sickness without rejecting the scientific view. We are simply going back another step. Some diseases are caused by viruses, but the very fact there is a malevolent relationship between humans and viruses is a manifestation of the work of the Evil One. Toothache is caused by decay, but the very process of decay is an example of the craft of Satan. If we are to recover the lost tradition of Christian healing, which we so desperately need today, if we are to learn to heal as Jesus healed, we must begin by adopting the worldview that Jesus held—and that would be a worldview that sees sickness and disease (and oppression and poverty and abuse and ignorance and heterosexism) as manifestations of the demonic forces that are alive and virulent in our world. It would be a worldview that holds that God opposes the very existence of all these things, that God casts out sickness and disease and wills healing, wholeness, and happiness for all creatures.

You need not necessarily envision an army of demons, each with a specific job description—the AIDS demon, the poverty demon, the homophobia demon, the racism demon. Rather, the very fact that these conditions exist in our world at all is due to the work of the satanic forces, the result of the entrance of evil into the world. This is the classical Christian distinction between the Creation and the Fall—the gulf between God's original perfect vision for the world and the flawed and broken reality in which we live. Sickness and disease and death, poverty and oppression and heterosexist privilege, all belong to the realm of the Fall. They are not a part of God's original creation. The scripture and the Christian tradition are quite clear that these conditions entered the world because evil had entered the world. Evil, then, evil as a force in the universe, is the source of any sort of suffering in our world.

The fact that the world has been flawed by evil means we are all born into the conditions of evil. That is the meaning of the much-misunderstood concept of "original sin." Original sin simply means that you inevitably are born into and live your life in the midst of a less-than-perfect universe. None of us is exempt from the effects of this imperfection. Original sin means we all, without exception, suffer from a diminished capacity to love. We hurt each other because it is in our very nature to do so; we wound each other because we are all wounded, because we are all literally "living in sin."

However, the "good news" of the gospel, the very basis of the Christian faith, is that "in Christ" we can be "redeemed" or "saved" from our inability to love. By accepting Christ's message that God loves us, unconditionally, just as we are, we can begin to learn to love others. That is why Norman Pittenger *defines* the theological concept of "redemption" as being *freed to love*.[12] It is only when you have been "freed to love" that you can begin to practice the "law of love" of situation ethics—to do whatever love requires.

To borrow a phrase from the title of a book by a Fundamentalist author, Satan is alive and well on planet earth. You see Satan's work wherever you see a ghetto, a street gang, homelessness, or disease. You feel the effects of Satan's craft whenever you are the victim of heterosexist privilege or queer-bashing. Your vocation, the vocation of all Christians, is to fight against evil, to do battle against Satan and its host of demonic forces.[13] The way to fight against evil in the world is by refusing to take it quietly, by developing what Carter Heyward calls "a passion for justice," by protesting and acting up. But what about the evil in yourself, the evil you cannot escape because you live in the web of evil?

Confession

In the baptismal covenant, which a person about to be baptized is asked to make, and which we renew annually at the Easter Vigil, we are asked:

> Will you persevere in resisting evil, and, whenever you fall into sin, repent and return to the Lord?[14]

[12]W. Norman Pittenger, *Freed to Love: A Process Interpretation of Redemption* (Wilton, Connecticut: Morehouse-Barlow, 1987).

[13]Taking a cue from Scott Peck, I believe the neuter pronoun is the most appropriate to refer to the Evil One, who is, in fact, neither male nor female and is opposed to the entire concept of any sort of individuation. This is also one of the most important reasons to protest the use of neuter pronouns in reference to God. Satan is neuter, God is androgynous.

[14]Book of Common Prayer, 304.

Just how do you do that?

The accumulated spiritual wisdom of centuries of the Christian tradition has been that we deal with our own occasions of personal evil through the spiritual tools of confession, forgiveness, and reconciliation.

Confession is simply admitting what is true, admitting that you have made a mistake—first to yourself, then to God, and then, if necessary, to any others whom you may have harmed in the process. If you're in recovery or have friends who are, you may recognize this as being, essentially, steps four through ten of the Twelve Step process.

The sacrament of confession (usually called "reconciliation" today) is available as a powerful spiritual resource, primarily when you have trouble forgiving yourself and accepting God's forgiveness. It can be very helpful to hear a priest, speaking in the name of Christ, remind you of what you already know: that "God has put away all your sins." Having grown up under the conditions of the original sin of homophobia, we as a people are riddled with self-hatred. We find it difficult to forgive ourselves. If you are lucky enough to find a confessor or spiritual director who is more or less free from homophobia and sex-negativism, sacramental confession can be a useful spiritual discipline. Even if you don't have a particularly troubling sin on your conscience, the sacrament can be a sort of spiritual housecleaning. You might want to consider making a confession just before Christmas and Easter, to help you prepare for these great festivals of the church year. And just before your birthday, when it seems natural to take a self-inventory.

Reconciliation

Reconciliation is at the heart of the Christian life. The mission of Jesus was to reconcile us with God, and our response is to be reconciled to each other, and to act as agents of reconciliation for the world. This, of course, involves forgiving those who have harmed you. Forgiveness of others who have harmed you is a more complex issue than forgiveness of yourself, particularly for oppressed minorities. We have experienced more than our share of injustice; we have a lot to be angry about. How do we learn, as the Lord's Prayer says, to "forgive those who trespass against us" without giving up our passion for justice?

It has been largely the insights of my friend Carter Heyward that have helped me come to a clearer understanding of forgiveness. Basically, what Carter says is, forgiveness doesn't have much to do with who is right and who is wrong. In fact, if you come to believe that what someone did to you wasn't so bad after all, "forgiveness" makes no sense. To forgive someone means to acknowledge that they have in fact hurt you, but to say you are not going to hold on to the anger, which is destructive to your own spiritual (and physical) health. In other words, it is possible to say, "You treated me like shit, and I forgive you." As Christians, our model is Jesus, who is recorded as having prayed from the cross, "Father, forgive them, they know not what they do."[15] To forgive someone, you don't have to deny the seriousness and evil of what they have done. You simply have to say, "I'm letting go of this now, and moving on to other things." Before you can let go of anger, however, it is often necessary to express it clearly. The most destructive kind of anger is that which you hold inside yourself.

The other aspect of forgiveness Carter taught me is to remember that we do live in a flawed world, where our ability to love is impaired, and those who exhibit destructive behavior against us are operating from their own "woundedness." Again, this does *not* mean you have to excuse their behavior, to take a "boys will be boys" attitude, but simply that you can say you forgive them for what they did to you.

Never forget that anger, for you, can be holy. But anger must be expressed—quickly, effectively, and to the people who can do something about it. Once you have expressed your anger, you need to let it go, for it is self-destructive to stew in it. Releasing anger does not mean giving in to injustice; it just means *releasing* it, and thus releasing its hold on you.

[15]Luke 23:34.

PART THREE

Finding
God in Gay
Experience:
The
Vocation
of Queer
Christians

12
COMING OUT

Responding to God's Call

Coming out is absolutely central to the queer experience. Most of us grow up knowing, instinctively sensing, that we are different in some way, long before we have a vocabulary to describe it. But to come out is to translate that private experience of difference into an affiliation with a community, to claim your citizenship in the queer nation. Coming out is a healing and self-affirming experience. It is the first step toward fulfilling your vocation, to claiming, owning, and celebrating the unique configuration of who you are.

I am still coming out. Coming out is a process with a beginning, but no end. It is nothing more or less than making a commitment to tell the truth, to live the truth, to "do the truth." I went through the first part of coming out, telling everyone I was queer, years ago. Once I had told my family, it didn't seem to matter who else knew. The circles in which I moved—a liberal Episcopal parish and the advertising industry—were easily accepting of my sexuality anyway, so it didn't take long until I was out almost everywhere I went. A few years later, the details of my sexuality and my relationships would be explored by the press—and it was simply the latest stage in a lifelong process.

I date the beginning of my coming out from my first visit to a gay bar. I had had sex with men a few times, but I had not dared to identify myself as "one of them." In fact, a man I had met through a personals ad in an ostensibly straight "swingers" magazine had given me directions to a bar where I could meet him. I carefully took down the directions before I realized where he was directing me. "Wait a minute!" I protested. "Is this a gay bar?" The man confirmed that it was. "I don't go to gay bars," I told him. I met him at a straight bar instead, and we went home and had gay sex. (It doesn't make any sense to me now, either, but at the time it seemed very logical.)

About two days later, I went to the garbage can, retrieved the directions to the gay bar, and decided to go there. I was petrified. I parked in the back in a dark spot where I couldn't be seen. I sat in the car and watched the men going in and out for over half an hour, until I had satisfied myself there were "normal" men (as opposed to flaming faggots) inside. Actually, as it turns out, it was a sort of semileather bar, so there were a number of conventionally mascu-line men there. Finally I got up the nerve to go in. My heart was pounding, and my chest was so constricted I was almost panting. My hand shook as I opened the door. Thirty heads turned to look—no, *stare*—at me. Part of me wanted to turn and run, but the other part, the part that won out, felt as if I had come home. "My God!" I thought. "I've wasted all this time pretending I'm not gay when I could have been here, with these handsome men, where I *belong*!" Suddenly, this twenty-three-year-old man who had grown up feel-ing like an outcast, a sissy, felt affirmed, attractive, *wanted*.

My first experience of visiting an Episcopal church, by the way, which happened within a few months of my first bar visit, raised almost exactly the same emotions. On the one hand, I felt out of place, awkward, and lost because I was unfamiliar with the cere-monial customs. A voice in the back of my head, the product of years of virulently anticatholic Fundamentalist upbringing, whis-pered that I would probably burn in hell for entering a church that had an altar and used candles and incense. Yet the overwhelming emotion I felt, the moment I stepped into the church, was *This is where I belong. This is where I was born to be.*

These two homecoming experiences, within a few months of each other, cemented forever the link between my sexuality and spirituality. In both cases, I had found a place where I had a sense of belonging, a sense that I was in the right place. After the initial visit, I was back in an Episcopal Church every Sunday and holy day, and back in the gay bar almost every night.

The Truth Shall Make You Free

There are other things to come out about, too, besides being gay. Most recently, I have had another coming out about the fact that I have AIDS. My experience with this latest coming-out process has been the same. It is a powerfully liberating experience to live a life without secrets.

A few years ago, I was very involved with a transformational workshop called the Life Training, which is often described as "Christian est." Since that time, I have included among my personal canon of scripture these thoughts by the Rev. Roy Whitten, one of the founders of the Life Training:

> *At each and every*
> *moment*
> *in our lives*
> *We do one of two things.*
> *Either we tell the*
> *Truth*
> *all the time*
> *all the way*
> *down*
> *Or we do something else.*
> *This something else,*
> *no matter how neatly disguised,*
> *is called*
> *lying.*
> *And the better the reasons*
> *we have*
> *for our lies,*

> *The more firmly we remain*
> *in their grip,*
> *And the more dearly we pay*
> *the cost*
> *of grounding our lives*
> *on anything but*
> *the Truth.*

Jesus told his disciples, "You shall know the truth, and the truth shall make you free."[1] As an out and proud queer, you probably understand Jesus' words more clearly than most people. To come out is to be free—free from shame, free from self-denigration, free from buying into the homophobia and sex-negative philosophy of the dominant culture. And once you have taken the first step of coming out, telling the truth about being gay, you see more and more opportunities for telling the truth about other aspects of your life. Having secrets, skeletons in your closet, can be stifling and restricting, but to live a life without secrets, a life that is 100 percent open and honest, is to be truly free.

The God Who Brings Us Out

As a matter of fact, the very urge to come out, to live the truth, is nothing other than a response to what is classically called "the will of God." To come out is to answer God's call to you. One powerful image of God for queer Christians is God as *the one who brings us out*. Most of us have in our personal histories the fond memory of the person who brought us out.

Having queer sex is the Rubicon point in the process of coming out, but while sex is the pivotal experience, it is not *just* sex that those who bring us out offer us. As a people whose culture is still in large measure underground and suppressed, we rely even more heavily than the dominant culture on the one-to-one handing on of our wisdom and traditions. Unlike the dominant culture, our history and mythology are not taught us by our natal families. Our early same-sex partners are often also the transmitters of queer

[1]John 8:32.

culture to us. Most lesbians and gay men understand the significance of being the one to bring someone else out. Contrary to the absurd homophobic notion of "recruiting," very few go *looking* for a neophyte to bring out, but if circumstances put you in that position, please recognize that it is a vocation, an important responsibility—and, at some level, an honor.

Judy Grahn begins her study of queer culture by paying homage to the memory of the woman who brought her out and introduced her to the lesbian subculture:

> Well, Vonnie, teaching-lover, here I am now so many years and such a distance later trying to fill out a picture from the shadow you passed on to me, an opera from the little whistled melody you first gave me with such curiosity and eagerness.[2]

Of course, not all of us have been fortunate enough to have a first-time experience that was positive. For some, the first homosexual encounter was spoiled by shame, or violence. Yet a surprisingly large number of us were brought out gently and carefully by someone with more experience. (Not necessarily older, just out longer.)

In contrast to the image of the straight/white/male god who delights in giving orders and imposing his "will" on his human subjects, the queer God is the God who brings you out; the God who, with tenderness and gentleness, introduces you to a dizzying array of new experiences and new possibilities; the God who allows you to glimpse what you might become and gives you the courage to leave behind what you were. God doesn't *force* you into anything, but rather allows you to come out at your own pace. He stands before you modeling what is possible, urging, coaxing, seducing—but never demanding. She doesn't become angry with you when you are slow to respond, for she knows you are afraid to expand your limited horizons; but she calmly and firmly insists that

[2]Grahn, *Another Mother Tongue*, 3.

the new horizons you will obtain will be wider and more breathtaking than ever.

The straight/white/male notion of a god who *demands* your "love," homage, and respect as his due is a patriarchal image shot through with violence and fear. To speak of "love" in such a context is to employ the same outrageously inappropriate euphemisms our society uses for rape and child sexual abuse. In fact, a cold, passionless God who makes you "love" him, and makes you prove that love with servitude, but offers you nothing in return, would be a rapist-god. Ironically, we know from human psychology how absurd it would be to demand that someone love us, yet we continue to project such an absurd characteristic onto God. The queer experience offers an important corrective to this macho god image—the God who wants to bring us out, the patient and gentle lover-guide who promises to initiate us into a new realm of possibilities. This God demands nothing, but offers much. This God does not give us orders or commandments, but rather offers possibilities.

Perhaps the fact that the person who brings us out is so often not only our guide to the queer subculture but also our first same-sex partner is more than circumstantial coincidence. It is interesting that the language chosen by those who attempt to describe God's enticing activity so often has a slightly sexual connotation. The process theologians Cobb and Griffin, for instance, frequently use the word *lure* to speak of God's influence on the world.

A most striking use of this metaphor of sexual allure is in the writing of a popular theologian, Robert Farrar Capon. In his book on "the problem of evil," *The Third Peacock,* Capon writes:

> Most analogies to the creative act of God are unfortunate. Our heads are filled with pictures of responsible little watchmakers and painstakingly careful craftsmen whose products, once brought into being, no longer have any connection with their maker. God's relationship to the world should not be expounded like that. It deserves an analogy that is—well, more intimate. What he does to the

world, he does *subtly;* his effect on creation is like what a stunning woman does to a man. . . .

So God with his creation. He makes it, yes. . . . But after that, he doesn't *make* the world; he *makes out* with it. He just stands there, flaunting what he's got and romancing creation around his little finger without moving a muscle. . . .

Human beings turn each other on because we are made in the image of a God who is always on the make.[3]

The heterosexual experience of flirting that Capon describes is one that is romanticized by our culture's literature and mythology to be always positive. Yet being flirted with (or, to use the queer term, "cruised") can also be a *frightening* experience. It is difficult for a straight person to comprehend the clash of strong emotions felt by a closeted lesbian or gay man who becomes aware of being cruised by someone of the same sex. There is the positive rush of excitement, of self-affirmation, you feel when you realize (or suspect) another person finds you attractive and desirable. Most straights associate this rush with their early adolescent flirtations. Yet for the closeted queer just beginning to emerge from the safety of the closet, becoming aware of the cruise of another person of the same sex carries not only that positive and self-affirming energy, but also fear. For a closeted homosexual man to notice that another man seems to be flirting with him, and to admit to himself the attraction is mutual, and finally to begin to tentatively entertain the idea of *acting* upon this mutual attraction, is very threatening. We, like straights, were conditioned from early childhood that queers are deviate, sinful, or, at best, sick and in need of help. Most of us learned our lessons well and became quite skillful at hiding our feelings. Sometimes we suppressed them so well as to hide them even from ourselves. And now here is this attractive stranger who seems to be giving you the eye, and to your horror you realize you are, at some level, flattered by the attention. A fleeting, hazy image

[3]Robert Farrar Capon, *The Third Peacock: The Goodness of God and the Badness of the World* (Garden City, New York: Doubleday, 1971/1986), 57–59.

passes through your mind—of what it might be like if you acknowledged the energy flowing between you and allowed yourself to
become sexually intimate with this stranger.

The emotions a closeted lesbian or gay man would feel are
conflicting. There is the enticement and excitement, the thrill of
erotic attraction; but there is also the risk of losing your security.
You have been taught that homosexuality is sinful, evil, weak, sick;
that homosexuals are dissolute, sad, and lonely people—and you
are in imminent danger of becoming "one of them." It is as though
you have been offered a chance to fly, but still fear falling off the cliff
to your death.

So when a straight theologian such as Capon uses the image of
flirtation and seduction to describe God's activity toward humanity,
queer experience fills in a missing element. When God attempts to
entice you into relationship, you may shiver with excitement, but
also shudder with horror. You fear losing your very identity. The
Christian tradition confirms this fear. Jesus spoke of discipleship as
being like death: "The one who finds her or his life will lose it, and
the one who loses his or her life for my sake will find it."[4] The first
time, from the closet, you acknowledged your erotic attraction to a
member of the same sex, there was the joyful thrill represented by
the possibility of finding yourself for the first time in "the mirror of
the love" of another who is like you, who understands, who *knows*.
But there was also the chilling fear that to pursue the possibility of
that love is to risk losing everything—family, friends, self-respect,
professional status, church standing, and, ultimately, your sense of
who you are. It is not easy to choose to die for the elusive *hope* of a
better life to come. My parish priest, who helped me through the
trauma of coming out, told me, "To come out in our society is to
become a nigger."

If you have chosen to come out, to be open and honest about
your sexuality, you may have lost much. You might have experienced the total rejection of your natal family. You might have lost
jobs, been dishonorably discharged from the military, been expelled from schools or excommunicated from churches. Queer

[4]Matthew 10:39, rendered inclusive.

clergy who came out have lost their parishes and sometimes been stripped of the authority of their ordinations. Many lesbian and gay parents have been denied the right to see their children. Coming out can be a costly process. On the other hand, most of us who have experienced life outside the closet would never go back if we could, despite the costs. We have created new lives, founded on integrity rather than pretense, and those new lives have proved rich and rewarding. There is not a closeted queer in the world who would not ultimately benefit from coming out.

Years ago, gay priest Malcolm Boyd wrote of his coming out, relatively late in life, after a long period of struggle and fear, in an experience he describes as being like taking off a mask:

> Beyond all expectations, I have discovered release and freedom, joy and love. Isn't the purpose of our lives to develop and evolve with every breath we take, in every second we live? I have been able to risk everything, and this at an age when many people begin to settle in for their end.
>
> With great zest I celebrate life. I have countless friends. I am filled with joy and gratitude. I love. I am evolving as a person. How could I possibly ask for anything more? I have learned that a mask is a lie, that it obscures deep truths, that it gets in the way of life. The time has come to take off the masks.[5]

The God who brings you out is patient and gentle, a teaching-lover who understands your fear as well as your excitement, and who is willing to go slowly, to bring you along gradually. When you voice your fears, God the teaching-lover acknowledges them— indeed God tells you you are right. You *will* die; you will lose everything that has given you security and meaning up to now—but God also promises you a new life, a new security, a new system of meaning.

"Just trust me," God whispers. A firm but gentle touch against naked skin sends shivers down the spine. "Just relax and enjoy."

[5]Malcolm Boyd, *Take Off the Masks* (Philadelphia: New Society Publishers, 1984), 178.

When you can find the courage to trust, God the teaching-lover tenderly brings you out to a new identity; you become a new creation.

I'm sure you've heard the following Bible passage dozens of times—hundreds, if you've been to church much—but put on your lavender-colored glasses and read it again in a queer context:

> *I am the Lord your God, who brought you out of the land of Egypt, out of the house of bondage.*[6]

[6]Exodus 20:2.

13
I Am What I Am

Claiming Gay Pride

Gay pride is the logical next step, the next growth stage after coming out. To come out is simply to acknowledge what is true, to admit to yourself and others that you are queer. To express gay pride, on the other hand, is to make a positive value judgment. It is a wildly radical act to say, "Not only am I queer, I am *glad* I'm queer."

The litmus test of queer pride is to ask yourself: *If I could take a pill or perform a ritual or do something that would suddenly transform me into a heterosexual, would I do it?* When you reach the stage at which you realize you really *like* being queer, you'd *rather* be queer than straight, you have made a quantum leap in your psychological—and spiritual—health.

From time to time, gay spokespersons addressing straight audiences will say something along the lines of "Look, believe me, I didn't choose this lifestyle. It's not easy being gay in our society, and I'd be crazy to choose it." Such a statement, however well-intentioned, comes from a deep well of internalized homophobia that is in need of healing.

I knew a gay bishop, now dead, who was over seventy when I met him. Having long since retired, he had more or less come out, but he had not progressed to the stage of proclaiming gay pride. He loved to socialize with other gay men, particularly younger gay men, and in restaurants and at dinner parties he would talk quite freely about his own gay life.

However, one day he shocked a number of us by saying, "I don't think being gay is anything to be proud of. It's rather like having a clubfoot. If you have a clubfoot, people shouldn't shun you, but neither should you hold up your condition as normative or desirable." Thereafter, he became known to some of us as Bishop Clubfoot.

We should not really be too hard on my friend the gay bishop, since his generation and the choices he made in his life (e.g., being a bishop in a straight-dominated church) made it much more difficult for him to be self-affirming—but I do see his case as rather sad. (I am happy to report that my former lover, much more patient than I, gradually coaxed this bishop along to the point that, just before he died, he celebrated a Eucharist for an Integrity chapter—something he had previously vowed he would never do. So maybe he did begin to reach the stage of pride, after all.)

If the choice were put to you, would you choose to be queer? I certainly would. Unquestionably, my life has taken a significantly different course than that of my heterosexual friends and college classmates. At times, of course, it has been painful—and certainly many negative experiences come to you *because* you are queer—but overwhelmingly, being queer is a positive, enriching experience. Surely you have gone places, met people, had experiences you would never have had as a heterosexual living under the same cultural and socioeconomic conditions. There is a Chinese saying, by now an American cliché: *May you live in the most interesting of times.* Not the best times or the most peaceful or the most prosperous, but the most *interesting* of times. Being queer, out, and proud may not guarantee you a peaceful, prosperous, or pain-free life, but it unconditionally guarantees you an *interesting* life!

Who Made You?

In the last chapter, we looked at coming out as being a response to the call of God. To express queer pride is to continue to follow that divine call, to deepen your commitment and relationship with the God who called you out.

The Baltimore Catechism, the basic outline of the faith with which a generation of American Catholics grew up, began by asking the child, "Who made us?" The answer was "God made us," which instilled in the child a wonderful sense of self-esteem and purpose. If God made you, then who you are is someone special, and what you do with your life matters. If you were like most gay Catholics, however, that sense of pride was tarnished as you began to discover your sexual identity. Not only Catholics, but all of us who grew up in traditional religious households, began to believe we were sick, twisted, sinful, "an abomination to God."

I would propose for queer Christians a variation on the first question of the catechism: *Who made you queer?* You can cut through all the various medical and psychoanalytic and folk theories that assign blame to someone (your parents, yourself, or some other corrupting individual) and affirm as an act of faith: *God made me queer.*

Being queer is much more than a simple "social construction," a label imposed on you against your will by society. It is an essential attribute of your very being. You were queer, in the words of the prophet Jeremiah, before God formed you in the womb.[1] To say "God made me queer" is to make a radical theological affirmation. It is to assert God *wants* you to be queer, and therefore queer must be a special thing to be, a wonderful gift. To say "I'm queer and I'm proud," then, is to pay God a compliment—which in theological language is to "praise God."

Pride and Shame

In conventional Christian spirituality, pride was seen as one of the seven deadly sins. Christians were admonished to meditate upon their insignificance so as not to get too exalted an idea of themselves. St. Augustine of Hippo wrote that pride (*superbia* in his original Latin; *hubris* in classical Greek) was, in fact, the first sin—

[1]Jeremiah 1:5.

the beginning of all sins. He described the sin of Adam and Eve not as their disobedience, but as their pride:

> They would not have arrived at the evil act if an evil will had not preceded it. Now, could anything but pride have been the start of the evil will, for "pride is the start of every kind of sin." And what is pride except a longing for a perverse kind of exaltation?[2]

Traditionally, "original sin" is seen as our desire to rise above human status, to attempt to achieve the status of God. The serpent tempted Eve to eat the forbidden fruit in the Genesis story with the promise "You will not die. For God knows when you eat of it your eyes will be opened, and you will be like God."[3]

It may in fact be true that for those to whom Augustine was writing—straight, white men—pride is the "original" sin, the most frequent, most troublesome, most basic sin. For those of us on the margins of society, however, the situation is very different. When people in positions of power and privilege speak to the marginalized of "humility," we should be suspicious. Liberation theologians Justo and Catherine Gonzalez caution, "It is significant that many of those who tell us that humility is the greatest virtue, or that the root of all sin is pride, are doing so from prestigious pulpits and endowed chairs."[4]

In recent years, feminist psychologists and theologians have begun to notice that what might be true for men's psychological and spiritual development is not necessarily true for women. Susan Nelson Dunfee, a feminist theologian, says the "original sin" for women is not pride, but "the sin of hiding."[5]

Dunfee's insight is true not only for lesbian and straight

[2] Augustine of Hippo, *City of God* XIV, 13, R. S. Pine-Coffin, trans. (New York: Penguin Books, 1961), 571.
[3] Genesis 3:4–5.
[4] Justo L. and Catherine G. Gonzalez, *Liberation Preaching: The Pulpit and the Oppressed* (Nashville: Abingdon Press, 1980), 23.
[5] "The Sin of Hiding: A Feminist Critique of Reinhold Niebuhr's Account of the Sin of Pride," *Soundings* (Fall 1982): 316–27.

women, but also for gay men. Pride is *not* our "original sin." The most basic and most frequent sin of our people is just the opposite—"the sin of hiding," low self-esteem, or *shame;* and our pride, by contrast, is our salvation. It is deliciously ironic that most of the tactics developed by our community as adaptive responses to society's hostility can be grouped under the term *pride.* Coming out, the celebration of gay pride week, and even dressing in drag (whether transgenderal or leather drag) are tools for us to resist the definitions imposed on us by society and to define ourselves on our own terms.

We are also learning to put *shame* in its proper place. At the prompting of the Rev. Elder Troy Perry, founder of the Metropolitan Community Church, the participants in the 1987 National March on Washington for Lesbian and Gay Rights turned to the Fundamentalist antiqueer protestors who were screaming Bible verses at us and began chanting, "Shame! Shame! Shame!" Queer activists now routinely use the shame chant. During the New York gay pride march, groups ranging from ACT UP to Dignity turn to the fanatical Catholic protestors in front of St. Patrick's Cathedral and chant, "Shame! Shame! Shame!"

Stonewall: The Queer Exodus

Gay pride week (or sometimes gay pride month), observed in some form in most cities in the United States during the month of June, began as a commemoration of a historical event: a riot at a queer bar in New York City, on June 27, 1969, that is seen as the beginning of (or at least a major turning point in) the modern queer movement. Stonewall has become a symbol and has taken on much greater significance than, at first glance, it would seem to warrant.

By recognizing the relatively insignificant event of June 27, 1969, as a decisive moment, a symbolic focal point in the struggle for our freedom, the queer nation has instinctively participated in the same religious impulse that has created most of scripture, liturgy, and religious practice.

The Judeo-Christian tradition is committed to a vision of a God

who *acts in history*. Particular historic moments come to be commemorated as evidence of God's intervention in human history—
and they are often events that would seem relatively insignificant to
an outsider or a historian who is striving to be objective.

Today's biblical scholars know that the Exodus from Egypt
probably bore little resemblance to the Cecil B. deMille version. To
an outside observer it may have been nothing more remarkable
than the Israelites, on foot, being able to pass through a shallow
body of water, while the Egyptians, with their horses and chariots,
were bogged down in the mud and then drowned by the rising tide.
Yet however it happened, the Israelites understood it as an example
of God's acting in their history, and they began to derive their
identity as a people from that event. An ancient hymn attributed to
Moses proclaims:

> *I will sing to the Lord, who is lofty and uplifted;*
> *The horse and its rider God has hurled into the sea.*[6]

It was not so much the actual event itself, but rather the remembering and retelling of the event, that makes the Exodus holy.

Every Passover, Jewish families gather to remember and retell
the story once again, and they tell it in the present tense, as *their*
story. *Why is this night different from all other nights?* The head of
the household answers, "Because on this night, the Lord led *us* out
of bondage." Christian liturgy adds another layer, linking Easter, the
feast that remembers and retells the death and resurrection of Jesus,
with the Exodus from Egypt. The Exultet, the hymn traditionally
sung at the Great Vigil of Easter, includes the words:

> *This is the night when you brought our forebears, the children*
> *of Israel, out of bondage in Egypt, and led them through the*
> *Red Sea on dry land.*
> *This is the night, when Christ broke the bonds of death and*
> *hell, and rose victorious from the grave.*

[6]Translation from the Book of Common Prayer (1979), 85, rendered inclusive.

> *How blessed is this night, when earth and heaven are joined and we are reconciled to God.*[7]

It is the very nature of Judeo-Christian ritual to tell the stories of the holy moments believers see as God's actions, and to use dramatic acts to bring those moments into the present. On the mundane level, the central Christian act of worship, the Eucharist, is a dramatic telling and acting out of the last meal Jesus and his disciples shared before his death. But on a more cosmic level, it tells of the birth, death, and resurrection of the Christ.

Since our God is the God who calls us out of the shadows of the closet and into the light, a gay pride march not only commemorates the Stonewall Rebellion, but also the Exodus from Egypt. We need liturgies that make this clear. Every year on June 27, we should pray:

> *This is the day when you brought our forebears out of bondage in Egypt and led them through the Red Sea on dry land. This is the day when our sister Rosa Parks refused to move to the back of the bus. This is the day when our lesbian mothers and gay fathers refused to submit to the yoke of oppression and began to fight back for our freedom. This is the day Christ overcame shame and death and gave us the gift of dignity and pride. How holy is this day!*

The Holy Moment

Queer historian Toby Marotta has described the Stonewall Inn as "a dimly lit dance bar that welcomed homosexuals with countercultural lifestyles."[8] In those days, the police routinely "raided" queer bars, an officially sanctioned form of harassment. On that June night in 1969, however, a number of those present in the Stonewall Inn decided not to take it any longer.

[7]Translation from the Book of Common Prayer (1979), 287, rendered inclusive.
[8]Toby Marotta, *The Politics of Homosexuality: How Lesbians and Gay Men Have Made Themselves a Political and Social Force in Modern America* (Boston: Houghton Mifflin, 1981), 71.

An important aspect of the Judeo-Christian tradition that liberation theology is beginning to recover is the fact that God is *not* equally concerned about everyone. That is, *God takes sides*. God almost invariably chooses to act through and on behalf of the most marginalized people in a society. The customers in the Stonewall Inn were those on the margins of even the queer culture itself. Marotta writes:

> Many of those present on the night of the raid were "dope smokers," "acid heads," or "speed freaks." Some wore their hair long and dressed in unconventional garb. Some were raggedly flamboyant homosexual cross-dressers known as street queens.[9]

Extremely butch lesbians who would now be labeled "bulldykes" were also among the patrons.

As Marotta suggests, it may even have been the extreme marginalization of most of the Stonewall customers that gave them the courage to fight back—they had less to lose than the more conventional closet queers who were "passing" in mainstream society. If you ever find yourself resenting the participation of drag queens, butch women, and leathermen in gay pride marches because they "confirm negative stereotypes," remember that without drag queens and bulldykes, there would be no gay pride march!

For whatever reasons, on that night, those harassed by the police chose not to run to safety when they were released, but gathered across the street to wait for their friends. At first, the mood of the crowd was playful. But then, when the paddy wagon arrived, something snapped, and this group of drag queens, "acid heads," and bulldykes became angry enough to challenge the police. An account of the event in the *Village Voice* reports:

> Three of the more blatant queens—in full drag—were loaded inside, along with the bartender and doorman, to a chorus of catcalls and boos from the crowd. A cry went up

[9] Ibid., 72.

to push the paddy wagon over, but it drove away before anything could happen. With its exit, the action waned momentarily. The next person to come out was a dyke, and she put up a struggle—from car to door to car again. It was at that moment the scene became explosive. Limp wrists were forgotten. Beer cans and bottles were heaved at the windows, and a rain of coins descended on the cops.[10]

The police became frightened and barricaded themselves inside the bar. A parking meter was uprooted and used as a battering ram on the bar door, and a garbage can full of burning paper was thrown inside. Eventually, the crowd (estimated by some reports to have grown to over two thousand) dispersed, but a profound and permanent change had occurred in the attitudes of the gay community. A New York underground newspaper reflecting upon the riot said:

> People hung around till 4 A.M. talking in little groups. People were excited and angry. In talking to a number of kids who had been inside, it was evident most understood at least rudimentarily what was happening to them. What was and should always have been theirs, what should have been the free control of the people, was dramatized, shown up for what it really was, an instrument of power and exploitation.[11]

You see, the Holy Spirit was at work among the drag queens and bulldykes in the Stonewall Inn that evening, empowering them to take a stand, to stop participating in their own oppression, and to begin to say, "We're not going to take it anymore." Upon reflection, we can see the liberating hand of God in the Stonewall Rebellion as clearly as in the Exodus from Egypt.

Stonewall was not, by any means, the beginning of the queer

[10]Lucian Truscott IV, *The Village Voice* (August 1, 1969). Excerpted in Marotta, *The Politics of Homosexuality,* 72.
[11]"Queen Power: Fags Against Police in Stonewall Bust," *Rat* (July 1969): 2.

movement. Some of the rioters were shouting "gay power," a slogan that was already in use, not created on the spot. There had been, at least in major cities, a large and somewhat visible queer subculture for generations. My friend Dan, now in his late fifties, lived a very queer lifestyle in New York before Stonewall, and he has trouble understanding the importance younger queers attach to the event. Several active "homophile" organizations in the United States and Europe had existed decades earlier.

Nor was Stonewall, in terms of its concrete political impact, the most important event in the history of the queer movement in the United States. Other events, such as the National March on Washington, October 11, 1987 (now commemorated annually by "National Coming Out Day"), or some of the actions staged by groups such as ACT UP and Queer Nation, may have more dramatic and more far-reaching consequences. But Stonewall is for the queer nation, in the language of liberation theology, what might be called "the exemplary liberation event."[12] The annual remembrance of Stonewall during gay pride week is as significant to queers as is the annual observance of Passover to Jews or Easter to Christians.

For those of us who have been in gay pride marches for years, they are a yearly remembrance, a liturgical reenactment of our coming out process. A gay pride march is a holy moment that literally recalls into the present the other moments of our personal "salvation history" and those of our people throughout the centuries. The political impact of a gay pride celebration is profound but indirect—it empowers us to go out and fight for our freedom (and everyone else's) the other 364 days of the year. Why is the day of the gay pride parade different from all other days? Because (even if you have been 100 percent out and publicly identified as queer for twenty years) *this is the day our God brought us out of the closet of fear into the sunlight of freedom.*

[12]For a discussion of the Exodus as an "exemplary liberation event," see Latin American liberation theologian J. Serverino Croatto's *Exodus: A Hermeneutics of Freedom* (Maryknoll, New York: Orbis Books, 1981).

14
SEX

Eros as Vocation

Recently, a member of the Denver branch of Queer Nation, Joe Lindsay, designed and marketed T-shirts celebrating queer sex. The male version features an outline drawing of an erect penis and reads:

> *I praise God with my erection.*
> *I thank God for all the men I've slept with.*
> *I praise God.*

The female version sports a stylized vulva and says:

> *I praise life with my vulva.*
> *I thank the gods for all the women who have kissed my lips.*
> *I praise life.*

"The design came about as a proclamation of my individuality as a gay man and realizing the power of my sexuality and spirituality," Lindsay told an *Advocate* reporter.

Many within the gay and lesbian community in Denver seem to find that "power" of sexuality and spirituality too frightening to celebrate. A letter to the editor in a Denver queer newspaper complained that the T-shirts reinforce the "stereotypes of gays being nothing more than lustful, sex-crazed creatures." We've certainly come a long way as a community—and not all of it has been forward movement. A few years ago, we didn't mind being thought of as "lustful, sex-crazed creatures"; we *celebrated* it.

You may or may not agree with me that *queer* is a positive word. How, I wonder, do you feel about the word *homosexual*? Usually, when people object to *homosexual,* they say it is offensive because it "defines us by what we do in bed." Personally, I prefer the words *gay* or *queer* to *homosexual,* but only for the same reason I tend to use *car* instead of *automobile. Homosexual* is clinical and cumbersome, but I have no objection to being "defined by what I do in bed." I hope you *like* what you do in bed, that you thank God you are not a heterosexual, that, like Lindsay, you praise God for your homosexuality.

Although the younger generation of queer activists is beginning to recover that frank celebration of sexuality and the sense of their vocation to be sex radicals, we are still a long way from the early gay activists (usually called the homophile movement) who saw the affirmation of "gay power" as being inseparable from the celebration of gay sex. What happened?

Sex and Germs

For one thing, the AIDS epidemic happened. There is no *rational* reason for AIDS to make us adopt sex-negative attitudes, but then attitudes about sex are seldom rational, anyway. The sex-negative element in our culture (which is the dominant element) has seized upon AIDS and is using it in a powerful way to further de-eroticize our society. But the existence of HIV is no more reason to stop having sex than the existence of salmonella bacteria is a reason to stop eating. As long as we take a few simple precautions, there is no *rational* reason why we should feel a need to "limit the number of our sexual partners." There is no reason we cannot be what the lyrics of a Tom Wilson Weinberg song describe as a "safe-sex slut." But especially when sex is involved, *irrational* fears are powerful.

All of us, without exception, were raised in a culture that believes same-sex activity is perverted, sick, and sinful, and that sex in general is dirty, base, a product of our "lower" nature. With the help of counseling and wiser friends and pride rallies, we began to overcome this homophobic and sex-negative conditioning. Just as we were getting over it, AIDS came along. It is all too easy for us to internalize the "AIDS is God's punishment" idea and say, "Well, I guess they were right all along. Sex, especially queer sex, is dangerous. I'd better find a lover, settle down, and live as straight a lifestyle as I can, and maybe, if I'm good enough, God won't let me die."

The fact is, you can have safer sex with a hundred sexual partners and not contract HIV, or you could never have sex with anyone but the one person to whom you have made a monogamous commitment, and still contract the virus. *There is no causal connection between number of sexual partners and getting AIDS.* None. Again, the younger activists seem to have understood, and I hope older queers will learn from them, the importance of returning to our vocation as being society's sex radicals. I would suggest yet another T-shirt slogan: *No, we're not "just like you," in bed or out!*

Since being diagnosed with AIDS and becoming a part of what is usually called "the AIDS community," I have been appalled at the numbers of gay men with AIDS I have met (usually in AIDS support groups) who have reverted to a profoundly sex-negative philosophy. Some gay men with AIDS, realizing their sexual needs have not changed, simply adapt by finding new ways to meet partners and practicing safer sex. But others become asexual, saying AIDS has led them to reorder their priorities, and they have decided sex is not that important. (Since impotence is often a side effect of AZT, I think AZT is to blame for many PWAs' lack of interest in sex.)[1]

Sex itself is powerfully healing. Not only are there the obvious-

[1]See Michael Callen, "The Case Against AZT," in *Surviving AIDS* (New York: HarperCollins, 1990). Callen recently said on the "Geraldo" show, "You couldn't pay me to take AZT." I share his feelings about AZT and believe my good health is in part due to my refusal to take this highly toxic drug. Impotence is not the only problem it causes—I am convinced the majority of people with AIDS who are sick are sick from AZT, not a virus. Nor am I certain HIV is *the* cause of AIDS.

ly therapeutic aspects of human touch and mutual caring, but the endorphins that are released in the body by sexual activity and especially orgasm can actually strengthen the immune system. The Eastern religious tradition of Tantra teaches that the erotic energy is synonymous with the life energy, and that when we consciously cultivate the erotic energy and keep it circulating through our bodies as long as possible, it has a powerful healing effect.[2]

If sex is draining your energy, you're doing it wrong—good sex *increases* your life energy. *Sex is life affirming.* Thanks to AIDS, we are bombarded more than ever with antisexual attitudes. I suggest using this little sentence as a mantra or, if you will, an affirmation: *Sex is life affirming. Sex is life affirming. Sex is life affirming.* Say it sixty-nine times a day, and you'll grow hair on your palms.

Integrating Sex and Spirit

The more need you feel to keep your religion and your sexuality in separate boxes, the more you need to heal a fundamentally sex-negative attitude.

For several years, the Episcopal Church Women have employed a unique method of fund-raising for various charities, called the United Thank Offering. Individual church members are given little cardboard-box coin banks to take home. The concept is, whenever you feel especially thankful for something, when you find yourself noticing how fortunate you are (which most Episcopalians have more than ample opportunity to do), you are supposed to drop a few coins or a dollar into the box as a "thank offering." Once a year, the ECW collect these little offerings, and they add up to a substantial amount. My decidedly sex-positive friend Bill Irby used to keep his bright blue United Thank Offering box on top of the refrigerator beside his kitchen door. "Whenever an especially hot trick leaves my house in the morning," he told me, "I drop a dollar in the box and say, 'Thank you, Lord!' " Every now and then, he'd have an overnight guest who moved him to make a five-dollar thank offering.

[2]In several places in this book, I make reference to the excellent work of Joseph Kramer and his Body Electric School of Massage. These concepts, about erotic energy as a healing energy, are among his teachings.

When you reach the point of integration at which you can truly thank God for sex, sex becomes, paradoxically, both less important and more important. It becomes less important in the sense that you realize it's not that big a deal—all the emphasis churches put on controlling and limiting sex begins to look silly. Yet at the same time, sex becomes more important, for you can celebrate it (just as you can celebrate good food or a beautiful sunset) as a gift from your loving God.

Most people, especially most religious people, are tremendously afraid of sex. Although much evidence suggests the earliest Christian church adopted a sex-positive philosophy (as they had been taught by Jesus), the church quickly became frightened of the implications of celebrating sex and began to make rules and place restrictions on its use. Paul, the formative Christian theologian, was profoundly uncomfortable with sex and left us a sex-negative legacy through his writings that has infected Christianity for centuries. In the fifth century, Augustine, bishop of Hippo, who had had traumatic and painful sexual and romantic experiences, plunged Christian teaching even deeper into a position of fear and loathing of sex. Late in his life, Augustine actually equated the act of sex itself with the "original sin."

Yet authentic Christianity, that is, Christianity more closely based on the teachings of Jesus and the practice of the earliest Christian communities, is in fact a very sex-positive religion. The early Christians realized that the central Christian doctrine of the Incarnation—that God became flesh—implied the human body is holy in God's sight. Sex, then, should be seen by Christians not only as one of God's more pleasant blessings, but as *sacramental*—as a pathway to God. The lure of *eros,* the urge you feel to merge with another person from whom you sense erotic energy, mirrors the urge you feel to merge with God (and the urge God feels to merge with you). Augustine's classic line "Our hearts find no peace until they rest in you"[3] can apply equally to your relationship to God and your relationship with a human lover. As long as you understand

---

[3]St. Augustine, *Confessions,* Book I, 1, R. S. Pine-Coffin, trans. (New York: Penguin Books, 1961), 21.

that what you are really seeking when you make love with another person is, ultimately, available only from God, then the erotic encounter with another person becomes an icon of and a pathway to your encounter with God.

In some rare exceptions, the Christian tradition has cautiously recognized the sanctity of sex. Generally, the teaching has been that sex can be good and holy—but only when it is contained within marriage. In fact, the most classic statement of this view is that sex must be contained not only within a marriage, but a *heterosexual* marriage, and then it must be used only to produce children.

Jack Spong is clearly one of the most sex-positive of Christian leaders—I grant him that—but being the most sex-positive bishop is rather like being the least racist KKK member! Spong's stance on sexual ethics is light-years ahead of most Episcopalian and virtually *all* Roman Catholic bishops, but it's still light-years behind the ethical understanding of truly self-affirming queers. For instance, when he learned I had said in a public forum that I did not consider monogamy to be a requirement for a Christian marriage, Spong sent a letter to his fellow Episcopalian bishops, declaring his condemnation of "promiscuous, predatory sexual behavior." The jump from nonmonogamy to "promiscuity" is a major leap; but *predatory*? (Actually, I've decided I think *predatory sex* sounds kind of hot!) A few months later, addressing the House of Bishops, Spong said, "I think that both the church and individual bishops should be in the position to say that predatory, promiscuous, or casual sex is wrong."[4]

I couldn't disagree more. Who made the bishops (not one of whom is out) experts on sexual ethics, especially queer sexual ethics? And why is "promiscuous or casual sex" necessarily wrong? In sharp contrast to Spong's insistence on regulating sex, the gay theologian Norman Pittenger, already cited in Chapter 11 on ethics, outlined a sexual ethic over a decade ago that is unflinchingly sex-positive, offering an ethical system for "the bars, baths, bushes, and bookstores." When you walk away from a sexual encounter,

[4]John S. Spong, address to the House of Bishops, September 1990; transcript printed in *The Witness* 79, no. 11 (November 1990): 24.

Pittenger asked, are you leaving a body that has given you pleasure, or are you leaving a human being with whom you have shared life? By Pittenger's standard, the former situation is sinful, regardless of the degree of "commitment," and the latter is good and holy, even if you don't know your partner's name.

Sex, like absolutely everything else in the created order, can be holy or sinful, depending on how you use it. The determining factors are not in external rules and structures, but within your heart. Sex is holy to the degree that it manifests *caritas,* love and concern; and sex is sinful to the degree that it fails to manifest that love and concern. (And as Pittenger pointed out in his essay "Some Notes Towards an Ethic for Homosexuals," even prostitutes who are good at their work learn to show some degree of concern for their clients.)

While marriage is a wonderful and holy thing, another of God's special blessings, it is highly misused when it is seen merely as permission to have sex. Marriage, a special commitment to another person as a life partner, includes sex as one of its components, but it is not synonymous with sex. We need to learn to separate our thinking about the two, so we can affirm that marriage is a positive, holy thing. But so is sex, inside or outside of marriage, a positive, holy thing.

I applaud the movement both within the church and within the governments and courts to recognize queer marriage, but we must approach it cautiously. It would be wonderful if our government would grant the same economic privileges to same-sex couples that it grants to opposite-sex couples; it would be wonderful if churches offered liturgical ceremonies to celebrate the goodness of lesbian and gay couplings—but the danger is that churches and governments may be doing the right thing for the wrong reason. Much of the rhetoric from those who support the recognition of gay marriage within the established churches, for instance, appeals to the values of monogamy. It would be great for parishes to hold joyful ceremonies to celebrate the love of the same-sex couples in their midst; but more often, such ceremonies are used as a way to extort from queer couples a public promise to be conventional and monogamous—i.e., to "act straight." Bishop William Swing of California (the diocese that includes San Francisco), another Episcopal bishop who thinks of himself as liberal, justified his support of the idea of liturgical blessing ceremonies for same-sex couples by saying, "I'm much more concerned about promiscuity than homosexuality."[5]

Sexual Friendships

Had the gay men of the sixties and seventies been monogamous, a visible "gay community" might not exist today. Had we all lived happily ever after in vine-covered cottages in the gay equivalent of nuclear families—exclusive pairs modeled on television situation comedies and the women's magazines of the fifties—we would have missed the tremendous power of bonding that this period of sexual exploration gave us. It literally created our communities.

Truly anonymous, "promiscuous" sex may not be advisable for many reasons, but a broad scale of possibilities exists between bathhouse or rest-stop tricking on the one hand and a "committed, lifelong, monogamous relationship" on the other. You may reject both of those extremes and yet still be committed, as a Christian, to using your sexuality responsibly and ethically. Lesbian ethicist Carter Heyward has recently written of the concept of "sexual friendships" as an ethical option:

> While we may not be monogamous, we may resist the
> pejorative connotations of promiscuity that originate in a
> culture of sex-negative moralism. We may prefer to think of
> ourselves as open to sexual friendships.[6]

Gay sex educator Joseph Kramer, acknowledging that unrestrained, anonymous "promiscuity" as such might be dangerous today, nevertheless speaks of the value—the *community* value—of having sex

[5]The Rt. Rev. William Swing, *The Bishop's Newsletter* (Episcopal Diocese of California) VI, 15 (November 21, 1986).
[6] Heyward, *Touching Our Strength*, 121.

with friends, which is more important than ever because of the AIDS crisis.[7] And Margo Woods, sex therapist and educator, writes of a type of relationship that is a midpoint between lovers on the one hand and one-night stands on the other, which she calls "friends who fuck":

> I'm not much into one-night stands, although they're fun occasionally, and I'm not a swinger. But I've found that I have several friends whom I deeply love, with whom I will never, for one reason or another, be *in love,* but with whom I can have great sex and great caring and fondness.[8]

In the late seventies and early eighties in Dallas, we called such friends "fuck buddies."

Sex as Play

A curious paradox in the traditional Christian sex-negative teaching is that, on the one hand, the church has tended to take sex too seriously, and on the other, it has not taken sex seriously enough.

By taking sex too seriously, the Christian tradition has missed the fact that sex can be playful, delightful, just plain fun. The phrase *recreational sex* has pejorative connotations only if you begin with a sex-negative assumption. Sex can in fact be one of the most pleasurable forms of recreation, whether it is with your long-term lover or a new acquaintance. As long as you both have the same expectations—that is, unless one of you is deeply emotionally invested while the other is not—sex can be a healthy and wholesome form of recreation *at least* as satisfying (and offering *at least* as much exercise) as a game of tennis. The church and our culture in general are suspicious of sex as play because we lack what gay philosopher Michel Foucault so passionately argued we need: *an ethic of plea-*

[7]Joseph Kramer, *Ecstatic Sex, Healthy Sex: A Seminar for Gay and Bisexual Men* (audiotapes) (Oakland, California: Body Electric Publishing Company, 1988).
[8]Margo Woods, *Masturbation, Tantra, and Self Love* (San Diego: Omphaloskepsis Press/Mho and Mho Works, 1981), 60–61.

sure.[9] The religious attitude that took its most virulent form during the Protestant Reformation, the "Protestant work ethic," leads most people in our society to question the value of anything that doesn't have a "higher purpose." Sex, in this view, is good (or at least tolerable) if it is *for* something else—usually for reproduction. Lately, among liberals, sex is okay if it is *for* love. But sex doesn't have to be *for* anything other than pleasure, because pleasure itself is a good thing. In process theology, *enjoyment,* especially the most possible enjoyment by the largest number of creatures, is the greatest ethical value. When you remember that God created the universe for your enjoyment, and not just for your survival, you can begin to understand that sex can be a sign of God's blessing *just because it is pleasurable.* As feminist ethicist Beverly Harrison has written, when we begin with a sex-positive stance, with an ethical system that values pleasure, the intense pleasure of a sexual orgasm can be seen as a "powerful metaphor for spiritual blessing and healing."[10]

Holy Sex

Ironically, in spite of all the energy the Christian church has invested in controlling and regulating sex, it has generally tended to underestimate how deeply important sex can be. By defining sex as being "for" reproduction, Christianity has forgotten the spiritual aspects of sex—that the sexual act itself can bring you into closer union with God. So sex *does* have a "higher purpose"—it is one of the most powerful and most accessible pathways to the divine.

Joseph Kramer, a former Jesuit who holds a master of divinity degree, has done important pioneering work in "sacred sexuality." Kramer, stung by the negative aspects of his early religious teaching, dismisses "the Christian imprint" as being irretrievably sex-negative. He has turned, instead, to the traditions of Taoism, Tantra, and Reichian psychology. In the Western Christian tradition,

[9]See Michel Foucault, *The History of Sexuality: Volume I: An Introduction* (New York: Random House/Vintage, 1978, 1980).
[10]Beverly Wildung Harrison, "Misogyny and Homophobia: The Unexplored Connections," in Carol S. Robb, ed., *Making the Connections: Essays in Feminist Social Ethics* (Boston: Beacon Press, 1985), 149.

Kramer says, "the body is not part of the divine."[11] By contrast, certain Eastern religious traditions and some Native American traditions see the body and sexual activity as a pathway to the divine.

Kramer's work is exciting and wonderful and healing, and I enthusiastically recommend his basic workshop, "Celebrating the Body Erotic," to all gay men.[12] The only thing I would add to Kramer's message is that there *is* a tradition of sacred sexuality in Christianity, too. True, it has been carefully repressed, and we must dig deeply to find it, but it does exist. As I have remarked before, Christianity offers an excellent theological framework for sacred sexuality, through the doctrine of the Incarnation, the en-flesh-ment of God. Let me just give three quick examples from the Christian tradition of where we can see glimmers of an understanding of holy sex.

First, there is the Song of Songs (or the Song of Solomon), which is actually a long love poem with explicitly erotic imagery. The book, in fact, is so overtly sexual that the rabbis felt the need to "explain it away" as a metaphor of the love of God for Israel, while Christian scholars declared it was a metaphor of Christ's love for the church. Brushing aside these feeble attempts to de-eroticize the book, what is remarkable is that it exists at all, as a part of the Judeo-Christian canons of scripture—that someone, somewhere down the line, took this erotic love poem, this work of "soft porn," and decided to call it scripture.

Much later in the Christian tradition, at the time of the Reformation, the poet John Donne, who was an Anglican priest, wrote this poem expressing his desire for a more unmistakable experience of God, using intense, if not violent, sexual imagery:

> *Batter my heart, three-person'd God; for you*
> *As yet but knock, breathe, shine, and seek to mend;*
> *That I may rise, and stand, o'erthrow me, and bend*

[11]Kramer, *Ecstatic Sex, Healthy Sex,* tape 1.
[12]Kramer's Body Electric School of Massage offers several workshops in sacred sexuality and bodywork training at their Oakland, California, location, as well as weekend workshops in various cities. To contact them: Body Electric School of Massage, 6527A Telegraph Ave., Oakland, CA 94609; (415) 653-1594.

Your force, to break, blow, burn, and make me new.
I, like an usurped town, to another due,
Labor to admit you, but oh, to no end.
Reason your viceroy in me, me should defend,
But it captived, and proves weak or untrue,
Yet dearly I love you, and would be loved fain,
But am betrothed unto your enemy,
Divorce me, untie, or break that knot again,
Take me to you, imprison me, for I
Except you enthrall me, never shall be free,
Nor ever chaste, except you ravish me.[13]

Donne is, in effect, praying that God will *rape* him!

The third example you've already seen in the discussion of the sacraments in Chapter 9. In the marriage liturgy of the 1662 Book of Common Prayer of the Church of England (which is still the official liturgy of the church, even though there are more contemporary "alternative" texts as well), the groom makes the following promise to the bride, which somehow managed to escape not only centuries of Christian antisexual thought, but also the usual English stuffiness:

> *With this ring, I thee wed,* with my Body I thee worship, *and with all my worldly Goods I thee endow: In the Name of the Father, and of the Son, and of the Holy Ghost. Amen.*[14]

It is your particular vocation, as part of the queer community, to help the churches and our culture recover a more balanced view of sex, to rediscover sex as *play* on the one hand, and sex as *holy* on the other. On the most mundane level, you can question the sexual values of the dominant culture, such as that marriages must be monogamous, or that celibacy is a more spiritual state than being sexually active. On a more profound level, your vocation is to teach others about the use of sacred sex. Many of us seem instinctively to

---

[13]John Donne, "Holy Sonnet XIV."
[14]Book of Common Prayer (According to the Use of the Church of England) (1662), 293. Intriguingly, only the man said these words—presumably for no other reason than that the custom in 1662 was for the woman alone to wear a wedding ring. The exchange of rings is a later development.

sense the holiness of sex. Kramer, speaking of his early gay experience, says:

> A tantric is somebody who cultivates erotic energy and lives in an erotic space. In other words, they keep that vibration going all the time. Now, my experience of big cities in this country in the late seventies, in the gay community, was that all kinds of gay men, especially, cultivated this energy and lived in an erotic space all the time—some compulsively, but some celebrating it. It was just fun to feel that erotic energy, in your body and out; and it made people younger, and more vibrant, and more healthy . . . so I knew lots of tantrics.[15]

One of the most intriguing descriptions of sex as a spiritual experience I have ever read is that of Larry Uhrig, an MCC minister in Washington, D.C. He describes an anonymous sexual encounter at Rehoboth Beach, which he calls "the beach of my childhood." From the first meeting, he knew his partner understood the sanctity of sex:

> There was something about him, a deepness in his eyes, the kind that makes you nervous. He had a penetrating power which stripped me naked, and seduced the spirit along with the flesh.[16]

He and his anonymous partner were on a blanket on the beach on a clear night, and his partner asked him to lie back and simply enjoy his attentions.

> I laid there, on my back, staring into an incredible sky while this man proceeded to give my genitals his attention with passion and commitment.
> Something beyond words began to happen. I felt the earth under me, solid, as I saw the heavens turning above

[15]Kramer, *Ecstatic Sex, Healthy Sex,* tape 1.
[16]Uhrig, *Sex Positive,* 86.

me. We felt like one unit, the earth, the heavens, and I. My mind began to expand the scene and my erect organ seemed to raise not just into my partner's mouth, but from the earth into the heavens. A high monument, stirring the stars. Tears filled my eyes as I began to feel God's presence with me, with us. I dared to pray. "God, it's me. I want you to have all of me. I want my semen to flow as a gift to you. My body fluid; intimate symbol of life, to pour out in gratitude. Receive all of me." It was as if my partner was God drawing life from me. I was loving both this man and God. Then I saw more keenly still the white flow of the Milky Way. My prayer went on. "Let my semen flow into the Milky Way. I want each sperm to add to the billions of stars." A pulse began to throb within me. The surging sea and my body rhythm were one. I began to seek to give myself to God. No longer could I differentiate between the sexual experience and my prayer life. In the spirit, I prayed. In a new language of ecstasy, I spoke. Some call it tongues, others the language of private prayer. I knew it to be a private communication between God and me.[17]

The experience of glossolalia, "speaking in tongues," is considered by charismatic Christians to be the most intimate connection with God, the ultimate act of receiving God's blessing, and a certain sign of the presence of the Holy Spirit. For Uhrig to have had such an experience simultaneous with a sexual orgasm was, for him, an experience of deep healing, driving out the last residue of internalized homophobia and sex negativism. He would never again put his sexuality and his spirituality in separate boxes.

Anthropologists and queer historians have begun to uncover fascinating data about the unique roles played by our people in various tribal cultures of the past. Quite often, the ceremonial role fulfilled by queers in tribal societies has been a specifically sexual role. Judy Grahn sees in these sexual rituals of the past the roots of some contemporary gay sexual behavior:

[17]Ibid., 86–87.

All indications are that tricking began as a sacred and tribal act and was performed in village ceremonies and in the temples and sacred groves of the gods and goddesses, an act of worship (and much tribal worship is raucous, humorous, erotic) on the part of strangers who were erotically captivated and "tricked" into giving their sexual energy to the priestesses and cross-dressed male priests of the temple as an offering, the offering of orgasm. These people had special titles. For instance, two Hebrew titles for such temple offices are *Kadosh* and *Kadosha*. The priestesses, or sacred Gay men dressed as the priestesses, accepted the energy on behalf of the Divine Being.[18]

That is a key to understanding the Judeo-Christian repression of sexuality in general, and queer sex in specific. The purity codes in the Book of Leviticus contain prohibitions against the Hebrew men engaging in the sort of ritual sex Grahn describes, because it constituted the worship of a foreign god. YHWH, the Hebrew God, had declared, "You shall have no other gods before me."[19]

Our particular vocation as queer Christians today is to recover the ancient ritual uses of sex, and to put them in a specifically Christian context. You need not become a devotee of the Syrian goddess Asherah in order to practice sacred sex; you can offer your sexual experiences, as the Rev. Larry Uhrig described, to the Christian God. I am exercising my Christian priesthood just as much when I have a respectful, transcendent, sacred encounter with another naked man as when I celebrate the Eucharist. As I once wrote in a poem to a lover, "I can worship God in the Sacrament of the altar or at the Temple of your body." I invite you, queer Christian, to begin to recover the ancient mysteries of sacred sex, to claim and celebrate your devotion to Eros, and to see your sexual encounters as offerings to Christ, to the God who sanctified human bodies by becoming incarnate in one.

[18]Grahn, *Another Mother Tongue*, 208–9.
[19]Exodus 20:3.

15
LOVERS

The Vocation of Commitment

Queer marriage pushes more buttons among straight religious people than any other single issue—with the *possible* exception of the ordination of self-affirming queers. You can be an active and visible member of a parish for years as long as you're single, and people can go through all sorts of respectable middle-class machinations to describe you as "a nice young woman who hasn't found the right man," or "a bachelor who hasn't settled down yet," but the moment you bring your lover to church, the entire parish must confront the fact that these two women or these two men are a *couple,* which means they are probably *doing it.* Suddenly, the parish feels threatened.

Sitting in church with your lover and showing affection in the same subtle, discreet ways heterosexual couples do—one of you putting your arm around the other's shoulders, an occasional touch, holding hands, a hearty hug and kiss at the Passing of the Peace—is one of the most radical educational acts you can perform. Unfortunately, what most queer couples do is sit together, but carefully avoid touching or showing any sort of affection—and that is very sad.

It would be ten times more radical and more educational for the parish to join in the liturgical celebration and blessing of your marriage. Imagine a queer wedding handled exactly the same way a large heterosexual wedding is—announced through formal invitations, as well as in the parish bulletin and newsletter (for a wedding is always a *parish* event, and the members of the parish should always be included). Imagine a male couple, in tuxedos, standing before the altar with hands joined, exchanging vows and then receiving the nuptial blessing from a splendidly vested priest. Few actions could be more affirming of the value and goodness of queer love.

One reason our marriages raise such heated emotions for Christians is that the church has traditionally taught that marriage is a sacrament, and a sacrament is, by definition, "the outward and visible sign of an inward and spiritual grace." Celebrating a lesbian or gay marriage as a sacrament sends the powerful message that God does in fact sanction, bless, and rejoice in same-sex love.

Sacramental Love

In the traditional teaching about sacraments, marriage has been classified as one of the five minor sacraments. The two major sacraments, Baptism and Eucharist, are expected to be used by all Christians, but the other five are used only by those who are "called" to them. Marriage, like ordination, is seen as a vocation, a special calling. Obviously, queers are called to the state of marriage (and to ordination) just as often as straights are, and the church has no right to deny the sacraments to those who have been called to them by God.

By the way, the teaching that marriage is a sacrament appropriate only for those who are called to it should help remind us not to use the growing acceptance of queer marriage to further exclude those who are single. What liberal churches are in danger of doing is creating an atmosphere in which queer *couples* are welcome, but queer singles feel even more left out. Remember, marriage is a good and holy thing. So is sex a good and holy thing, inside or outside of marriage. We can celebrate queer marriage without implying that the state of being single is second class.

A Christian marriage, by definition, is an intentional, mutual, long-term (presumably lifelong) commitment between two people to live together in an ever-deepening union of body, mind, and spirit. A summer romance in which the partners see each other every day for a few months, but know they are going their separate ways in the fall, is *not* a marriage. Nor should the relationship between two roommates who love each other deeply and have lived together for twenty years in a nonsexual relationship be called a marriage. A Christian marriage necessarily includes elements of companionship, mutuality, commitment, and sex.

Companionship

The Roman Catholic Church (still) defines marriage as being for the purpose of procreation, but mainstream protestantism has not used this definition of marriage since the Reformation. In the protestant tradition, the primary purpose of marriage is companionship. For instance, Martin Bucer, arguing for changes to be made in the new protestant liturgy in 1551, said that in the part of the marriage liturgy where the priest lists the purposes of marriage, the first item on the list should be "mutual society, help, and comfort," for it is the most important.[1] Another Reformation theologian, Jeremy Taylor, made the same argument about the order of the list of the reasons for marriage;[2] and a contemporary theologian who specializes in the theology of sexuality, James B. Nelson, says this ranking of companionship over procreation is one of the "commonalities" of all mainstream protestant approaches to sexual ethics:

[1]Martin Bucer, "The Order of Service for the Consecration of Matrimony," *Censura;* E. C. Whitaker, trans., *Martin Bucer and the Book of Common Prayer* (Alcuin Club Collections No. 55, 1974).
[2]Jeremy Taylor, "The Marriage Ring," Sermon XVII in *A Course of Sermons for All the Sundays in the Year,* vol. 4 in Reginald Heber and Charles Page Eden, eds., *The Whole Works of the Right Rev. Jeremy Taylor, D. D.* (London: Longman, Brown, Green and Longmans, 1850–59).

Protestantism rather early abandoned procreation as the primary purpose of marriage and sexual expression. Instead of procreation, the fundamental aim became the expression of faithful love.[3]

A protestant theology of marriage is rooted in the biblical affirmation that it is not good to be alone, and so God has given us the gift of loving companionship.[4] Don't hold your breath waiting for the Roman Catholic Church to bless queer unions. It's not going to happen in my lifetime or yours, because the Roman definition of marriage makes same-sex marriage a non sequitur. But protestant churches could be brought around to seeing that their own theology of marriage inevitably implies a same-sex marriage is just as valid and holy as a heterosexual marriage. Marriage is a "remedy against loneliness," and certainly we are just as prone to loneliness as straight people.

The Genesis myth, that God created a companion for the first human so that Adam would not be lonely, is a beautiful image of the gift of human companionship, but it has been so shot through with heterosexist assumptions it can be used against rather than for us. I'm sure you've heard Fundamentalist evangelists say, "God created Adam and Eve, not Adam and Steve!" However, another ancient myth of the origins of human companionship is much more inclusive, a myth that should be a part of the canon of queer scripture. A version of it is found in Plato's *Symposium*. Plato's character Aristophanes, attempting to win a contest by telling the best story about love, expounds the story of "the other half." He claims the original human beings were double—with two heads, four arms, and four legs. When they became arrogant and tried to be "like gods," the gods split them in half to reduce their power, which "left each half with a desperate longing for the other."[5] What we would today call "sexual orientation" depended upon the gender of one's

---

[3]James B. Nelson, *Between Two Gardens: Reflections on Sexuality and Religious Experience* (New York: Pilgrim Press, 1983), 66.
[4]Genesis 2:18–24.
[5]*Symposium* 191a.

other half—some of the original beings were male and female, some were male and male, some were female and female. All three go through life seeking and longing to be reunited with their "other half." To be human is to experience a "desperate longing" for a lover, for our "other half," and Christian marriage is the church's sacramental celebration when we find that person.

Mutuality

The assumption that a marriage should be a *mutual* relationship is a relatively late development in Christian history. For centuries, marriages were not transactions between social equals—they were property contracts, often between a man and his wife's father, detailing the distribution and exchange of property (including the wife) from one to the other. The contemporary church, however, has moved away from the "wives, obey your husbands" mentality and has insisted a Christian marriage should be a covenant between two equals, not a relationship of dominance and submission. It is difficult to find suitable biblical passages to be read at heterosexual weddings because no heterosexual marriages in scripture were covenants between two social equals.

It is deliciously ironic, then, as you read in Chapter 4, that the only two descriptions of truly mutual covenant love to be found in the Bible are of same-sex relationships—David and Jonathan, and Ruth and Naomi. In fact, the words of Ruth's covenant with Naomi are so beautiful and compelling they are read or sung at hundreds of heterosexual weddings, with no one giving a second thought to the fact they are inspired by a lesbian love affair.

Perhaps it is not so ironic, after all, because in fact gay and lesbian pairings are often more truly mutual relationships than most heterosexual marriages. While it is difficult if not impossible for a straight couple to shake off totally their gender-role conditioning, we have no such role images to follow. We must make our own decisions and do our own negotiating about who's going to be responsible for which tasks, how finances are to be handled, and how to weigh the demands of one partner's career against the other's. In fact, straight couples could learn a lot from us.

Commitment

A Christian marriage is not just a random pairing of two people; it involves an intentional, well thought out, formal commitment to each other. One of the biggest problems among queer couples is that since we do not have structures, such as marriage ceremonies and licenses, to mark the beginning of our relationships, we tend to slide into them without much intentionality or consciousness about the parameters of the relationship we are creating. Then, a few months or a few years down the road, we may find that our assumptions about the "rules" of the relationship clash with our partner's assumptions. All this could be avoided by sitting down together at the beginning of a new relationship and spelling out those assumptions and expectations. When a same-sex couple ask me to bless their relationship, I take advantage of the opportunity to ask them a lot of questions about their arrangement, making sure they have at least considered the right questions about possible future situations: What if one of them becomes seriously ill? What if one becomes unemployed? What if one dies—what financial arrangements do they need to make? What if one's elderly mother wants to come live with them? What if one's offered an excellent job on the other coast; would the other quit her job to go along? Et cetera.

A key element of a successful marriage is *the ability to make and keep intentional agreements.* To a large extent, it doesn't much matter what the agreements are, as long as they are carefully discussed and mutually agreed upon. Before any two people enter into a marriage, they need to sit down and have a long, serious talk about such issues as living arrangements, finances, division of household chores, relationship to each other's family, career goals and decisions, and feelings about sexual exclusivity. You know the old saying about *assume:* It makes an *ass* out of *u* and *me.* Never assume that your values, goals, and expectations are the same as your partner's. Discuss them.

I lost my job for saying this, but I still believe it is true: Monogamy, an agreement to be sexual with no one except your primary partner, is an agreement a couple may or may not choose to make. It is an option. As long as you and your partner agree which option you choose, it has no more moral value attached to it than whether you prefer vanilla or chocolate ice cream. Marriage is not defined by sexual exclusivity. I have had sex with lots of male couples, as well as with many men whose lovers were out of town or simply home for the evening while my partners enjoyed a night out. I have even had sex with some couples both separately and together. Many of these couples have been together for decades. In fact, it may just be that relationships that are not sexually exclusive last *longer* than those that are.

What is immoral is the not-uncommon situation in which someone with whom you've had a sexual encounter suddenly remembers he (or she) has a lover back home, a lover who would be deeply hurt by knowing of this affair. If a couple's agreement includes the possibility of outside sexual relationships or threeways, then such sexual play is an ethical fulfillment of that agreement. But when a couple agrees to (or more often, assumes) sexual exclusivity and one partner has a secret sexual encounter with someone else, that is unethical, for the agreement has been broken.

I will officiate a marriage ceremony for a couple whether or not they intend to be sexually exclusive. However, I will not do so until they have carefully outlined for me just exactly what their agreement is, and I am satisfied they both have the same understanding and assumptions. When we bless a marriage, we bless the love and the covenant between two people, so it is imperative they be as clear as possible about what that covenant is.

An important distinction is to be made between a covenant and a contract. Although marriage in our society remains primarily a legal contract about the transfer of property, a distinctly *Christian* marriage is not a contract, but a covenant. A contract is worded, "If you do A, then I'll do B," and it implies that if you fail to do A, I am no longer obligated to do B. A covenant, on the other hand, is worded, "I will do A and you will do B, and if you do not do B, I am not released from my obligation to do A." That is, if your covenant includes an agreement for sexual exclusivity, you cannot say, "Well, you had an outside affair, so now I'm going to have one, too!"

Sex

All sorts of covenant relationships exist, but I am absolutely adamant about insisting that a relationship cannot be called a marriage unless the partners intend to be sexual with each other. Sex is not all a marriage is, but it's not a marriage without sex. It is, in fact, sex that makes a marriage sacramental.

If our God has ordained it is not good to be alone, and has provided us with marriage as a remedy against loneliness, it is especially through sex—the embrace of another warm body—that our loneliness is alleviated.

Mystics for centuries have made the connection between the longing for union with God and the longing for union with another person that is the sexual urge. In fact, our embodied sexual longings—the intense and inevitably frustrated desire to transcend the boundaries of our skin and be truly at one with another person—can be seen as an icon, even as a manifestation, of our desire to experience union with God. We do not ever totally achieve this union, either with another person or with God, in any lasting way in our present existence, yet we can occasionally catch glimpses of the promise of such union in the afterlife. A primary occasion for such foretastes of the Realm of God is the fleeting sense of union we can feel during sex, and particularly during a shared orgasm, when we feel, for a moment, the boundaries have dissolved and we have truly merged with our lover. This orgasm, powerful sign of God's blessing, makes sex within marriage the sacrament of a sacrament—a rich sacrament of the Incarnation, the doctrine that God is present in human flesh.

Marriage: A School for Love

According to the classical definition, a sacrament is not just a *sign* of God's grace, but a *means* of grace—a channel by which God's power and presence come to us. How is a marriage a channel of God's grace?

As we saw in Chapter 11, the concept of "original sin" primarily means we all have a diminished capacity to love. God's redemption, her saving act, is simply to make us aware of her unconditional love for us, so that we are, in Norman Pittenger's words, "freed to love." When we come to understand that God loves us, unconditionally, just as we are, "warts and all," then it becomes easier to believe and risk that another person might love us and we them. And it is cyclical: The more we experience the love of another human being, as unconditional as it is possible for human love to be, the more we can understand and experience God's love for us.

Love is not just a warm fuzzy feeling; love is taking action, making decisions, negotiating, sometimes altering your needs and desires in order to accommodate those of another. Marriage, the experience of living intimately with another human being whose needs, wishes, and preferences daily confront and conflict with your own, gives you practical experience in dealing with other decisions and conflicts on a larger scale. So through marriage, you can learn justice, you can learn to love others. Through marriage, through the act of working out an equitable partnership between two adults with different needs, wants, abilities, and gifts, you put into practice the communal (and Christian) principle *from each according to ability, to each according to need.*

When a marriage is good and healthy, it becomes a source from which the partners draw as they go out into the world to do the work of justice and love to which we are all called by God. In the liturgy I use for a same-sex marriage, one of the prayers says:

> Give them such fulfillment of their mutual affection that they may reach out in love and concern for others; with a passion for justice and a particular concern for the marginalized and oppressed.

Queer Weddings

You've already heard at some length in Chapter 9 about the liturgical ceremony of a same-sex wedding. At this point I simply want to reiterate how important such ceremonies are. A marriage, whether queer or straight, whether Christian or not, is not a private affair; it is a community event. One important reason for having a marriage ceremony is that it is (or at least should be) a very public declaration of the covenant the two people are making together. In the queer wedding liturgy I use, after the couple have made their vows to each other, I turn to the congregation, their friends, family, and support community, and ask, "Will all of you witnessing this covenant do all in your power to uphold these two persons in their life together?"

Although homophobia sometimes demands certain concessions to privacy, in general I am uncomfortable with queer weddings that are clandestine affairs, held in secret in the couple's living room. A closet wedding is a contradiction in terms. A wedding should be a public affair. It should certainly be known to all the members of your parish, announced in the parish bulletin and newsletter, and recorded in the parish register of services. Your family, friends, and coworkers should be invited, so they can witness the covenant and pledge to help you uphold it.

Of all the same-sex weddings I have officiated, my favorite was a double ceremony for a male couple (one of whom is a porno star!) and a female couple that was held on the upper deck of *The Spirit of New Jersey,* a boat that sails around the Statue of Liberty in the New York harbor. It was a very formal wedding, with many attendants, and careful attention to detail. Hundreds of guests attended, including queer and straight friends and many family members. Clearly, the couples were surrounded by the people most important to them, their wedding being an act of their community. I felt proud to have been a part of it, and proud of both couples for having the courage and vision to arrange such a ceremony. We need more large, visible, public queer weddings.

The Healing Power of Queer Love

I want to turn again to the works channeled by Andrew Ramer, which I mentioned earlier. Remembering that all of the universe is made up of vibrating, pulsating energy, we can then see that love itself is an energy, and *Two Flutes Playing* teaches that it can be a healing energy. In fact, according to the spiritual guides responsible for that book, different energies are created by woman-woman love and man-man love than those created by man-woman love—and all three are necessary to create the web of energy that sustains our universe:

> We knew this before. You will know this again: that same-sex loving is the cross-fibering on the loom of humanness; that without it, no weaving can happen; that without it, humanity cannot exist. For same-sex loving holds the cross fibers, the cross song. For same-sex loving is the other half that makes a whole be more than itself.[6]

If you are fortunate enough to be living in a same-sex marriage, remember that your relationship itself is a vocation, a holy vocation that can help heal the world. Our world certainly needs all the love it can get, and the love you express for your partner is literally a healing and sustaining energy. You two are doing God's work.

[6]Andrew Ramer, *Two Flutes Playing* (Oakland, California: Body Electric Publishing), 35.

16

HOLY ANGER

Protest as Vocation

Multiple-choice quiz:
Which of the following could be a way of living out your
Christian faith?

A. Making an effort to be in church and receive Commu-
nion every Sunday without fail.
B. Telling off a coworker who just told a racist joke.
C. Participating in an ACT UP "action" at a cathedral.
D. All of the above.
The correct answer is D, all of the above.

According to the classical Christian tradition, anger is one of the
seven deadly sins. Since Thomas Aquinas, Christians were coun-
seled to avoid the expression of anger, for it was seen as an emotion
that could easily get out of hand and put your soul in danger.

While Thomas Aquinas may not have been wrong about *everything* else, he was certainly wrong about a number of other things.
Pride was also considered one of the seven deadly sins—number
one, in fact—and yet as we discussed in Chapter 13, gay pride is
not sin, but salvation for our people. Just as pride is not a

sin but a virtue for you, anger, when thoughtfully expressed and carefully directed, is not a sin but a virtue. Claim for yourself the power of *holy anger*.

With the AIDS crisis as a catalyst, many queers have learned to claim and celebrate the positive use of anger, through such organizations as ACT UP and Queer Nation. Yet queer religious groups still tend to be profoundly uncomfortable with anger, seeing it as "non-Christian."

Bullshit. Christians generally accept that we should pattern our lives after Christ, and he was anything but shy about showing anger. We tend to forget this because the church hierarchy, concerned to keep us docile and controllable, has wanted us to forget it. The propaganda has been so effective that most people have an image of "gentle Jesus, meek and mild," and honestly believe Jesus never showed anger. The life-of-Christ novel *The Greatest Story Ever Told* went so far as to claim Jesus never stepped on a bug. *Puh-leeze, Mary!*

Jesus Gets Riled

We have to go no further than the Bible itself to be reminded that Jesus exhibited quite a talent for pitching a bitch. First of all, we have the descriptions of his tirades against the Pharisees and Sadducees. In the English translation, several centuries removed from their cultural context, Jesus' words sound relatively tame. He calls them such names as *blind fools, children of hell, hypocrites, white-washed tombs full of dead men's bones, open graves, sons of those who murdered the prophets, serpents,* and *brood of vipers.*[1]

What we miss is that in the original language and in the original cultural context, these words were as strong as such words as *you sons of bitches* or *you shitheads* would be for us. What we also usually miss is that these diatribes were addressed to the religious leaders of the day. The cultural equivalent of Jesus standing in the temple courtyard calling the Pharisees a brood of vipers today would be your walking into a gathering of bishops and calling them a bunch of murderous assholes.

[1] See Matthew 23; also Luke 3:7–9.

218

The most vivid picture of Jesus venting his holy anger is an incident that has come to be known as "the cleansing of the temple." The courtyard of the temple had the flavor of a busy town square. Vendors set up tables selling sheep, oxen, and pigeons for sacrifices. Others exchanged (at a profit) the Roman currency for Jewish "temple money," which was to be used to buy the sacrificial animals.

Jesus walked into the courtyard one day and was so angered by the contrast between the bustling commercialism he saw and the atmosphere of reverence and devotion he felt the temple should have, he literally threw a fit. He began screaming at the vendors, calling them "thieves," as he turned over their tables, scattering the coins and stampeding the livestock. According to the account in the Gospel of John, he used a "whip of cords" to drive both the animals and the vendors out of the temple.[2] That is, he was hitting people with a rope whip. It was undeniably an act of violence.

If you are to pattern your life after the life of Christ, why isn't that image just as valid as the image of "turning the other cheek"? The account of Jesus' angry, even violent, outburst, which appears in all four of the gospels, is all the documentation you need for a justification of protest and holy anger. Critics try to treat anger as though it somehow cancels out your message. They are wrong. ACT UP's strident protests have gotten more press coverage than any gay pride parade ever did. I wish I had a dollar for every time someone said to me, "You're such an *angry* young man!" As I have gotten older, I have learned the proper response (to Christians, anyway) is, "Hell yes, I'm angry. Why aren't you?" Anger about injustice is not a "deadly sin" but a "cardinal virtue" for Christians. We must have the self-confidence to reject the dominant culture's labeling of anger as "sinful" or psychologically "unhealthy," and claim and celebrate our anger as holy, a response to God's call to us.

When ACT UP stages a "die in" on the steps of a government building, when Queer Nation hands out condoms at a religious shrine in upstate New York, when angry queers confront Cardinal O'Connor in St. Patrick's Cathedral, they are expressing their holy anger, just as our brother Jesus did that day at the temple.

[2]Matthew 21:12–13; Mark 11:15–19; Luke 19:45–46; John 2:13–22.

Cleansing the Temples

A popular notion is that while protest might be a constitutional right for Americans, staging protests in religious settings is inappropriate. The judge who sentenced the "Safe Sex Six" for their role in the "Stop the Church" action at St. Patrick's Cathedral cited the violation of the worship space as their real crime. Yet if we follow Jesus' example, we come to see it is *especially* religious institutions and religious leaders that are the most appropriate targets of our rage. In most examples in the gospels of Jesus expressing anger, the targets of his rage are religious leaders. Besides, in the case of St. Patrick's Cathedral, the protestors were using the cathedral to voice a demand for justice, and since justice is an attribute of God, theirs was an inherently holy act. They were not desecrating a holy space; the cardinal had already desecrated it by using the cathedral pulpit to preach intolerance and hatred.

Our valuation of religious freedom and pluralism has led many people to believe that everyone is entitled to the expression of whatever religious beliefs and practices they choose, and that one person's religion is no one else's business. That is a dangerous belief. The Ku Klux Klan makes use of religious language and Christian symbols. Does that mean, in the name of tolerance and pluralism, we must stand back and let them proclaim their message of hate? And who has been responsible for more queer suffering and death in the past fifty years—the Ku Klux Klan or the Roman Catholic Church? *The protestors who disrupted the worship service in St. Patrick's Cathedral were following in Jesus' footsteps, by expressing holy anger.*

"You shall not make my Father's house a house of trade!" Jesus shouted at the temple vendors.[3] I have no doubt he would shout at Cardinal O'Connor or Cardinal Law, "You shall not make my church a house of homophobia!"

Staging dramatic, powerful expressions of queer rage is what the various queer religious groups such as Dignity, Integrity, Affirmation, and Lutherans Concerned *ought* to be doing with their time

---

[3]John 2:16.

and resources. The fact that these groups have failed to take such action, leaving it to a "secular" group such as ACT UP, is a sad commentary on their spiritual bankruptcy. Ten years ago, most queer religious caucuses were radical action groups; today, they have almost all sold out to the patriarchal power structures they were created to confront. When a bishop invites you to an elegant luncheon at the church headquarters, you are less likely to stage a noisy protest on the front lawn the next time he does something homophobic. Most of these organizations are so busy "playing church" they have little energy for demanding justice.[4]

Holly Near's haunting and popular song is the closest thing we have to a queer movement song. Her lyrics beautifully describe the place of anger in the queer psyche: "We are a gentle, angry people." We are, by nature, a *gentle* people, but we are also, by necessity, an *angry* people—angry at the injustice we have been dealt by governments and churches. Although pacifism and tolerance have always been central to our collective soul, we are mad as hell and we aren't going to take it anymore!

We're All in This Together

It is important that we recognize our holy anger as a function of our *community,* in order to avoid the unhealthy manifestation of misplaced anger. When you express your anger on an individual rather than a collective level, it can easily give rise to the stereotypical images of the "bitchy queen" and the "humorless lesbian," taking out anger on anyone nearby, often those who have little to do with the issue. When you feel frustrated at a lack of power and control over your life, you are likely to become abusive to those who are placed in subservient positions to you, such as waiters, flight attendants, and utility company employees. In its darker man-

---

[4] I am, however, happy to report the recent founding of an organization called Presbyterian ACT UP, which stages powerful "actions" at Presbyterian Church events. I have also had some conversations with an energetic young man who wants to found a similar organization for the Episcopal Church. In England, a creative protest group called the Whores of Babylon, an affinity group of OutRage (similar to ACT UP), has begun utilizing techniques such as drag and street theater to protest Church of England homophobia. I pray other denominational caucuses in this country and elsewhere will get angry enough to follow suit.

ifestations, such misplaced anger may be directed at children or spouses and can become physical violence. Organizing and focusing your anger collectively can help you to retain your sense of humor as an individual.

I am not suggesting you should not take action as an individual, but when you do so, you should not be acting in a vacuum. Both you and your message benefit greatly from a sense of standing with the community, of being in solidarity with your queer brothers and sisters, of feeling their support behind you, of acknowledging the great cloud of queer witnesses who have struggled before you, and pausing to remember those who will take up the fight after you. Lesbian theologian Carter Heyward has suggested, in the light of a relational ethic, that the answer to Rabbi Hillel's classic questions, "If not you, who? If not now, when?" might in fact be, "If not now, then later; and if not me, then others, representing me."[5] You are not, of course, excused from the responsibility of individual action, of doing what you can, but you need not act alone. You are not an island, but part of a network, a community, a great queer nation.

In fact, when action is taken in community, the protests that are designed often exhibit a healthy sense of humor. One of my favorite examples was a creative statement made using the life-size Christmas crèche on the Boston Common a few years ago. (The very existence of the crèche on public property is an inappropriate violation of the concept of separation of church and state; thoughtful Christians should protest it on those grounds alone.) This particular year, however, Governor Michael Dukakis had made headlines with his veto of the possibility of lesbian or gay people serving as foster parents, based on his incorrect assumption that children are healthier when they grow up in a traditional mommy-and-daddy household. (Since many of us are in recovery from precisely such upbringing, we know how ridiculous the notion is!) That Christmas, someone stole the baby Jesus from the scene and left in its place a sign explaining that since the holy family did not meet Governor Dukakis's standards for foster care, the kidnappers

[5]Heyward, *Touching Our Strength*, 31.

were holding the baby until a *married* heterosexual couple with previous child-rearing experience came forward to claim it.

The now-defunct Sisters of the Perpetual Indulgence, who staged hilarious protests in nun drag, were effective without losing their sense of humor. Dave Hurlbert, a founder of the Whores of Babylon, an affinity group within London's OutRage, explained, "What we try to do is to take what we call camp, but which is really sacred ritual, and use it for the positive good of all. Why should the church hierarchy have a monopoly on camp?"[6] Another example of humor in protest, albeit biting humor, was a sign carried by an activist during the "Stop the Church" action at St. Patrick's Cathedral. The sign, divided into two panels, featured a large photo of Cardinal O'Connor on the left, wearing his bishop's miter. On the right was a photo of an unrolled condom, which has roughly the same shape as a bishop's miter. The caption: *Know your scumbags.* I would venture to guess the person who designed that sign was operating from a much healthier personal space than the person at the same event who shocked the nation by desecrating the consecrated Communion host.

Crumbling the Communion wafer, although unfortunate, was certainly an understandable act of rage, but it has the flavor of *blind* rage and therefore is potentially self-destructive to the protestor and to the community. Both the organizers of the action and the individual who crumbled the wafer have said it was the individual's idea, not a planned part of the protest. He was, clearly, acting without that sense of community solidarity.

Christian Idealism

Being dissatisfied with the state of the world is a profoundly Christian attitude. Jesus taught us to pray for the Realm of God to be manifest "on earth as in heaven." As a Christian who holds a mental image of the world as it *should be,* you cannot help but be shocked and dismayed at how the world *really is.* If you are not deeply moved by war, hunger, disease, poverty, and injustice, you are not

[6]Chris Woods, "Activists Exorcise Church of England," *The Advocate* 586 (September 21, 1991): 51.

really praying "the prayer Jesus taught us to pray." To complain about the state of the world is to follow the command of Christ—provided you follow through by taking action, by doing something to help make the Realm of God come to the here and now.

A Christian dissatisfaction with the world as it is should not be confused with a sub-Christian disregard for the world. Any dualistic philosophy that concentrates on "the spiritual" and sees the real world as unimportant or evil is not authentic Christianity. The Christian response is to feel dissatisfied with the reality precisely because we have a vision of how it could be, should be, in the Realm of God. The Christian stance toward the world is to confront the evil and imperfection, and to live our lives as though the Realm of God had in fact come on earth. To focus on what is wrong in the world and work to correct it is diametrically opposed to seeing the world as the realm of the Evil One (as do many Fundamentalists) or as a meaningless illusion (as do many New Age practitioners).

In the musical *Man of La Mancha,* Cervantes is on trial by his fellow prisoners for being an idealist. His accuser shouts, "A man must come to terms with life as it is!" Cervantes replies, "When life itself seems mad, who knows where madness lies? Perhaps to be practical is madness; and maddest of all, to see life as it is, and not as it should be."

Solidarity

Nor should you be stirred to action only about queer issues. The very fact that you have a firsthand experience of injustice should move you to stand in solidarity, and act in solidarity, with those who are denied justice in any quarter. The radical Christian ethicist Joseph Fletcher has suggested that Jesus' enigmatic teaching to his disciples to "be perfect" as God is perfect can only make sense if we understand it to mean, as suggested by the context, "be as all-inclusive in your *agape* [love] as God is."[7]

I frankly do not understand or appreciate gay Republicans. The Republican Party has for several years embraced a highly individual-

[7]Fletcher, *Situation Ethics,* 108.

istic, survival-of-the-fittest economic policy, and a social policy that favors those already in positions of power and privilege. I do not believe any self-respecting queer can, in good conscience, adopt such a callous stance to the injustice suffered by other minorities, nor do I believe that anyone can who takes seriously the teachings of Jesus the Christ. For a queer Christian, it is unthinkable. Economically advantaged (and usually closeted) homosexuals who vote against social justice and for their own selfish economic interest are (let's not mince words) committing a grievous sin. They are being particularly ungrateful to those in the past who have struggled, suffered, and even died so that they might enjoy the relative freedom to achieve that economic success, rather than being systematically imprisoned or burned at the stake. As a Christian, you have a special vocation to work for justice for all people. As a queer you have a special vocation to work for justice for all people. As a queer Christian, then, you have that vocation, that call to justice making, particularly clear-cut. You can support the unjust dominant culture only by denying both your religion and your essential personality.

17
BEING A BERDACHE

The Vocation of Being Queer

One of the reasons I prefer the word *queer* over *gay* is that it has a delightfully double meaning. Not only does *queer* mean homosexual, it also means unusual, different, abnormal, aberrant. When you call yourself queer, you are claiming both constellations of meaning, and claiming them proudly. *Why be normal?* If you are homosexual, you have a special vocation to be queer.

In Andrew Holleran's novel about urban gay life of the seventies, *Dancer from the Dance,* he describes a group of gay friends driving through the small towns of New York to Fire Island, and feeling a sentimental longing for that heterosexual small-town life.[1] To the extent that you do in fact wish for the trappings of the straight, white American suburban lifestyle, you are denying your very self and ignoring your unique queer vocation. It is not that you have to live in a city (although the vast majority of us do choose to do so), but rather that, wherever you live, you must not sell out to the value systems of the dominant culture. The American dream of

[1] Andrew Holleran, *Dancer from the Dance* (New York: William Morrow & Co., 1978), 24.

the nuclear family, living in a space symbolically marked off by a white picket fence, is foreign territory for us. It is not *our* dream, and we imitate it at the peril of losing our very identity, of losing our queer souls.

Roughly since the Christian church began to usurp political power in the early fourth century, we as a people have suffered incredible maliciousness at the hands of homophobic and antipleasure "Christian" organizations. Governments, churches, and medical professionals have subjected us to humiliation, imprisonment, torture, castration, shock therapy, and burning at the stake. Yet the worst crime that has been committed against us has been to make us forget who we are; to make us forget that we are an ancient nonfamilial tribe with a unique function and purpose in the larger society. Today, we are on the verge of recovering our lost tribal consciousness, and thus on the verge of again fulfilling our sacred destiny.

Being a Berdache

In virtually all tribal societies that had not yet received the Christian imprint, our people were highly valued for our uniqueness and singled out for special cultural and religious roles. In these pre-Christian societies, men who did not want to be warriors and women who rejected "women's work," far from being despised, were honored and given special duties and functions for the good of the tribe. Often, we were chosen to be the priests and shamans of the community.

Anthropologist Walter Williams, working with more recent Native American tribes, found remnants of this special queer office, although it had largely gone underground thanks to the harassment of Christian missionaries.[2] Years ago, anthropologists and ethnographers coined the term *berdache* to describe the man who was "not-man, not-woman," who was often a cross-dresser. The term *amazon* is sometimes used to describe the same phenomenon among women.

Most aboriginal American tribes had some form of the institu-

---

[2]Walter L. Williams, *The Spirit and the Flesh: Sexual Diversity in American Indian Culture* (Boston: Beacon Press, 1986).

tion that has come to be called the berdache. A berdache or amazon was often described by outside observers as an "effeminate" man or a "masculine" woman, but more careful ethnographers have insisted the berdache constituted, in the view of the culture, a *third* gender category. The genders were male, female, and berdache—or, sometimes, male, female, berdache, and amazon. These gender roles were as clearly defined as our two. A berdache, for instance, could marry a conventional male warrior, but two berdaches or two warriors could not marry—they were the same gender.

Horrified whites described berdaches as transvestites, but in fact their dress was often either a blend of male and female clothing (more akin to "gender fuck"), or quite distinct from either—as are church vestments today. Berdaches dressed according to their ceremonial role as "not man/not woman."

Native American societies, being matriarchal, were less oppressive of women and less homophobic, and they simply accepted the fact that the Great Spirit created some people who do not fit into conventional gender roles. If you were a young boy who exhibited a distaste for "masculine" pursuits and an interest in the tasks usually done by women, or a young girl who showed a preference for masculine-identified tasks, you would simply be encouraged to follow your inclinations. (Imagine our parents having *approved* of girls playing with trucks, or boys with Barbies!) Rather than bringing shame and pity on themselves, those who became berdaches/amazons were highly esteemed, and their families considered to be unusually honored (in the same way a highly catholic culture honors the family of a man who becomes a priest). Precisely because berdaches were rarer than conventional women and men, the society assumed they must have been singled out by God for special attention.

The Shamanic Vocation

The primary religious functionary in most tribal societies was the shaman. Caricatured by whites as a "medicine man" or "witch doctor," a shaman is the mediator between the tribe and the realm of the Spirit. Shamans are to be found among Native American tribes, as well as in African, Tibetan, and Eskimo cultures. Something at least similar to the shaman can also be found in the pre-Christian history of most European cultures. Typically, healing is a major part of the shaman's work, as is offering guidance to others about the spiritual path. Not all berdaches were shamans, and not all shamans were berdaches, but many tribes did seem to prefer berdaches in the shaman's role. The reasoning is that if a berdache is "that way" because of the special attentions of the Spirit, then he must be unusually close to the Spirit, and thus uniquely qualified to instruct others in spiritual matters. Even when berdaches were not shamans as such, they usually fulfilled special roles in religious ritual and ceremony, often ceremonial sexual roles.

In general, the role of a shaman is to serve as a go-between for the spirit world and the physical world. The shaman served as a messenger from the spirits to the people and, when necessary, went to the spirit world with messages or requests from the people, or to seek healing or guidance. It is the shaman's function as an intermediary, a go-between, that links shamanism and berdachism. A berdache, already the mediator between masculine and feminine roles, was deemed especially suited to being a mediator between the seen and unseen, the spiritual and the mundane.

Anthropologist Victor Turner coined the term *liminal* to describe that which is on the limits, on the cusps, between two realities or alternatives. Jungian psychology uses the term to describe, for instance, a powerful dream that is a *liminal* experience because it brings us to the edge of a nonmundane spiritual reality. Queers are by nature a highly *liminal* people. We live our daily lives in the liminal spaces between society's perceptions of "masculinity" and "femininity." In our homophobic culture, we also inhabit the liminal spaces between respectability and criminality. How many gay men have I known who go to the opera in a tuxedo in the early evening, then stalk the dark and smoky leather bars in the city's warehouse or meat-packing districts a few hours later! Your very nature, your sexual nature as "not man/not woman," guarantees your liminality. You are, then, almost a *natural* shaman. Since you can move freely in the liminal spaces between male and female, and between what is socially respectable and what is despised, it is an easy step into the liminal space between the mundane and the spiritual, the seen and the unseen. Thus, you are also, by nature, a deeply spiritual person.

Agents of Change

Our spirituality is not, however, of the otherworldly variety. One of the reasons we frighten straight people, especially straight religious people, is that we seem to have a knack for living with one foot in the spiritual realm and the other planted firmly on the earth. In a culture that keeps its sexuality and spirituality in separate boxes, we blend the two together in ways they often find confusing and frightening. We inhabit the liminal space between the sacred and the profane, and enjoy both immensely. If straight people often hate and fear us, it is because we threaten their carefully guarded boundaries.

But threatening boundaries is our *job*. In an astounding variety of cultures and time periods, our people have held the office of liminality. We are ordained by nature to be agents of change. It is no accident that we are so prevalent in the fashion industry—we have a knack for seeing, predicting, and creating trends. Creating change is our special gift. Even the colors associated with the queer nation, lavender and pink, are the colors of the liminal periods of the day, the dawn and the dusk, the periods of change between night and day.

Judy Grahn has created a monumental work documenting the tribal and spiritual roots of our people, *Another Mother Tongue: Gay Words, Gay Worlds*. She presents mounds of evidence that, in countless societies, we have functioned as the liminal people, the change agents for the larger society. She says queer culture is not a "subculture," but rather a *metaculture*:

> Transculture is what we have, crossing every imaginable border with our functions, qualities, and philosophical stances intact, with, of course, intercultural and interracial

variations. The qualities of gayness are metacultural, they transcend eras of historical time, they transcend national borders, and they transcend social systems. . . .[3]

The particular function of this queer metaculture, Grahn says, has always been mediating between intersecting worlds or lifestyles. That is why, she points out, gay ghettos are so often in "transitional," economically and racially mixed neighborhoods, and why the largest concentrations of queers are to be found in major cities—especially port cities (such as New York, San Francisco, Amsterdam, Copenhagen), or in resort communities, particularly those near the sea (such as Provincetown, Key West, and Fire Island)—where the interchange of cultures is most evident. It is also why we as a people so love to travel—experiencing foreign cultures is in our blood.

Queer Priesthood

Because queer people were traditionally associated with the Mother Goddess, often as her priests and votaries (the word *gay*, remember, is probably derived from Gaia, the Greek name of the earth goddess), we were especially targeted for destruction by Christian "missionary" pogroms, which were hell-bent on presenting God as all-male. The residual racial memory of the ancient enmity between the queer priests of Gaia and the Christian crusaders may well be the source of much of the irrational hatred of queer people that continues to infect most branches of the Christian church today.

Our forgotten history as the priests and priestesses of Gaia also explains why gay men, and more recently lesbian women, represent such a high percentage of the clergy of all major denominations today (although most of them are closeted).[4]

Q: How many straight priests does it take to screw in a light bulb?

A: Both of them.

---

[3]Grahn, *Another Mother Tongue,* 270.
[4]Polls in the United States have suggested that around 25 percent of Episcopal priests, and 50 percent of Roman Catholic priests, are gay. A recent study of the Church of England reported that 15 to 30 percent of their priests are gay, but almost none of them are out.

Nor is the phenomenon limited to the liturgical churches (although we do have a penchant for smells and bells, not to mention lacy vestments!). I had a friend who was the organist in a large Southern Baptist church in Texas, and he was part of a large network of highly closeted but highly active gay Southern Baptist clergy and musicians. The image of the priest performing the marriage ceremony at the end of *La Cage aux Folles,* prissily turning the page of the prayer book, is indelibly printed in our memory because it is such a common archetype.

Since the memory of our ancient ceremonial office has been suppressed, it has tended to manifest in more mundane ways. Queers are disproportionately represented in the visual and performing arts because the creation of art requires entering a liminal space, which we do almost effortlessly. We practically *are* the fashion and design industries because of our centuries of experience as agents of change. The number of queers, both out and closeted, to be found in the "helping professions" is legendary; and it recalls our ancient liminal role as shamans and healers. Even the well-organized gay political organizations are a remnant of our role as society's change agents—and before there were gay political organizations, closet queers were instrumental in other justice movements, especially the black civil rights movement of the sixties.

As Grahn has shown, most of the signals and codes our people used to identify each other in more repressive times have their roots in our tribal religious roles, although most queers have employed them without realizing their historical significance. Pinky rings, for instance, once a form of gay identification, can be traced to the occult tradition that the little finger is associated with Mercury/Hermes, the trickster god of change.[5] Ironically, since we are harbingers of fashion, the symbols we invent for our own community are soon imitated by the straight culture. Almost as many straight men as gay men wear earrings today, for instance, and black leather and colored bandannas have become universally fashionable. Still, we do have a penchant for symbolically marking our

[5]Grahn, *Another Mother Tongue,* 15.

bodies, and if straights imitate us, we simply find other, more radical markings.

Tattooing remained popular among leathermen and bulldykes at a time when it was considered distasteful by "respectable" people. Piercing of the earlobes and other body parts, recalling ancient religious ceremonies of piercing, often in honor of Eros, may have become widespread today, but we did it first. Grahn writes:

> The fact is, of all the people in my assimilated Swedish family who could wear a bright gold tooth in the front of their mouths for decoration, I am the only one who does. And if I did not have a gold tooth, I would certainly get a tattoo.[6]

I got my tattoo (which is a rose over my heart) while I was still in the process of being "screened" for ordination in the Episcopal Church. That year I attended the Diocese of Newark annual convention, which was held in a hotel with an indoor swimming pool. I remember a moment of sheer panic when one of the members of the Commission on Ministry suggested we go for a swim. Tattoos may be becoming more popular among straight society, but they are still considered a little *too* liminal for Episcopal priests.

Grahn says that since she lives in a straight, working-class neighborhood, her very presence is a fulfillment of the office of the "ceremonial dyke":

> You may be wondering what impact my mere presence could possibly have. Firstly, by my clothes and bearing I model a certain freedom for women. Secondly, as two women living together, my lover and I strengthen the position of every married woman on the block, whether she knows and appreciates it or not. (Her husband probably does.) Thirdly, by parenting a child we present an obvious example of alternate family structure.[7]

[6]Judy Grahn, "Flaming Without Burning: Some of the Roles of Gay People in Society," in Mark Thompson, ed., *Gay Spirit: Myth and Meaning* (New York: St. Martin's Press/Stonewall Inn Editions, 1987), 5.
[7]Ibid., 7.

Grahn is clearly unusual. She has made the recovery of queer cultural history her life's work, and so she is aware of the deeper significance of her contemporary "ceremonial" behavior. Most queers operate without this sense of historical, transcultural connection. We as a people are suffering from a cultural amnesia. We have literally lost our memory.

From time to time, queer visionaries have intuitively sensed this lost tribal history and have attempted to articulate it and to reconstruct it imaginatively. One of the most outstanding was Walt Whitman. Living in a period much more homophobic (and generally sex-negative) than our own, Whitman wrote boldly of the special significance of same-sex love. At a time when there was no vocabulary to speak positively of queer love, Whitman coined the term *adhesiveness* to describe male-male love, "the dear love of comrades." Many of Whitman's poems speak in spiritual terms of the erotic energy exchanged between two men. For instance:

> *Camerado, I give you my hand!*
> *I give you my love more precious than money,*
> *I give you myself before preaching or law;*
> *Will you give me yourself? will you come travel with me?*
> *Shall we stick by each other as long as we live?*[8]

or:

> *Love divine and perfect Comrade,*
> *Waiting content, invisible yet, but certain,*
> *Be thou my God.*
> *Thou, thou, the Ideal Man,*
> *Fair, able, beautiful, content, and loving,*
> *Complete in body and dilate in spirit,*
> *Be thou my God.*[9]

[8]"Song of the Open Road," 15, in *Leaves of Grass*.
[9]"Gods," in "By the Roadside," *Leaves of Grass*.

Whitman often spoke of male-male love as though it were a religion in itself:

> *I hear it was charged against me that I sought to destroy*
>   *institutions,*
> *But really I am neither for nor against institutions.*
> *(What indeed have I in common with them? or what with the*
>   *destruction of them?)*
> *Only I will establish in Manhattan and in every city of these*
>   *States inland and seaboard,*
> *And in the fields and woods, and above every keel little or*
>   *large that dents the water,*
> *Without edifices or rules or trustees or any argument,*
> *The institution of the dear love of comrades.*[10]

Harry Hay, the founder of the Mattachine Society, the first modern queer organization, also operated from a vision of the spiritual significance of being queer. He described the forming of the Mattachine Society as "a call to me deeper than the innermost reaches of spirit, a vision-quest more important than life."[11] Although for three years Hay and a small group of friends held discussions about the spirituality of homosexuality, almost from the moment the Mattachine Society became a national organization, it lost its spiritual roots. Hay left the organization he had founded because it had become concerned "with being seen as respectable—rather than self-respecting."[12] Hay had envisioned Mattachine as a "brotherhood," a group that would use ritual to celebrate its queerness. He was deeply disappointed when it degenerated into a political organization instead:

> I myself was no longer willing to retrogress back to that
> hetero-imitating, subject-object, white-man, middle-class

[10]"I Hear It Was Charged Against Me," Calamus in *Leaves of Grass*.
[11]Interview with Hay by Mark Thompson in *Gay Spirit*, 186.
[12]Ibid., 187.

obsolescence. I never joined any of the conventional hetero-imitating type of gay organizations again: I vowed that I would never have to submit the golden treasure of my heart, my vision of gay consciousness, to the ugly and distorting vicissitudes of *Robert's Rules of Order . . . ever again!*[13]

Other visionaries who have written of the unique queer spirituality have included writer Mitch Walker, who coined the term *ROIKA* for "the nonrational, nonlinear spirit-essence lying at the source of our gayness."[14] Recently, the Radical Faerie movement, a grass roots movement of gay men, has come together to celebrate queerness through erotic and spiritual rituals,[15] and another organization, called the TBS Network, puts gay men who are interested in exploring spirituality in touch with each other.[16]

Our Souls Are Queer

I recently discovered a book that so reverberated within me, that struck such deep chords within my soul, it has taken on the significance of scripture for me. This channeled work by Andrew Ramer represents the contributions of three discarnate entities, all of whom identify themselves as gay. The three works, published in one volume, are titled *Two Flutes Playing, Spiritual Love/Sacred Sex,* and *Priests of Father Earth and Mother Sky.*[17]

Conventional Christians tend to look askance at "channeled" works, but it is a silly prejudice. After all, what is the Book of the Revelation to St. John if not a "channeled" work? What were the

---

[13]Ibid., 195.

[14]Thompson, *Gay Spirit,* 214.

[15]By choice, the Radical Faeries are rather loosely organized, and somewhat difficult to get in touch with. A place to start is a newsletter called *The Faeriegram,* published by Vince Collazo, 234 8th St., Apt. 2F, Brooklyn, NY 11215; or *RFD: A Country Journal for Gay Men Everywhere,* Rt. 1, Box 127-E, Bakersville, NC 28705.

[16]TBS is an abbreviation for "Touching Body and Spirit." A subscription to the newsletter is $10; membership in the network (which includes a personals ad listing) is $20. Write for a membership application to the TBS Network, Box 957, Huntington, NY 11743-0957. The newsletter is edited by Robert Lynn Kazmayer.

[17]Available from Body Electric Publishing, 6527A Telegraph Ave., Oakland, CA 94609. (415) 653-1594.

Hebrew prophets doing if not channeling communications from spiritual entities? I do suggest one caveat about channeled information: remember that just because it is channeled doesn't mean it is true or accurate. Those who have died no doubt have access to information we do not have, but they do not suddenly become perfected beings. Just because someone is dead doesn't mean she is *wise*, so information channeled from discarnate or nonincarnate entities should be subject to at least as much critical analysis as any other information. Please take such works, just as you should take the Bible, with a large grain of salt.

I do, however, trust the validity of most of what is contained in these three books because the first time I read them, somewhere deep down inside myself, I just *knew* they were true, they were scripture. These books were written specifically for gay men. (Yamati, the entity who is the source of the first book, says, "Here were women who loved women, and I leave it to others to channel their glorious history.") I recommend them highly. I wish every gay man in the world could read this glorious vision of the purpose and meaning of gay love, and I wish a lesbian psychic would channel a similar work for women. For instance, *Two Flutes Playing* says:

> All through the ages there have been gay men, though never a word existed, though many were celibate or married. It is the loving that has always existed, since time began. Who is now gay, has almost always been gay, in life after lifetime. Our tribe is ancient, and we carry its history; both the love and the torturous pain. So let us remember the loving, and use the pain as a lever in our transformation.[18]

The book presents a vision of gay nomadic tribes roaming the earth at the end of the Ice Age and tells the story of Tayarti, "the greatest saint of the gay tribes," who first discovered that gay men have a particular gift for healing and who trained other gay men to use their healing powers. Yamati admonishes contemporary gay men

[18]Ramer, *Two Flutes Playing*, 12.

that we are still healers, although we block and deny our power, "and our power to heal is needed more than ever now."[19]

A prerequisite for the renewal of the queer shamanic office is to give up the urge for "respectability." Your shamanism is based upon your being queer. To the extent you try to assimilate yourself into mainstream society, to the extent you buy into the notion that "we're just like you, except what we do in bed," you destroy the possibility of exercising your unique gifts. If you join this grass roots movement, then, you must step outside the current tide of opinion even within the queer community itself. Virtually all gay and lesbian organizations—with a handful of exceptions—have as their goal the assimilation of our people into the dominant society. We cannot have it both ways. We cannot be a liminal people unless we live on the edges of society.

A fascinating group in Los Angeles, called Treeroots, is exploring gay spirituality through Jungian-oriented dreamwork. They have found that we gay men have different archetypes in our dreams (such as the figures of the diva and the leatherman) than do women or straight men. Their conclusion is that being queer, far from being a strictly sexual identity, runs deep down to the unconscious level, the level of soul. Don Kilhefner, one of the founders of Treeroots, says:

> The intrapsychic material of gay men—particularly when it's compared to the intrapsychic material of straight men— does not support the idea that gay people are just like straight people except for what we do in bed. I would say basically our souls are gay, our vision is gay, and we move in the world in very different ways than straight men.[20]

The Shaman's Path

The Holy Spirit is moving among our people today to call us to rediscover and renew the ancient office of the queer priest/shaman/

[19]Ibid., 35.
[20]Interview in "Gay Soul Making: Coming Out Inside," by Mark Thompson, in *Gay Spirit*, 246.

healer. Hundreds of queers all over the world are independently coming to this consciousness, beginning to reclaim the role of the shaman and the healer. Judy Grahn reminds us of our religious roots and urges us to be "ceremonial dykes and faggots." Mitch Walker calls for the institution of the ROIKA shaman. Joseph Kramer wants to develop a network of "heart-centered gay healers." The Radical Faeries gather to practice ancient queer rituals. I have a friend, a gay priest, who has opened a "shamanic practice" that combines bodywork, healing, and pastoral counseling. A grass roots movement is springing up in many places at once, a movement to remember who we are and what our purpose is.

The recovery of queer shamanism is not incompatible with the enlightened practice of Christianity. In fact, it can be deeply enriching for the Christian church. As Christians who remember our ancient role as votaries of Gaia, the mother goddess, we can bring about a renewal of fervor for devotion to Mary as the symbol of the divine feminine. As a Christian who recalls your ancestors' servitude to Eros, you can insist that Christianity expunge itself of every trace of sex-negative and antipleasure thinking. As a very old people with a long tradition of healing, we can help the Christian church rediscover and renew its lost traditions of healing. We can teach them what they have forgotten, for by nature we are healers.

PART FOUR

The Resurrection of the Body: Life, Death, and Healing

18
LETTING GOD BE GOD

Addiction and Recovery

I was having a beer recently with a lesbian friend of mine, a seminarian who envisions a lesbian/gay ministry.

"I think Twelve Step programs are the dominant spirituality of the lesbian and gay community," she said.

"God, I hope not!" I said, choking on my beer.

But actually, I think she's right—Twelve Step programs have become immensely popular in our country in general, and they are even more popular among lesbians and gay men. When the churches failed to offer us any spiritual sustenance, many of us turned elsewhere—and more of us turned to Twelve Step programs than any other single resource. I think it is safe to say that more queers attempt to meet their spiritual and religious needs through the meetings of Twelve Step groups than through *any* church or religious organization.

For the most part, this is a positive thing. Twelve Step programs have been a valuable resource for our community. Thousands of our people have been helped by Twelve Step programs; many have literally had their lives saved by their participation in a Twelve Step program. Still, the suggestion that the particular brand of spirituality espoused in Twelve Step programs should be the dominant gay and lesbian spirituality makes me nervous.

To begin with, I don't think the Twelve Step methodology in itself is adequate as a system of spirituality. The program is clearly a spiritually based approach. In fact, one of the most valid criticisms of the Twelve Step method, and particularly of the tendency to tout the program as the *only* way to recovery for everyone, is that it is so spiritually oriented it doesn't work for honest atheists. Seven of the Twelve Steps specifically mention God or spirituality. Because the Twelve Step program is so undeniably religious, it seems to me that when a judge *orders* someone (such as a DWI offender) to attend AA meetings, that person's civil right to the freedom of religion is being violated.

But the fact the program has a heavy emphasis on spirituality does not mean it can stand alone as a complete spiritual system. The wording of the official Twelve Steps, as contained in the Alcoholics Anonymous "Big Book," was carefully designed (for its time period) to be as inclusive of various religious traditions as possible, so that, for instance, a Jew and a Christian could attend the same AA meeting and discuss the Steps together without getting bogged down in differences of faith and doctrine. Yet it is that very vagueness, that attempt to be all-inclusive, that largely prevents the program itself from being a self-contained spirituality. If you are "working the program," a mature spirituality requires getting more specific than the necessarily vague language of the Steps—it depends upon giving the "Power greater than yourself" a name. If, in a meeting, you talk about the "Higher Power," and in your own mind you translate that phrase to mean the Jewish YHWH or Christ or Krishna or almost any name for God that implies a complete religious system, then it works. If you simply stop there, without questioning who this amorphous "Higher Power" is, what her/his attributes might be, and how exactly you can relate to him/her, then although the recovery process may be working for you, your spiritual growth will be stunted.

It was my friend and teacher Naomi Lake who taught me this lesson. Naomi, who describes herself as an "energy healer," draws her spirituality and her healing techniques from a variety of sources, from Hinduism to Christianity to contemporary science. But her primary spiritual tradition is Native American spirituality. She taught me how important it is—especially if you want to combine several approaches—to be grounded in one tradition, and to practice that tradition with integrity. The problem with most New Age spiritual approaches is that their practitioners have no primary religious tradition at all. When you have a tradition and are true to it, you can branch out into limitless other approaches and still keep your feet on the ground.

As an aside, let me point out that the language of the Steps, which was remarkably inclusive for its time, isn't inclusive enough today, particularly not gender inclusive. If you are a lesbian feminist at an AA meeting, and you have to sit through hearing someone read the third step, "Made a decision to turn our will and lives over to the care of God *as we understood Him*," you are having reinforced for you deep within your psyche, however much you may disagree on an intellectual level, that God is yet another male you are being asked to obey. To add insult to injury, the traditional version of the Lord's Prayer, said at the close of every Twelve Step meeting, begins "Our Father, who art in heaven . . . ." You can, of course, amend the words when you say them ("the care of the Goddess as we understood her"), but why should you be forced to make such translations? A gender-inclusive edition of the Big Book is long overdue.

Abstinence Is Not Spirituality

Another problem with a Twelve Step–based spirituality is that it is based on abstinence, and as you read in Chapter 10, such an approach is antithetical to authentic Christian spirituality. Christian spirituality is about celebrating life, and celebrating God's gifts. It is a spiritual stance of saying "Yes!" to life, not saying no. A person who is truly addicted to a chemical substance such as alcohol might have to abstain from that substance, but for the rest of us, alcohol is a gift from our loving creator, to be gratefully enjoyed. Remember Psalm 104, which praises God for giving us the gift of wine "to gladden the heart."

Precisely because Twelve Step programs are taking the place of spirituality for so many of us, we are seeing a glorification of abstinence among queers. It's not uncommon to hear people describe their "spirituality" by listing all the things they don't do: *I don't drink alcohol or use recreational drugs, eat meat (or at least not red meat), use sugar, salt, or caffeine, or have sex when I want to. See how spiritual I am?* The political manifestation of this abstinence-based "spirituality" can be seen in the notices about meetings and events held in gay community centers. For instance, there might be a dance described as "drug and alcohol free and smoke free," and more recently, "scent free," meaning you aren't allowed to wear cologne. The divisive message is that unlike us "bad queers," the unhealthy, insensitive, politically incorrect queers, the "good gays" stay away from all those nasty things.

My Higher Power or *the* Higher Power?

The most serious problem with what might be called a Twelve Step spirituality is its tendency to make God too small. Although the third step in the Big Book describes God as "a Power greater than ourselves," in recent years this "Power greater than ourselves" has been reduced to "my Higher Power," with a heavy emphasis on the *my*. The transcendent God, who is radically other than yourself, has been replaced with a power that is entirely located within yourself. You do have a "higher power," but your higher power is not God. What most people mean when they speak of "my higher power" is what we might call spirituality itself—or to be more precise, your *spirit*. Your spirit is that spark of the divine within you, the part of you that makes it possible to relate to God—*but it is not God.* If you confuse your own spirit, which is a component part of who you are, with God, then you have precluded the possibility of having a true relationship with God. You can't have a "relationship" with yourself.

Possessive language can be used as the language of love. As a Christian, you can legitimately speak of Christ as "my Lord and Savior," in the same way you can describe a romantic partner as "my lover." But possessive language can also be an attempt to control, to imply that you literally *own* your lover or your "higher power." The

Jewish and Christian scriptures are filled with warnings that God will not tolerate our attempts to define, control, and limit God. The prophet Isaiah describes God as saying:

> *For my thoughts are not your thoughts,*
> *neither are your ways my ways . . .*
> *For as the heavens are higher than the earth,*
> *so are my ways higher than your ways*
> *and my thoughts than your thoughts.*[1]

In fact, the almost universal human tendency to identify one's own spirit, a mere aspect of oneself, with God is the very behavior almost all world religions label the beginning of all sin. It is the classic flaw of *hubris,* or *superbia,* a human trying to be God. In the myth of the "fall" of humanity in Genesis, Adam and Eve are driven out of paradise not because they disobeyed a command (and certainly not because they ate an apple!), but because they strove to "be like God."[2] God is not *your* Higher Power, but *the* Highest Power, with her own personality and her own agenda, which may or may not match yours.

Homesick for God

The reason addiction and recovery are spiritual issues is as basic as the message of Christianity itself. Precisely because this spirit, this "higher self," is an important part of who you are, you cannot be complete and fulfilled if you ignore the spirit. No one has ever said it more poetically than St. Augustine: "You made us for yourself and our hearts find no peace until they rest in you."[3] Centuries later, the monk Thomas Merton rephrased it as "There is a natural desire for heaven, for the fruition of God in us."[4] It is as though we all have a God-shaped hole in our hearts, a longing that only God can fulfill. If you do not allow God to fill that hole in your

---

[1] Isaiah 55:8–9.
[2] Genesis 3:5.
[3] St. Augustine, *Confessions,* Book I, 1, 21.
[4] Thomas Merton, *The Sign of Jonas* (New York: Harcourt Brace Jovanovich, 1953), 112.

heart, then you will find something else to try to fill it—alcohol, food, career, sex, relationships—the list is endless. The good news is, if God is in fact in that space (evangelicals would say if God is "enthroned" in your heart), then all those other things—alcohol, food, career, sex, relationships—can be used and enjoyed as gifts of your loving Creator. Some of these gifts (i.e., sex and relationships) can actually be used as *pathways* to God—as long as you don't assign them the significance of God.

The beginning of addiction, the underlying spiritual problem that can eventually lead to compulsive behavior and to chemical addictions, is that unfulfilled spiritual longing, that desire for God that seems to be built into all human beings. Christian psychiatrist Gerald May calls it the "displacement of spiritual longing":

> We try to fulfill our longing for God through objects of attachment. For example, God wants to be our perfect lover, but instead we seek perfection in human relationships and are disappointed when our lovers cannot love us perfectly. God wants to provide our ultimate security, but we seek our safety in power and possessions and then find we must continually worry about them. We seek satisfaction of our spiritual longing in a host of ways that may have very little to do with God. And, sooner or later, we are disappointed.[5]

The problem is worse for us for two reasons. First, queers are, by nature, even more spiritual than the general population. You might say that the "God-shaped hole" in your heart is bigger than it is for straight people. Second, since we have been largely rejected and despised by the Judeo-Christian religious establishment, we have, with very good reason, tended to stay the hell away from all religious institutions and everything associated with them, including God. Often the very words *God* or *Christ* or *prayer* are enough to push all our negative buttons, and so we naturally look for other things or behaviors to fill that void. It is no wonder our addiction

[5]Gerald May, *Addiction and Grace* (San Francisco: Harper & Row, 1988), 92–93.

rate is so high. Currently, no accurate studies document the incidence of drug and alcohol abuse in our community, but some past studies have suggested it is as high as 33 percent.[6]

Being Addicted to Recovery

Not only is there a disturbing recent tendency among those "working" Twelve Step programs to substitute the program for a spiritual tradition, there is also a much more serious problem—a tendency to put the program itself in that "God-shaped hole." Rather than treating the program as a tool for recovering from an addiction, many people make the program the center of their lives—for the rest of their lives. You can actually replace your addiction to alcohol with a dependency on the program—which is, granted, not as self-destructive as a chemical addiction, but it still cannot lead you to true maturity and spiritual growth. As Dr. Stan Katz has argued, such groups "do not promote full recovery. They promote dependency under the guise of recovery." If, after all, you went to a therapist who told you therapy would help you, but only if you came once a week for the rest of your life, you would report that therapist to the local licensing boards. Yet that is exactly the rhetoric of the Twelve Step recovery program.

Sometimes, the people who turn to AA for help not only feel a spiritual void, but evidently feel a void in most other areas of their lives as well. Without meaningful relationships, a challenging career, or satisfying recreational outlets, they turn to the program and the groups for all these things. They don't just use AA as a program to help them recover from addiction; they make it an entire way of life, a primary identity. Twelve Step programs themselves encourage this sort of total dependency on the program, through promoting a dogma that recovery is necessarily a lifelong process. As Katz points out, such a philosophy is the opposite of therapeutic—it encourages the former addict to focus on past problems rather than

---

[6]The Pride Institute, a lesbian and gay substance abuse treatment center (14400 Martin Drive, Eden Prairie, MN 55344, 1-800-54PRIDE), warns that the only available studies were based on a flawed sample—a population found in bars—and so the actual percentage may be lower. What is clear is that the incidence of drug and alcohol problems is *at least* as high as among the general population, and I for one have no trouble believing it is considerably higher.

moving beyond them. Katz's message is "we do *not* all need to spend our lives under the shadow of former experiences, relationships, and behaviors. Complete recovery *is* possible."[7] By the way, because I believe literally in the possibility of Christian healing, I believe there are no "incurable" diseases. Just as you should reject the notion that AIDS is always fatal, because you affirm God is greater than AIDS, so should you reject the notion that addiction cannot be totally cured. God is also greater than addiction and can certainly effect a total recovery.

Powerless or Empowered?

Because it has become fashionable to be "in recovery," it has become unfashionable to be emotionally healthy. If you have managed to develop a strong and self-confident personality, you are labeled "arrogant" or "abrasive," not only by straights, but by other queers. The vast majority of queers today seem to resent the very traits of self-esteem and self-confidence that we should admire and aspire to.

It doesn't take a brilliant social analyst to notice that the tendency to imply that all queers are addicts has serious negative sociopolitical consequences. AA's original first Step (which, remember, was designed for use by alcoholics, not by those with problem behaviors) says, "We admitted we were powerless *over alcohol* . . ."[8] In practice, however, more and more of the participants in Twelve Step programs have begun to describe themselves as "powerless" not just over alcohol, but over everything in their lives. Stores that cater to the growing recovery market sell bumper stickers and T-shirts that are emblazoned "Powerless." The implications of an ever-growing percentage of a marginalized community beginning to adopt "powerless" as a primary self-identity are astonishing. For over twenty years, queer activists have struggled to empower us, while staggering numbers of us are blithely labeling ourselves "powerless."

[7]Dr. Stan J. Katz and Aimee E. Liu, *The Codependency Conspiracy: How to Break the Recovery Habit and Take Charge of Your Life* (New York: Warner Books, 1991), 4.
[8]Big Book, 59. My italics.

Someone addicted to a chemical substance may in fact be "powerless" over that substance—over the chemical and physiological damage it has done to her body and brain—but no human being is "powerless" in the general sense. It seems to me that true recovery is about regaining your personal power, not giving it up. We, more than anyone, need to proclaim and celebrate the fact that *we are powerful.*

When responsible adults label themselves "powerless," particularly when they are speaking of behaviors rather than chemicals, they promote a spiritual and ethical infantilism, a sort of "the devil made me do it" mentality. People stop taking responsibility for their own actions; they blame it on "the disease." It is increasingly popular for those in recovery to say things like "I didn't mean that; that was my disease talking."

I was shocked to hear Ann Rule, author of *If You Really Loved Me,*[9] a book about convicted murderer David Brown, and other books about sociopathic killers, say on the "Joan Rivers" show, "Serial murder is an addiction, just like any other addiction."[10] You see where this can lead. If virtually any human behavior can be labeled "addiction," and if addiction is described as a "disease," then no one has to take responsibility for any of his or her actions. A serial killer can say, "My disease killed those people." On a less serious note, when Boston Red Sox player Wade Boggs finally pissed off his mistress enough that she called the media and told them of her long-term affair with Boggs, he denied responsibility by labeling himself a "sex addict." The woman had been traveling with him, and sleeping with him, for years. In fact, they had a fairly steady relationship. Yet *when he got caught,* Boggs suddenly diagnosed himself as a "sex addict," an announcement I have no doubt was orchestrated by the Red Sox public relations consultants. (All I can say is, if Wade Boggs is sexually addicted, I volunteer to be co-dependent with him!)

---

[9]Ann Rule, *If You Really Loved Me: A True Story of Desire and Murder* (New York: Simon & Schuster, 1991).
[10]September 12, 1991.

The Myth of "Sexual Addiction"

Which brings us to the whole sticky subject of "sex addiction." Let me begin by stating my bias up front: I think it's bullshit. I don't believe "sex addiction" exists—or at least, if it does, it is much rarer than such groups as Sex and Love Addicts Anonymous (SLAA) would have you believe. As sexologist and sex therapist Marty Klein said, in an address to the Society for the Scientific Study of Sex (Quad-S), "Those who are *really* sexually compulsive are typically psychotic, sociopathic, character disordered," and such seriously disturbed people would not benefit from a Twelve Step program. They need "medication, deep therapy, structured behavioral interventions, or other intensive modalities" (such as lithium).[11] As Klein points out, those who self-diagnose as "sex addicts" are not in fact addicted at all, or even truly compulsive, in the classic, clinical sense of the word. Although they may describe their sexual drives as being "out of control," this is, Klein says, a metaphor. What they really mean is they find it *painful* to control their sexual urges—but that is a far cry from saying they are incapable of doing so ("powerless"). Except for that handful of true sexual compulsives, the psychotics and sociopaths, the rapists and serial killers, Klein declares, "virtually everyone has the ability to choose how to control and express their sexual impulses. The concept of sexual addiction colludes with people's desire to shirk responsibility for their sexuality."[12] And you, remember, have a special calling to take responsibility for your sexuality.

Much more disturbing, the entire concept of "sex addiction" is inherently based upon—and helps promote—a profoundly sex-negative philosophy and ethical stance, a stance you as a queer Christian should reject. When does sex become "compulsive"? How much sex is too much? Who decides and on whose behalf?

The official literature of the "sexual addiction" movement promotes a highly conservative ethic, a sexual value system that sounds suspiciously like that which churches and governments

[11]Marty Klein, "Why There's No Such Thing as Sexual Addiction—And Why It Really Matters," address to the Annual Meeting of the Society for the Scientific Study of Sex, Toronto, Canada, November 10, 1989. Klein can be reached at 881 Thornwood, Palo Alto, CA 94303.
[12]Ibid.

have tried to impose on us for centuries. Since SLAA is pressing the Twelve Step model (which was meant for alcoholics) into service to help people "recover" from a problem behavior, they have to ignore the fact that the AA model was based on total abstinence. Not even Patrick Carnes, the guru of the "sex addiction" movement, is willing to come out as promoting total abstinence from sex, so he has modified the AA model. Those in the program are encouraged to abstain from sex until they are in a committed, monogamous, loving relationship. Sound familiar? In July 1991, the Episcopal General Convention once more "affirmed" for the umpteenth time that "the teaching of the church is that physical sexual expression is appropriate only within the lifelong, monogamous relationship of marriage." Presbyterians and Lutherans made similar statements around the same time. The Roman Catholic Church, of course, won't even debate the issue. As Klein puts it, "The sexual addiction movement is not harmless. These people are missionaries who want to put everyone in the missionary position."[13]

I hope you don't believe sex can only be healthy and "good" within a committed, monogamous relationship. The SLAA stance, like that of the churches, is based on the assumption that sex is dangerous, that it must be carefully controlled and regulated. Sex can be healthy, good, and even holy with a stranger whose name you don't know and whom you will never see again. Sex, like tennis, can be engaged in *just because it's fun*.

Another tenet of the "sex addiction" movement is that it is unhealthy to use sex to feel better about yourself. In fact, you can use sex, quite consciously, just for that purpose. What's wrong with saying, "I'm feeling lonely and depressed. I need to get laid"? You can make an intentional decision to use recreational sex in just such a way, and such a decision can be totally moral and psychologically healthy. As always, the catch is that you don't use sex to try to fill in that "hole in your heart" that only God can fill. But if God is in fact filling that void, you can enjoy recreational sex, "sport fucking," without being compulsive—and give thanks to God for having given you the *gift* of sex.

[13]Ibid., 12.

What is particularly ironic is that the Big Book of Alcoholics Anonymous, the "bible" on which not only AA but SLAA and all Twelve Step programs are based, presents a very sane, balanced approach to sexuality that should preclude the use of its methods to cure "sexual addiction" (with delicious irony it is found on page 69!):

> We want to stay out of this controversy. We don't want to be the arbiter of anyone's sex conduct. We all have sex problems. We'd hardly be human if we didn't.

The Big Book goes on to offer a wise and open-minded sexual ethic. The test of the goodness of a sexual encounter, it says, is "was it selfish or not?" This is exactly the sexual ethic promoted by "situation ethics," as discussed in Chapter 11.

We've got enough trouble on our hands with the straight churches and governments trying to tell us what to do with our bodies and when and with whom to be sexual. We don't need to hear the same thing from the self-proclaimed prophets of "sexual addiction," especially from our queer sisters and brothers.

Slaves of Love

The concept of "love addiction" is even more bizarre. Robin Norwood started the craziness with her best-selling book *Women Who Love Too Much*.[14] The flaw in the concept of "love addiction" is the same as with "sex addiction"—it is impossible to be *addicted* to a behavior. Addiction is a physiological, chemical process. Certainly many women and men feel trapped in abusive relationships, but as Klein said about "sex addiction," the problem is that they find it *painful* to end those relationships, not that they are *incapable* of doing so.

What particularly bothers me about the "women who love too much" concept is its unexamined use of language. If Norwood had titled her book something like *Women Who Find Themselves*

[14]Robin Norwood, *Women Who Love Too Much: When You Keep Wishing and Hoping He'll Change* (New York: Pocket Books, 1985).

Trapped in Self-Destructive Relationships, it would be much less objectionable. Promulgating the notion that it is possible to be addicted to love leads people to confuse good old-fashioned *passion* with addiction. In *Unusual Company,* a lesbian love story written by my friend Margie Erhart, one of the characters says to another, "I resent you for being in love with someone as great as me and then not treating me as the most important thing in your life."[15] That is what romantic love is: treating your partner as the most important thing in your life, a partner who is treating you as the most important thing in her or his life.

Well, actually, not the *most* important thing. We're back to the "God-shaped hole." You can't expect your lover to fill the void in your soul that only God can fill. Erotic writer John Preston portrayed this tendency in a haunting way in his story "I Once Had a Master." The protagonist of the story describes in great detail his intense sexual and romantic obsession with another man. The last paragraph of the story says, "Finally, I went to his farm no more. I was frightened that I would forget that he was not God."[16]

But, if you remember your lover is *not* God, if you let God be God and be "enthroned" in your heart, then your lover can certainly be the *second* most important thing in your life, and your love for her can even be a pathway to lead you to a deeper love of God. As Chris Glaser wrote:

> Anyone in relationship with me would have to deal with another jealous lover, the church. Better to find someone who shared a similar, passionate commitment to the church; any marriage for me would have to be a ménage à trois, the third party being the church."[17]

(Personally, I would prefer to name the third party of the ménage à trois as Christ, not the church. If the church was Glaser's lover, it

---

[15]Margaret Erhart, *Unusual Company* (New York: Dutton/Penguin, 1987), 113.
[16]John Preston, *I Once Had a Master and Other Tales of Erotic Love* (Boston: Alyson Publications, 1984), 9.
[17]Chris Glaser, *Uncommon Calling: A Gay Man's Struggle to Serve the Church* (New York: Harper & Row, 1988), 66.

was a lover who was unfaithful to him, who shafted him, as it has shafted *all* of our people. The church cannot fill the void in your heart, either—only God can; and God is seldom if ever to be found in the church.)

In a way, as a Christian who understands this concept, you are in a position to have healthier relationships than people of no faith, whose natural tendency is to put a human lover in the "God slot."

But as long as God comes first, it is impossible to "love too much." The very phrase should strike you as an unfortunate oxymoron, anyway. If your *vocation* is to love your neighbor as yourself, and to extend that love even to your enemies, then it would be hard to imagine loving your marriage partner "too much."

One of the local Provincetown papers runs a campy pseudo-advice column I love, called "Dear Darla." Darla dishes out advice and opinion on virtually any topic, but waxes most poetic when giving pointers on romance. A recent issue carried this interchange between Darla and a querent:

> *Dear Darla:*
> *I was listening to my favorite Supremes song, "Ain't No Mountain High Enough," recently, and realized that the lyrics are incredibly co-dependent. Darla, is it OK to feel like "nothing could keep me, keep me from you" or should I be reading* Co-Dependent No More *and* Women Who Love Too Much? *Signed: No Wind*

> *Dear No Wind:*
> *Darla has just about had it with all this co-dependent talk. What ever happened to good old-fashioned passion-driven desire?*[18]

I couldn't agree more.

[18]*Provincetown Magazine* 1, no. 14, 19.

TRUSTING THE GREAT PHYSICIAN

AIDS and Christian Healing

John Fortunado has written a book attempting to assess the spiritual implications of AIDS, titled *AIDS: The Spiritual Dilemma.*[1] Fortunado's title is profoundly important. If you are religious in any way, AIDS does raise some extremely complex and troubling theological issues.

Basically, the "spiritual dilemma" posed by AIDS is the same religious question that has troubled people throughout the history of all religions. Today, the specific form of the question is, *Why would an all-powerful God allow AIDS to exist?* Technically, the exploration of this question is called theodicy, from the Greek words for *god* and *judgment,* so it is defined as "the vindication of God's judgment."

In classical theology, one of the primary attributes of God was *omnipotence:* God was seen as being powerful without limit. Since you probably grew up with an image of God as a stern, demanding father and judge, you probably also grew up with an image of God as powerful and controlling. Absolutely everything that happens in the world, from an earthquake to a toothache, is seen as being "the will of God." Most Christians imagine God as a cosmic puppeteer,

[1]San Francisco: Harper & Row, 1987.

pulling the strings of the entire universe, making everything happen according to some mysterious divine plan, a god who could well wear a T-shirt emblazoned, "Because I'm the Daddy, that's why!"

Did God Create AIDS?

In this model of an omnipotent God, God is the creator of disease and uses illness to punish you if you overstep his "will" (even though his "will" is so impossibly vague, you often don't even know you have violated it). The fact that God is the author of disease, however, was supposed to be both good news and bad news: If God made you sick, God could also make you well, as soon as you repented. Christians began to see sickness this way in the medieval period, and from about the ninth century until very recently, the arts of Christian healing were almost lost. The rites for the sick came to be used only as "last rites," as a preparation for death. Although in the early church, Christians were instructed to call the elders of the church to anoint them with healing oil whenever they were sick,[2] the former rites of healing became so associated with death that if you saw a priest come into your sick-room, you would assume you were about to die. The liturgies no longer spoke of healing, but of sin and confession, repentance and contrition. One form of rite for the visitation of the sick called for the priest to begin by making a cross of ashes on the sick person's chest and then to cover the patient with a hair shirt—a symbol of repentance.[3] From 1566, the Roman Catholic Church would not allow physicians to obtain a license to practice medicine unless they swore they would not treat for more than three days a patient who had not made a confession to a priest.[4]

Such an attitude toward sickness may seem perverse, but it is the inevitable outcome of a view of God as "omnipotent." If God controls everything in the world, from viruses to people, then God could easily choose to make you well, and the fact that you are sick, then, must mean you have displeased God.

[2]James 5:14–15.
[3]Morton Kelsey, *Psychology, Medicine and Christian Healing* (San Francisco: Harper & Row, 1988), 163.
[4]Ibid., 166.

The Freedom of All Creation

An alternative is to affirm that God is *not* omnipotent—at least not in the way that word is usually meant. God is not a cosmic puppeteer pulling your strings and controlling every last detail of the universe—not because God isn't capable of doing so, but because our God *chooses not to*. Instead, the Creator has endowed the entire universe with an awesome freedom of choice. Christians have always insisted that human beings are endowed with free will. That, in fact, is generally agreed to be the meaning of "let us make human beings in our own image," which, according to the Book of Genesis, God said while creating the first humans. Because of the high value God places on free will, God never forces you to do *anything*. God may try to coax you into a particular path, may hold up possibilities before you and invite you to take a particular action, but God never *requires* you to do anything—even to believe in or love God.

As queer Christians, we should stand with the many feminist theologians of liberation who reject an "anthropocentric" theology—a theology that sees human beings as the center of the created universe, and therefore having a God-given right to use and abuse other creatures as we see fit. Once you admit that we are only one order of the creatures of God, you can begin to entertain the possibility that "free will," too, might be extended to nonhuman beings. In fact, you can come to understand that God endows *all* creatures with some degree of free will—a greater or lesser degree depending upon the degree of consciousness. Therefore, there is a sense in which the gift of "free will" extends down to the cellular and molecular levels. Certainly a virus can exercise its free will— which would be, primarily, its will to survive.

The fact that HIV, then, is choosing to survive at the expense of its human hosts does not in any way implicate God. In fact, as we discussed in Chapter 6, you can assume God is not pleased with the way things have turned out, either. You can be quite certain God is working overtime to heal the malevolent relationship between humans and HIV, and you can rest assured God is as heartbroken as you are at the suffering and death that has resulted. But you cannot expect God to wipe out one creature that is causing another creature distress. In classical language, it is not in the nature of God to do so. In more direct language, God simply does not work that way. Still, God's will is for all creatures to live together in harmony, as the account of the original paradise in the Book of Genesis poetically affirms.

Did We Create AIDS?

The danger in affirming the concept of your freedom of choice, coupled with an anthropocentric view of the universe, is that you can forget that other creatures who also make free choices interact with you and affect your life. Many New Age systems are so extremely anthropocentric, they affirm, "You are at cause in your universe." While attempting to correct the classical view of God's direct control over all things, they have offered a concept that is an *over*corrective. Rejecting the traditional view that God creates disease, many New Age practitioners, say, No, *you* create your disease.

Louise Hay, a controversial but popular healer, has been severely criticized by some segments of the queer community, who feel she is adding to a PWA's guilt when she insists "you can heal your life" if you first "take responsibility for your disease." Whether the problems with what is assumed to be "the Louise Hay approach" stem from ideas that are actually taught by her or from the misunderstanding and misreporting of her ideas by those who read her books and listen to her tapes is difficult to assess. (Carl Jung once said, "Thank God I'm not a Jungian," and Louise Hay, too, might be horrified to hear some of the things her followers are claiming she says. Many of Louise Hay's most committed fans have suggested that Hay has heard the assertions that her ideas create guilt for people with AIDS, and lately has either modified her position or at least chosen her words more carefully.)

Unfortunately, human beings have a tendency to be Fundamentalists. We are not comfortable with ambiguity and uncertainty; we want clear, simple *answers*. Many people flee from the frying pan of evangelical Christian Fundamentalism, only to land in the fire of the New Age Fundamentalism. "Disease is God's punishment" is a Fundamentalist view, but so is the most extreme insistence upon "you can heal your life." The authentic Christian position is neither of these. You can't heal your life, but God can—and God's healing requires your cooperation. You don't single-handedly create disease for yourself—there are certainly external and environmental factors—but your attitudes and beliefs can help create the conditions for disease to flourish.

The Fatalistic View

Another way of approaching disease is to shrug your shoulders and say that's just the way life is. Unfortunately, this position is currently in vogue among pastoral counselors, and most hospital chaplains express some form of this view to their patients. Rather than praying with you for healing, most current hospital chaplains are more likely to "help you face reality," to "come to terms with your disease," and to deal with such practical (and admittedly important) matters as making out a will and expressing your wishes regarding extraordinary medical care.

I was in the hospital recently, and a parade of priests and bishops visited me. Most of them offered to do anything they could for me, but with very few exceptions, they never suggested that what they might do is pray for my recovery. They almost never brought with them the holy oil for the anointing of the sick. They all had been trained in the current school of pastoral counseling, that the purpose of hospital visitation is not to offer healing, but to offer comfort and to help the patient "face the reality of the disease."

God's will for you and for all of us is health and wholeness, and as a Christian you should reject the notion that suffering and illness are an inevitable part of life.

Remember Satan?

The authentic Christian position is none of the above. God does not send disease, you do not bring disease on yourself, and disease is not "just the way life is."

In order to make sense of AIDS, queer Christians need to recover a basic Christian affirmation: There is a force of evil alive and well in our universe. This malevolent force, while not as strong as God, is often stronger than you are. While God is coaxing all creatures toward greater good, the Evil One is constantly coaxing creatures toward evil. While God is tirelessly urging all creatures to form harmonious relationships with each other, the Evil One is encouraging discord. Wherever there is an adverse relationship between two or more creatures, we can see the handiwork of the evil force that is alive and well in the universe—disease is just one example.

Many of the New Age philosophies want to reject a belief in evil. According to this view, there is no evil—only our misperception. If something appears evil to you, you are not seeing it correctly; you need to stand back and get the larger picture. *A Course in Miracles,* a popular three-volume work supposedly channeled by the Holy Spirit, the basis for countless study groups and even therapies, teaches that evil is an illusion. As psychologist M. Scott Peck has pointed out in his book about evil, *People of the Lie,* the danger in viewing evil as an illusion or a human misperception is that we allow evil a free rein. As Peck says, "Perhaps Satan's best deception is its general success in concealing its own reality from the human mind."[5] Hinduism, also, teaches that evil is an illusion, and the extreme manifestation of that view is the pious Hindu who will step over a dying leper in the gutter because it is not his business to interfere with the leper's karma, and it is, after all, only meaningless illusion.

I believe that Christ can heal—and is healing—AIDS. But we cannot begin to understand or practice Christian healing, we cannot hope to heal as Jesus healed, unless we understand (and adopt) Jesus' basic worldview. Jesus clearly saw disease as a result of evil forces in the world, the work of Satan, which he was called to destroy. Jesus never told people they were sick because God sent disease to punish them; but neither did he ever tell a sick person, "love your disease" (which is the title of a currently popular book). Jesus saw the work of healing as a struggle against the evil forces

[5]M. Scott Peck, *People of the Lie: The Hope for Healing Human Evil* (New York: Simon and Schuster, 1983), 208.

that hold human beings in bondage. Any sickness, Jesus believed, was demonic.

Developing a healthy respect for Satan goes a long way toward helping you make sense of AIDS, as well as other diseases and other tragedies. God didn't create AIDS, nor did we create AIDS. AIDS is the creation of the force in the universe that attempts to pull all creation away from life and God—the force we know as Satan, the Evil One, Lucifer, the fallen archangel. Just as we can see the hand of God in much of the creation, we can see the hand of the demonic in disease, and particularly in AIDS.

When my friend Malcolm Boyd learned I had been diagnosed with AIDS, he wrote me a letter expressing his concern, in which he referred to AIDS as "the monster, the enemy." Since I had just come from a series of New Age–oriented seminars on AIDS and healing, my first reaction was that Malcolm was being old-fashioned and unenlightened by viewing AIDS in this way. I had been taught to view disease as an "opportunity," even as a "blessing." I had just attended a workshop in which people imagined HIV writing them a letter, and some of them sounded like *love* letters! Now, upon reflection (and a rereading of the gospels), I understand Malcolm may indeed have been expressing an "old-fashioned" view of disease, but he was expressing an authentically *Christian* view. I have no trouble imagining that Jesus would have referred to AIDS as "the monster, the enemy," because Jesus saw all disease as the work of *the* Enemy, the Evil One.

Christian Healing

Jesus was a healer. If you read the gospels, that fact is inescapable. He spent at least as much time healing the sick as he did teaching. Father Morton Kelsey has tabulated the scriptures of the gospels, verse by verse, and concludes that accounts of miracles of healing make up one-fifth of the gospels.[6] Laurence H. Blackburn, getting at the same idea a different way, calculates that one-third of the gospel accounts of Jesus' public ministry deal with healing

[6]Kelsey, *Psychology, Medicine, and Christian Healing*, 42.

miracles.[7] If Jesus spent at least as much time healing as he did teaching, doesn't it seem silly for us to adopt his teachings and ignore his healing?

The early Christians simply *expected* healing as one of the promises of Christ to his followers. If they got sick, they called the elders of the church to come heal them. When Jesus commissioned his disciples to carry on his ministry after he was gone, he told them not only would they be able to heal the sick as he did, but:

> *Truly, truly I say to you, you who believe in me will also do the works that I do; and greater works than these will you do, because I go to the Creator. Whatever you ask in my name, I will do it, that God may be glorified in the Christ; if you ask anything in my name, I will do it.*[8]

Sharing Energy

Recently, I became deeply involved in the study and practice of the almost-lost tradition of Christian healing. I celebrated a healing Mass every week, and taught a class on healing to a group of lay Christians who are attempting to develop their own healing gifts. In addition, I have been studying and taking classes myself, exploring every avenue of the healing arts I can find. I want to know all I can about healing—how African shamans heal, how witches heal, how charismatic Christians heal.

What I have come to believe is that Jesus was basically what might today be called "an energy healer." Although it appears he used several methods of healing, most of the time he seems to have employed some method of transferring biomagnetic energy to the person who was sick, to balance and restore the sick person's own body energies.

The practice of energy healing is based on a view that everything in the universe is composed of energy—that the true "basic building block" of all matter is energy; that rocks, trees, and human

---

[7]Laurence H. Blackburn, *God Wants You to Be Well* (New York: Morehouse-Barlow Co., 1974), 48.
[8]John 14:12–14, rendered inclusive.

bodies are formed by energy vibrating and pulsating at various rates and frequencies. Once you accept this energetic view of the universe (which, actually, Einstein demonstrated half a century ago, and contemporary physicists continue to confirm), it is easy to understand how various forms of "esoteric" healing work. Music and color and light and emotions, such as love and anger, are also energy vibrations—and so they can have a direct effect upon the harmony and health of your body. The use of crystals and gemstones in healing is similarly based upon the conviction that each stone has a particular vibrational frequency, and that those vibrations can be applied to your body for balancing and healing. Methods such as acupuncture and shiatsu seem to be designed to remove blockages of the energy flow within your body. Other methods, such as Reiki, macrobiotic palm healing, and the Christian laying on of hands, seem to be importing energy from an outside source into your body.

The most basic form of energy healing is simply the transfer of balancing energy from one person to another, usually done by touching the sick person, allowing energy to flow through the healer's hands into the patient's body. This is, essentially, the Christian healing method. This seems to be the method that Jesus most frequently employed.

In addition, Christian healing makes use of holy oil, which is simply a fine oil that has been blessed and set apart for the work of healing. Usually olive oil is used, though a good case can be made for using castor oil, which has a long history of use in the healing arts. In fact, another name for the castor-oil plant is the palma Christi, or hand of Christ. Often the oil is scented with a substance such as balsam. Recently developed technologies, such as Kirlian photography, have been able to document the flow of energy from the healer to the patient. In fact, Kirlian photography has shown that all living things, including plants, have an energy field around them, a field that fades when the animal or plant dies. In addition, it has shown that when a person touches an object, some of that person's energy remains in the object for a while. Some objects and substances seem to retain the energy longer than others, and oils hold it longest of all. So technology has confirmed the ancient wisdom of the church—that blessed oil is a valuable aid to healing. The very act of blessing the oil, in fact (like blessing the bread and wine at the Eucharist), is similarly a transfer of energy from the priest to the object being blessed.

An intriguing and largely unanswered question is exactly where the energy channeled in the healing process comes from. Is the energy that flows into your body simply that from the body of the healer, or does it come from some outside source? The answer, I believe, is often both. It is possible for a healer to transfer some of her own energy to you—but if she does so often, she will probably deplete and unbalance her own energy fields. Christians have always believed that the most effective healing occurs when the healer relies not just on his own energy, but acts as a channel, a conduit, for the healing energy of the Holy Spirit. Certain non-Christian healing methods make similar claims. The Japanese word *reiki* literally means something like "God energy" or "universal life force," and Reiki healers speak of their healing process as "delivering" this universal life force to the client.

Christian healers, Reiki healers, and various other energy healers all use different vocabularies, but when you strip away the words and the belief systems, you begin to see an amazing similarity in many of the healing methods. I have recently been studying with an energy healer who is grounded in the Native American tradition, and I have become increasingly convinced that her healing method is almost identical to the healing method Jesus used and taught his disciples.

The liturgical form of Christian healing today is, like many of our sacraments and ceremonies, the distillation of what was once much more elaborate—a sort of remnant of the ancient practice. Most likely, in the early church, if you were sick and called on the priest to come heal you, the priest would spend about an hour praying (perhaps praying "in tongues") and laying hands on you—and especially laying hands on the parts of your body that were diseased. The holy oil, also, would most likely be applied to the areas of your body that were most in need of healing—in fact, the oil might be applied to your entire body, a sort of holy massage. Today, in a liturgical setting, such as a healing service, what is most often done is that the priest or healer lays hands on your head or face, makes a small cross of holy oil on your forehead (on your brow chakra, if you will), and says a prayer that lasts about thirty seconds. While this scaled-down, symbolic anointing is helpful, and should be offered in a public service of healing, it is not appropriate, not enough, for the visitation of the sick. If I went to see someone in the hospital with pneumonia, for instance, I would lay my hands on and anoint not only his brow, but also his chest.

The Healing of AIDS

Since, as Christian healers, we affirm that the healing energy is not simply that of the healer, but the power of the Holy Spirit, we can also affirm as a matter of faith that there is no such thing as an "incurable" disease. If all we had to give was our own energy, our own healing power, then we might have to acknowledge we cannot heal some diseases and conditions. But we channel the awesome and unlimited healing work of God's Holy Spirit, and God is greater than any disease or illness.

Christianity, like Judaism, is based upon a theological stance of radical monotheism: There is only one God. While other world religions contemporary with the founding of Christianity often believed in a pantheon of gods, or at least in two gods—one responsible for good, one responsible for evil—the Judeo-Christian tradition insists there is only one God, who is the most powerful force in the universe. This is not to deny the existence of other spiritual entities—and we stand within centuries of catholic tradition when we affirm the literal existence of "angels, archangels, and all the company of heaven," of both benevolent and malevolent spiritual beings—but as a matter of faith and doctrine, we must insist that none of these beings is as powerful as the one God. In fact, in the Christian tradition, to suggest that any other force or being is equal to God is to commit the classic sin of *blasphemy*.

Yet in practice, most Christians commit blasphemy every day because they believe certain diseases and conditions (such as AIDS and addictions) are in fact stronger than God. In spite of the words they parrot in the liturgy, very few Christians (and even fewer clergy) today actually believe that literal, physical healing is possible—and almost no one believes the healing of AIDS is possible.

In the greater Boston area, an organization called the Ecumenical Task Force on AIDS sponsors what are called "AIDS healing services" in churches of various denominations. I have been to many of these services; in fact, for two years, I was a member of the task force. I have yet to have been present at one of these services where I had the sense that anyone involved really expected anyone to be *healed*. Recently, one of these task force "healing" services was held nearby, and the members of our healing study group thought we should attend. I wasn't excited about the prospect, but told them I would go, if only so I could later say, "I told you so." After the service, one of the members of the healing class said, "You can say it, a thousand times over!"

These monthly services, like the vast majority of what are called "healing services" in mainstream churches, are not really about healing. They are something closer to *comfort* services, with a goal of making those who come up to receive the laying on of hands feel loved and supported and cared for—but not literally *healed*. Those specifically billed as AIDS healing services also have a tendency to degenerate into something closer to grief and bereavement services. They more closely resemble a requiem Mass for the dead than a service offering the hope of Christian healing.

Let me offer you a three-part affirmation to assert as a matter of faith:

There are no "incurable" diseases.
AIDS can be healed.
God is greater than AIDS.

Our Provincetown healing ministry, the Palma Christi Institute, was unusual. I do not know of any other Christian healing ministry anywhere that is willing to proclaim AIDS can be healed. But why not? Christ's promise to his followers was "If you ask anything in my name, I will do it." He didn't say, as most contemporary Christians seem to believe, "If you ask anything in my name—except to be totally healed from AIDS or Alzheimer's or substance addiction, or any of a number of other incurable illnesses—I will do it."

Part of the problem is that most of the Christian communities that take healing seriously tend to be evangelical or charismatic—and that almost inevitably means they adopt radically conservative social and ethical policies. If you go to the average charismatic Christian church and ask to be healed of AIDS, they are much more likely to try to "heal" you of homosexuality. They will insist you "repent" of your sexual "sin" before you can be healed. No wonder they're not having much success with healing AIDS! On the other hand, if you go to a church that is open-minded enough not to view homosexuality as a sin, you are unlikely to find anyone there who really believes actual, physical healing is possible—especially healing from a disease such as AIDS, which the medical establishment and the media have labeled "fatal" and "incurable."

When I was in seminary, *no* courses in Christian healing were offered in any of the nine schools of the Boston Theological Union. On my own, I read Morton Kelsey's wonderful book, *Psychology, Medicine, and Christian Healing*,[9] and I was intrigued. I was intellectually convinced—I believed it in my head, but not in my heart. I set up a healing ministry in my parish in Hoboken, offering the sacraments of healing at the side altar during Communion. I set up a similar ministry in Provincetown, and I did some teaching about the renewal of the Christian healing ministry—I even led a seminar on that topic—but like most priests, if I had laid my hands on someone who was then actually *healed,* I would probably have fainted.

What finally moved belief in Christian healing from my head to my heart was that it ceased to be an interesting theological issue and became personalized for me, on a life-and-death basis. In November 1990, I was diagnosed with pneumocystis pneumonia and AIDS. In January 1991, I was diagnosed with Kaposi's sarcoma. I shrugged my shoulders and prepared to die. I started making out a will, joined the right-to-die Hemlock Society, planned my funeral, and warned all my friends that I would choose suicide over a messy death.[9]

Then, I went to a seminar called "Beyond AIDS: A Journey into Healing," led by George Melton, a man who is in the process of healing from AIDS through his faith in God.[10] It wasn't exactly anything he said, but just the fact of who he *was*—a person who refuses to believe AIDS is always fatal, who believes AIDS can be healed. Then I began searching the literature, and I found there are many long-term survivors of AIDS.[11] A few people have even sero-converted from HIV-positive to HIV-negative.[12] Finally, I learned to pray again and began, for the first time in years, reading the Bible in a devotional context, rather than a strictly intellectual context.

God doesn't speak to me in complete sentences, but from time to time—very rarely—I have had an experience that I knew was God communicating with me. I can't describe it very well: It is a strong feeling of conviction, deep down inside myself, an idea that so reverberates in my heart and soul that I simply *know* it is true, and I *know* it is God's voice. I felt it several years ago when I heard God calling me to be ordained to the priesthood as an openly gay man. At the time, it seemed the odds against my being ordained were insurmountable, but I approached the entire process with a sense of confidence, knowing that since God was calling me to do this, God would find a way around the obstacles.

I had that same experience again in January 1991 when I felt, from deep within my heart and soul, that God was telling me I don't

[9]Please don't take anything I am saying here as an indictment of the Hemlock Society or of the morality of rational suicide. I remain a loyal member of the Hemlock Society, and I believe Christians should lobby for the right of terminally ill people to choose the time and method of their own death. The Hemlock Society, which I recommend joining, can be reached at P.O. Box 11830, Eugene, OR 97440-3900. (503) 342-5748.

[10]See George Melton, with Will Garcia, *Beyond AIDS: A Journey Into Healing* (Beverly Hills, California: Brotherhood Press, 1988).

[11]See especially Michael Callen, *Surviving AIDS* (New York: HarperCollins, 1990). Callen interviewed several long-term survivors for the book. Callen himself has lived over ten years since his diagnosis—without taking the highly toxic antiviral AZT. Another book that includes interviews with AIDS survivors is *They Survived AIDS* by Scott Gregory and Bianca Leonardo (Palm Springs: Tree of Life Publications, 1989). Also, the January 1991 issue of *East/West* magazine included interviews with several long-term survivors.

[12]The most well-known is Niro Markoff Asistent, who has just published a book called *Why I Survive AIDS* (New York: Simon & Schuster/Fireside, 1991). The book is excerpted, as the cover story, in the October 1991 issue of *New Age Journal*.

have to die of AIDS, that I can be healed—and I don't mean to survive a few extra years, to cope with my illness, to "live powerfully with AIDS"—I mean that I can be *healed*. At the same time, I felt an equally strong conviction that God is calling me, at this moment in my life, to be a healer, and to help renew and restore the lost tradition of Christian healing.

You might think I am doing this out of a sense of desperation, whistling in the dark, clutching at straws. The editor of the newsletter of the American Gay Atheists Association, who had read of my interest in what the press called "faith healing," wrote, among other things, "This reversion to religion as a cure-all . . . demonstrates the inadequacies of the religious person."[13] But I wasn't desperate in January 1991; I was quite prepared and ready to die. It is not desperation, but *faith*.

And is it working? I believe it is. I believe Christ is healing me from AIDS now. I am not relying *solely* on the laying on of hands; I also use several holistic healing methodologies as well as more conventional drugs. The medical establishment—with the exception of the rare physician of faith, such as Bernie Siegel—would insist I will eventually die of AIDS anyway. The satanic forces have done their work quite well. The demonic voices constantly whisper in our ears to give up, to give in to the lie that AIDS is always fatal. But I choose to believe the inner voice I hear instead—God's voice, telling me I can be healed; I *am* being healed. I not only reject the label "AIDS victim," I equally reject the label "PWA." I refuse to make AIDS the center of my identity. Ninety-nine percent of the time, I don't even think about AIDS. Sometimes, I honestly *forget* that I was ever sick. I am *not* a "person living with AIDS," I am a person *healing from AIDS*. This sort of personal testimony is what evangelicals would call "witnessing." It is an excellent term: to be a *witness* to the power of Christ. I am an eyewitness, a *body*-witness, if you will, to the healing power of Christ; and I tell you what I know: This power is real. It works. It is available now to you and those you love. I bear witness to the fact that Christ continues to heal his people, just as he has for two thousand years.

[13] *The American Gay & Lesbian Atheist* 9, no. 3 (March 1991): 6.

If you are HIV-positive or have been diagnosed with AIDS, or care about someone who has, I hope you will believe that healing is possible—not just comfort, not just acceptance of the disease, but literal, physical healing. Your belief is of profound importance. What was fascinating about Michael Callen's interviews with several long-term AIDS survivors in his book *Surviving AIDS* is that their approaches to healing are so varied. Some take AZT, others refuse all drugs and opt for holistic approaches. Some practically became disciples of Louise Hay, others would not go near a Hay seminar. Some adopted macrobiotic diets, others eat at McDonald's. Some gave up all alcohol, others drank heavily and used other recreational drugs. The only trait all the survivors had in common was *believing that they could survive.* This belief in the possibility of healing is not even religious belief—Callen himself is an atheist. Those who are beating AIDS are those who refuse to accept the medical establishment's prognosis and insist on surviving. If you give in to the messages you hear all around you from the medical profession, from the press, and even from the AIDS support community, that AIDS is inevitably fatal, then that prophecy will definitely come true for you. But if you can find the courage—the faith—to dismiss those dire predictions and trust in your own "inner healer" and the healing power of Christ, I believe you can hold AIDS in remission indefinitely.

What must you do to be healed? First and most important, learn to pray and meditate, and be diligent about meditating daily. All healing comes from that place where we (and all creatures) are connected, where we are one with God. Daily meditation helps you truly come to know that you are one with God. Second, find healers who can transfer the healing energy to you on a regular basis—Reiki practitioners, energy healers, et cetera. Even lovers and friends who are not trained as healers can transfer some energy to you just by touching you.

Try to attend Christian healing services, if you can find services where those involved really expect *healing* to occur. Even if they don't, receiving the laying on of hands regularly, and especially anointing, can be useful, but you may have to use affirmations to overcome the negativity and pessimism that characterize some Christian "healing" services. Ask people to pray for you, but make sure they are praying for healing, not for comfort and "acceptance of your disease." Pray for yourself, and be bold about asking for total healing. Look for a healing circle you can become involved in. Most major cities have holistic health and education centers (such as the New York Center for Living) that offer workshops on various healing methodologies—check them out. Read every book about healing you can get your hands on, and especially those that offer testimonies of people who have been healed from life-threatening illnesses. If you have a chance, do enroll in positive workshops such as the AIDS Mastery[14] or SHARE.[15]

Some sort of support group would probably be helpful, but you must choose it carefully. Try to find a group that is made up of people who plan to be healed, not one of people who are waiting to die. If you visit a support group, and all they talk about is disease and drugs, don't go back. A group sponsored by a holistic health center is more likely to take a positive approach.

Become informed about AIDS and various treatment alternatives, but beware of becoming obsessed with disease literature—reading too much of it can be overwhelmingly depressing. Ask your physician lots of questions and make up your mind to be a stubborn, difficult patient. Bernie Siegel says "difficult" patients are the ones who survive. Don't take a Fundamentalist stance that rules out the use of any drugs, but don't take any drug anyone suggests to you until you are *sure* it is best for you. Don't take your physician's word for *anything* if it goes against the wisdom of your heart. Learn to say no to the medical profession when you need to. Use meditation to draw from your own inner wisdom to make decisions about various treatment methodologies.

[14]The AIDS Mastery Workshop, an affordable weekend of positive reeducation experiences developed by Sally Fisher, is offered in several locations by Northern Lights Alternatives, 150 West 25th St., Suite 503, New York, NY 10001.
[15]SHARE stands for Self-Healing AIDS-Related Experiment, an organization founded by Niro Asistent, the AIDS survivor who seroconverted to HIV-negative. She offers workshops in New York and occasionally other cities. Write to her for information on the workshops at 215 East 95th St., #21B, New York, NY 10128; or SHARE on the Road, an umbrella for workshops offered by her associates, 740-A 14th St., Suite 448, San Francisco, CA 94114.

The healing process seems to be made up of paradoxes. For one, it seems you must come to an acceptance of death before you can be healed. Many survivors of life-threatening illnesses went through a stage when they "made their peace with death," were prepared to die—and often at that moment, they felt the major turnaround toward healing. If you have any life-threatening illness, you should "put your affairs in order." Make sure you have a current will (which is extremely important if you have a current or ex-spouse or children). You should also file a document granting your partner or a good friend "medical power of attorney," to make medical decisions on your behalf if you are not able to do so, and also a general power of attorney, authorizing someone to make financial decisions on your behalf. You might also want to sign a "living will," stating your preference that extraordinary life-support systems not be used if you are unlikely to recover. You can save your survivors a lot of stress and grief if you make funerary arrangements in advance, and write down your wishes for your funeral ceremony—your favorite hymns, which friends should be asked to do readings, et cetera. Of course, what's really important is not the legal paperwork, but the fact that you come to terms with the emotional impact of facing your own mortality. Filing the legal documents, however, can help you do that.

Michael Callen says that one of the most important things you can do is fall in love; and my own experience confirms this. And don't give up sex. Sex is healing and life-affirming. Don't assume your life is over, and if you are single, don't assume you will never have another partner. Both Callen and I met our lovers *after* we were diagnosed.

There are documented cases of people recovering from all sorts of illnesses through the healing power of Christ. If God can cure cancer, then God can cure AIDS, because our God is greater than AIDS. No disease in the world is stronger than the power of God. This is gospel, this is literally Good News, so spread the word: *Christ is healing AIDS now!*

Remember, you can't heal yourself, but God can; and paradoxically, in order for God to heal you, your total cooperation is required. As healer Margo Adair says, "The choice to live—to deny medical prediction—must be a *total* one, one in which you engage every thought, feeling, and cell of your being."[16] Believe it: Christ can heal you.

[16]Margo Adair in Jason Serinus, ed., *Psychoimmunity and the Healing Process: A Holistic Approach to Immunity and AIDS* (Berkeley, California: Celestial Arts, 1986/1988), 155.

20
Sure and Certain Hope

Death and Afterlife

When I was growing up in heavily Fundamentalist Abilene, Texas, my grandfather's siblings, all ten of them, with all their children and grandchildren, used to gather on Sundays for dinner at my great-grandparents' house. After dinner, we would sit on the big front porch of their old house, the guitars would be brought out, and we would all sing gospel hymns. Since many of those hymns have rousing tunes, it was a lot of fun—as long as you didn't listen too closely to some of the lyrics. One of them says:

> *This world is not my home,*
> *I'm just a-passin' through.*
> *If heaven's not my home,*
> *then, Lord, what would I do?*
> *The angels beckon me*
> *from heaven's open door,*
> *and I can't feel at home*
> *in this world anymore.*

You've probably known people like that. The fact they "don't feel at home in this world" is all too painfully obvious. Don't you see that hymn as being rather macabre? I wonder whether the person who wrote it suicided shortly after, in response to the beckoning of those angels.

From about the medieval period until the recent rise of rationalism, Christians became so obsessed with the afterlife they were positively morbid. This existence came to be seen as a "vale of tears," a necessary evil, something to be patiently endured so you could get to heaven, where your real life began. Many Fundamentalists still exhibit this unhealthy fixation on heaven, being "so heavenly minded they're no earthly good."

But as with most other aspects of Christianity, the modern church, wanting to move away from this otherworldly stance, has tended to throw out the baby with the bathwater. Now, most mainstream Christians, especially clergy, don't even believe in heaven. But just as with the healing arts, what mainstream Christianity has abandoned as superstitious, science is beginning to investigate and confirm.

The Evidence for Life After Life

The most striking evidence available is the experience of those people who have had "near-death experiences," who have come very close to dying—and some of them even *have* died, according to the clinical definition, and yet they have been revived, they have "come back," you might say. Some of these people have some fascinating stories to tell.

The most widely read telling of these stories is in Raymond Moody's three books, *Life After Life, Reflections on Life After Life,* and *The Light Beyond.* Moody, a physician, became fascinated with the stories a few of his patients told him about their "near-death experiences," when they appeared to die momentarily. He began investigating and asked other people who had had such experiences to contact him. He found that the experience was much more common than he had suspected—a 1982 Gallup poll found that 8 million Americans had had "near-death experiences"—but people are reluctant to talk about it, particularly with their physician, because they are afraid of being thought crazy. People are, evidently, even *less* willing to talk to their clergy about such experiences.

Moody catalogued nineteen separate elements or aspects of this experience. Not everyone reported all of these elements, and some of them were described differently. Almost all of Moody's subjects spoke of the difficulty they have in putting the experience into words. Since the experience was beyond the ordinary senses, in order to talk about it they had to translate—and most felt frustrated by how poorly they were translating. (This is exactly the way the Christian mystics speak of the difficulty in communicating their experiences of God.)

Almost all of Moody's subjects reported hearing themselves described as dead, either by a doctor or nurse or a passerby. Often, they were surprised to hear this, for they didn't "feel" dead. Next, they usually describe a feeling of great peace or calm or quiet—with no pain and no fear.

What happens next is variously described, but most report some sort of loud sound—either a ringing or a rushing or a roaring or a buzzing. Then most described a feeling of being drawn through a narrow, dark tunnel, or a narrow hallway or a cave. These two phenomena seem to accompany their becoming less attached to their injured physical bodies. From this point, they are often able to see their own bodies, as a spectator—often from a point slightly above. They watch the scene, the scurrying around, the lifesaving attempts, with a sort of detachment and fascination. One of the most compelling bits of data here is that often these people, when "brought back," report words that were said, or procedures that were done, that they could not have known otherwise, *even if they had been awake.*

Then the next stage—which only happens to those who remain in this "near-death" or "clinically dead" state for a longer period of time—is what is most commonly described as a meeting with a "being of light." Many of these people reported seeing other people, often people they knew who had died—a parent or a relative, or a close friend. If they don't know someone who has died, other people, with whom they are not familiar, are there to greet them. These other people seem to serve as guides, taking them to this "being of light." Sometimes, depending on their religious background, they might call this "being of light" God or Christ or an angel; but most of the time, even if they do profess a particular religion, they use more vague terms—just a being of light or a being of pure love. Almost all of those who encountered this "being of light" felt they were being questioned about their lives—but in a very nonjudgmental way. They seemed to be asked probing questions, but they did not feel condemned. Many people at this point report what might be described as the cliché of "your whole life passing before you," as if they are being given a chance to review their entire life. Finally, many of them are given a choice—either to go or stay. The bottom-line question seems to be, "Are you finished with your life?" All of Dr. Moody's subjects, of course, came back— many of them because they felt they *weren't* finished with their lives, that someone they loved really needed them. For instance, mothers often felt they had to return until their children were grown. And so, gently, they return to their bodies; the feeling returns, and they often make spontaneous recoveries.

That *is* evidence of life after life. Oh, there are other ways you can explain it. You might, for instance, suppose that when bodily sensations are suppressed by any means—whether hypnosis or meditation or the shock of an accident or surgery—then mental images take over and become more vivid. But you would still have to account for the striking similarities in these accounts—and the similarities, by the way, are not dependent on the subjects' religion, or even whether they *are* religious. Whether the patients are Christian, Jewish, Buddhist, or atheist, they all seem to have the same experience. So you *can* find other ways of explaining it—but why? Why not take the simplest explanation, the one that is the most logical, the one that just happens to match the ancient wisdom of almost all major world religions. If you read the Tibetan Book of the Dead or certain parts of the Jewish or Christian scriptures, you will find descriptions of the afterlife that are uncannily similar to what Dr. Moody's interviewees describe. If miracles or angels or afterlife are not a part of your perceptual field, you will not see them, no matter what evidence you are presented. If they *are* in your perceptual field, that is, if you admit the possibility, the evidence is there.

There is other evidence. There are the experiences of people who report having had some sort of encounter with someone who is dead. Again, most people are reluctant to talk about these experiences, but a survey by Andrew Greeley, the priest trained as a sociologist, showed that 44 percent of the American public report having had some type of communication with a person who had died. Almost none of these people *sought* the experience—it came spontaneously.

Why Does It Matter?

What difference does it make? It makes a hell of a lot of difference—and it makes more difference in the 1990s than it did in the 1950s. Among other things, being queer today means that, unless you are truly isolated from your community, you have been to a lot of funerals and memorial services lately. It used to be that, except for wars and a few accidents and rare diseases here and there, no one except the very old really had to deal with his or her mortality. In fact, an entire industry (an industry I consider a parasite on our society) grew up around creating the illusion that death is not real. We're not content to just bury our dead, we have to use grossly unnatural chemical means to preserve their bodies, cover their faces (and any signs of disease) with so much makeup they look like they belong in a wax museum, and put them on display in outrageously expensive coffins under pink lights to the accompaniment of cloyingly sweet music—all so that they will look what we perversely refer to as "natural."

Please! As a Christian priest who occasionally officiates funerals, I beg you, write it into your will that you are to be cremated, not buried; and unless the laws of your state require it (which they do in states where the funeral-industry lobby has been especially aggressive), state that you refuse embalming and a coffin. As Christians, we should treat human bodies with respect and reverence and even awe—but I don't think *pickling* a dead body is showing respect.

Maybe without years of having seen the pounds of makeup under the pink lights, we might be more prepared for the reality that has slapped us in the face in the past few years: People do die. All people die. Death is part of the human experience.

That's the bad news; but the good news is that death is only a *part* of the human experience. On either side of death, there is life. When you do come face-to-face with death—your own or someone else's—you are forced to ask those "ultimate questions" that are often the catalyst for the spiritual journey. Above all else, you are forced into the task of *making meaning*. If a human life only lasts a quarter of a century, what is life for? What does it mean? Is it worth it? The Christian affirmation is yes, it's worth it, because death is not the end, only a transition. The Roman Catholic burial liturgy says, "For your faithful people, life is changed, not taken away."

I, for one, frankly couldn't deal with the reality of AIDS in our community (not to mention in my own body) if I didn't have faith in "the sure and certain hope of the resurrection." What a faith in the resurrection of the body means to me is that I have not seen the last of my best friend Bill Irby, my mother, or any of the dozens of other friends and relatives who have died. In fact, when I cross over to the other side, I expect to find them there to greet me.

It also means, by the way, that you can continue to have some forms of communication with the people you love who have died. Through prayer and meditation, you can commune with St. Aelred, St. Joan of Arc, or your relatives or your old friends. I don't know why conventional Christians get so upset by channeling when every Sunday they declare they believe in "the communion of the saints." (Well, actually, I *do* know why—because they don't stop and think about what they're saying.) Channels of communication exist between this world and the other side. That isn't a New Age concept; it's an ancient and venerable Christian concept.

Now, you may be "just a-passin' through," but for the time being, this world *is* your home. I hope you're fond of life on earth and want to live it as fully as possible and have it last as long as possible. But when "death, a necessary end," does come, you, as a Christian, can be much less afraid of it than you would be if you thought it meant total oblivion.

To me, Moody's research and these other data offer "proof," all the proof I need that human existence does in fact continue after death, just as Christianity and most other religions have for centuries taught it does. But I presented a workshop on this topic once in Provincetown. I talked about how Moody's findings confirm what Christians have always believed as a matter of faith. In the evaluation sheets after the workshop, one of the participants wrote, "This is all very interesting, but I don't think it proves anything." And, you know, that person was right. You can read Moody's books and say, "Wow! Here's *proof* of life after life," or you can read Moody's books and say, "Isn't it interesting that when people are dying, when their normal sensory data is blocked, they tend to hallucinate?" It is, in the final analysis, a matter of making a choice.

So we've come full circle about this faith business. We're back where we started in Chapter 1, in the discussion about how to acquire faith. The bottom line is, you just *choose*. You can choose to believe or not to believe. It is commendable and responsible to pile up all the data you can find (such as Moody's research), but it still doesn't "prove" anything—and it never will. In order to believe in the afterlife, just like to believe in God, you've got to "make believe," *make an act of faith*.

Into Paradise May the Angels Lead You

You've already heard me, in earlier chapters, on my soapbox about liturgical integrity: Either we should *mean* and *believe* the words we say in liturgy, or we should stop saying them. The close of the burial liturgy of the Episcopal Church is a perfect example of words the vast majority of clergy blithely recite without believing them:

> *Into paradise may the angels lead you. At your coming may the martyrs receive you, and bring you into the holy city Jerusalem.*[1]

I'm not suggesting we should stop using these words; I'm saying we should *believe* them! Most contemporary clergy are so

[1]Book of Common Prayer, 500.

rationalistic they don't even believe in angels, not to mention paradise. What seems to be happening today, though, is that more and more people are recovering the old beliefs about the afterlife, because of experiences in dealing with AIDS. This is just one part of the great spiritual awakening for which AIDS has been the catalyst.

I know a Methodist minister named Tom who worked in AIDS ministry in California. Now, modern Methodists, as I'm sure you know, tend to be fairly rational in their approach to religion. And they certainly don't want to say or do anything that might sound "catholic." But Tom told a story to a large interfaith group about being in the hospital room of a man with AIDS who was dying. This man was having a vivid experience of the other side, and he was narrating it to Tom. Tom was so blown away by the experience he reported it to his bishop, who is more than a little homophobic. What Tom said, I'm sure, must have grated on the bishop's ears, and must have caused him a little twinge of embarrassment, going against everything the bishop had been taught about rational religion in seminary. Tom told his bishop the only way to describe this PWA's experience was to say that he had crossed over to the other side, and that the angels and saints had come to carry him home.

A similar story is told by George Melton, the long-term AIDS survivor who has written about his experience in the book *Beyond AIDS: A Journey into Healing*. When George's lover, Will Garcia, died, George was with him. George's feelings were hurt a little, at first, because Will, as he was dying, seemed to be paying little attention to George. He was too busy talking with "the others" who, George is certain, "came for him."

So your answer to the Big Question—*Is* there life after death?—is: You bet your life there is!

Harp Lessons in Heaven?

While the Christian scriptures do teach us there is "life after life," they don't tell us much about what existence on the other side is like. Some images are in the Book of Revelation, but these are little vignettes, not intended to provide a complete picture of life in heaven. I offer you, drawn as much from Moody, Edgar Cayce, and other trance channelers as from "canonical" scripture, a concept of the afterlife not as a static existence of "eternal bliss" (doesn't that remind you of the spooky, spaced-out manner of Moonies, Jehovah's Witnesses, and assorted Fundamentalists?), but as a life of continued growth and learning.

In *Huckleberry Finn,* Huck decides, after Miss Watson teaches him about heaven and hell, that he'd rather go to hell—it sounds like a lot more fun. Heaven sounds boring: "She said all a body would have to do there was to go around all day long with a harp and sing, forever and ever. So I didn't think much of it."[2] If you image heaven as a place where you loll around on clouds and stroke harps, you probably agree with Huck. Even the idea of standing around the throne of God constantly singing hymns sounds a little boring, doesn't it? I mean, I *like* to sing hymns—but for eternity? The idea of continual learning and growth and increasing consciousness, on the other hand, sounds more like heaven. But if you *want* to sing hymns all day in heaven, I'm sure that could be arranged.

My friend Bill Irby always said he fully expected that when he got to heaven, God would let him sing alto in the heavenly choir. He felt that in the gospel and evangelical hymns that he loved, the altos always had the best parts. Bill is in heaven now, and when I get there, I expect to hear his new alto voice welcoming me.

Is There Sex in Heaven?

A few years ago, country singer Larry Gatlin enraged the Salvation Army, among others, when he recorded a song about the street people who attend a gospel mission and get "saved" several times weekly. After the mission closes, they acquire a bottle of wine and stand outside and sing, "Do they have Mogen David in heaven, Sweet Jesus? If not, who the hell wants to go?"

You may not be particularly interested in drinking Mogen David in heaven, although you might want to know whether they have Dom Pérignon. Actually, what you probably *really* want to

[2]Mark Twain (Samuel Clemens), *The Adventures of Huckleberry Finn,* in Lawrence Teacher, ed., *The Unabridged Mark Twain* (Philadelphia: Running Press, 1976), 749.

know is, do they have *sex* in heaven—and if not, who the hell wants to go?

The controversial and flamboyant late Episcopal Bishop of California, James Pike, was, just before he died unexpectedly, about to be put on heresy trial by the other bishops because he had begun to explore forms of spirituality outside the jurisdiction of the church. Most notably, since his son, Jim, had suicided, Bishop Pike had gone to trance mediums in order to communicate with Jim. In Pike's book, *The Other Side,* he prints the transcripts of many of the channelings through which his son (and the theologian Paul Tillich) spoke to him. If you accept the validity of channeling, you will find these accounts provide a fascinating picture of the afterlife.

In one of the sessions, Bishop Pike, worried about his son, who had had considerable trouble with relationships, asked him about his relationships on the other side. The bishop stammered around using vague language about "intimate expression," until finally the voice of his son cut in to ask if what he really wanted to know was whether the people on the other side have sex. Jim's answer was:

> Sex? Yes, there is sex. But it is not like it is there. It's not physical, of course, but actually there is less limitation. It is more obviously like what sex really means. Here you actually can enter the whole person. It's like you are in fact merging—becoming one.[3]

Phew! You can go to heaven, after all!

[3]James Pike and Diane Kennedy, *The Other Side* (Garden City, New York: Doubleday & Co., 1968), 151.

AFTERWORD

Taking Stock

In the first chapter, I asked you to "make believe" with me, to make an act of faith, to play the "what if" game for the amount of time it took you to read this book. So now it's time to check in with you, to find out how you feel now.

Above all else, I hope I have conveyed to you my *passion*—a passion for the truth, a passion for justice (especially within the church itself), a passion for the inherent goodness and holiness of the queer lifestyle, and, above all, a passion for Christ. If I have successfully done that, all that's left is your decision, your choice to "take it or leave it"; or as they say in AA, "take what you like and leave the rest."

The preacher at my ordination reminded us, "The church is not synonymous with the Kingdom of God," and that only at rare moments do the two coincide. The established institutional church likes to think it is the Body of Christ, but in fact it is seldom if ever worthy of that title. Those currently in power in the churches do not have a monopoly on the Christian faith. Please remember that, and don't give up on Christianity because of the stupidity and abusiveness of those who hold the power in the institutional church. Remember Jesus' words, "Blessed are you when they revile you and persecute you and utter all kinds of evil against you falsely on my account. Rejoice and be glad, for your reward is great in heaven, for so they persecuted the prophets who were before you."[1]

Being an authentic Christian, a true follower of Jesus the Christ, is never easy. Being a self-respecting queer in our society is even more difficult. Being out, proud, queer, and Christian is almost impossible. It's not going to be easy, I can guarantee that—but it can also be glorious.

In the Name of Christ, I wish you well, queer Christian.

[1]Matthew 5:11–12, rendered inclusive.

SUGGESTIONS FOR
FURTHER READING

PART ONE
Who Says?
Sources of the Truth

Chapter 1
Faith:
The Starting Point

Holmes, Urban T. *Turning to Christ: A Theology of Renewal and Evangelization*. New York: Seabury Press, 1981.

Jones, Alan W. *Journey Into Christ*. New York: Seabury Press, 1977.

Kelsey, Morton T. *Companions of the Inner Way: The Art of Spiritual Guidance*. New York: Crossroad, 1983.

Leech, Kenneth. *Soul Friend: The Practice of Christian Spirituality*. San Francisco: Harper & Row, 1977.

Lewis, C. S. *Mere Christianity*. London: Geoffrey Bles, 1952.

Merton, Thomas. *The Seven Storey Mountain*. New York: Harcourt Brace Jovanovich, 1948/1976.

Miles, Margaret R. *Practicing Christianity: Critical Perspectives for an Embodied Spirituality*. New York: Crossroad, 1988.

Needleman, Jacob. *Lost Christianity: A Journey of Rediscovery to the Center of Christian Experience*. New York: Doubleday/Bantam, 1980, 1982.

Pittenger, W. Norman. *Life in Christ*. Grand Rapids, Michigan: Eerdmans, 1972.

Chapter 2
Prayer and Meditation:
Trusting Your Inner Voice

Bloom, Anthony. *Beginning to Pray*. New York: Paulist Press, 1970.

*Kelsey, Morton T. *The Other Side of Silence: A Guide to Christian Meditation*. New York: Paulist Press, 1976.

* = most highly recommended

Merton, Thomas. *Thoughts in Solitude*. New York: Farrar, Straus and Giroux, 1956/1981.

Nouwen, Henri J. M. *Behold the Beauty of the Lord: Praying with Icons*. Notre Dame, Indiana: Ave Maria Press, 1987.

Puryear, Herbert B., and Mark A. Thurston. *Meditation and the Mind of Man*. Virginia Beach: ARE Press, 1978.

Underhill, Evelyn. *Practical Mysticism*. New York: Dutton, 1915/1943.

———. *Abba*. Treasures from the Spiritual Classics series. Wilton, Connecticut: Morehouse-Barlow, 1981.

Chapter 3
The Bible: The Bad News
and
Chapter 4
The Bible: The Good News

*Boswell, John. *Christianity, Social Tolerance, and Homosexuality: Gay People in Western Europe from the Beginning of the Christian Era to the Fourteenth Century*. Chicago: University of Chicago Press, 1980.

Collins, Adela Yarbro, ed. *Feminist Perspectives on Biblical Scholarship*. Society of Biblical Literature Centennial Publications. Atlanta: Scholars Press, 1985.

Countryman, William. *Biblical Authority or Biblical Tyranny? Scripture and the Christian Pilgrimage*. Philadelphia: Fortress Press, 1981.

———. *Dirt, Greed, and Sex: Sexual Ethics in the New Testament and Their Implications for Today*. Philadelphia: Fortress Press, 1988/1990.

Edwards, George R. *Gay/Lesbian Liberation: A Biblical Perspective*. New York: Pilgrim Press, 1984.

Horner, Tom. *Jonathan Loved David: Homosexuality in Biblical Times*. Philadelphia: Westminster Press, 1978.

*Russell, Letty M., ed. *Feminist Interpretation of the Bible*. Philadelphia: Westminster Press, 1985.

Schussler Fiorenza, Elisabeth. *Bread Not Stone: The Challenge of Feminist Biblical Interpretation*. Boston: Beacon Press, 1984.

Uhrig, Larry J. *Sex Positive: A Gay Contribution to Sexual and Spiritual Union*. Boston: Alyson Publications, 1986.

Chapter 5
Holy Mother Church vs. the Queer Nation:
The Authority of Community

Cone, James H. *God of the Oppressed*. New York: Seabury Press, 1975.

———. *A Black Theology of Liberation*. 2d ed. Maryknoll, New York: Orbis Books, 1987.

Cromey, Robert Warren. *In God's Image: Christian Witness to the Need for Gay/ Lesbian Equality in the Eyes of the Church*. San Francisco: Alamo Square Press, 1991.

Daly, Mary. *Beyond God the Father: Toward a Philosophy of Women's Liberation*. Boston: Beacon Press, 1973/1985.

Denman, Rose Mary. *Let My People In: A Lesbian Minister Tells of Her Struggles to Live Openly and Maintain Her Ministry*. New York: William Morrow, 1990.

Glaser, Chris. *Uncommon Calling: A Gay Man's Struggle to Serve the Church*. San Francisco: Harper & Row, 1988.

Nugent, Robert, ed. *A Challenge to Love: Gay and Lesbian Catholics in the Church*. New York: Crossroad, 1984.

Perry, Troy, with Thomas L. P. Swicegood. *Don't Be Afraid Anymore: The Story of the Reverend Troy Perry and the Metropolitan Community Church*. New York: St. Martin's Press, 1990.

Reuther, Rosemary R. *Women-Church: The Theology and Practice of Feminist Liturgical Communities*. San Francisco: Harper & Row, 1985.

Sacred Congregation for the Doctrine of the Faith. *Letter to the Bishops of the Catholic Church on the Pastoral Care of Homosexual Persons*. Washington: United States Catholic Conference, 1986. *Note: This is a negative, nasty document, with a grossly inappropriate title. You should be familiar with what it says, but it is not pleasant reading.*

Sherwood, Zalmon O. *Kairos: Confessions of a Gay Priest*. Boston: Alyson Press, 1987.

Zanotii, Barbara, ed. *A Faith of One's Own: Explorations by Catholic Lesbians*. New York: Crossing Press, 1986.

PART TWO
I Believe:
Basic Christian Doctrines

Chapter 6
God:
Healing Our Images

*Cobb, John B., Jr., and David Ray Griffin. *Process Theology: An Introductory Exposition*. Philadelphia: Westminster Press, 1976.

Jordan, Merle R. *Taking On the Gods: The Task of the Pastoral Counselor*. Nashville: Abingdon Press, 1986.

Rizzuto, Ana-Maria. *The Birth of the Living God: A Psychoanalytic Study*. Chicago: University of Chicago Press, 1979.

Trible, Phyllis. *God and the Rhetoric of Sexuality*. Philadelphia: Fortress Press, 1978.

Chapter 7
Mary:
The Divine Feminine

Atkinson, Clarissa W., Constance H. Buchanan, and Margaret R. Miles. *Immaculate & Powerful: The Female in Sacred Image and Social Reality*. Boston: Beacon Press, 1985.

Berger, Pamela. *The Goddess Obscured: The Transformation of the Grain Protectress from Goddess to Saint*. Boston: Beacon Press, 1985.

Eisler, Raine. *The Chalice and the Blade: Our History, Our Future*. San Francisco: Harper, 1987.

*Mollenkott, Virginia Ramey. *The Divine Feminine: The Biblical Imagery of God as Female*. New York: Crossroad, 1983.

Ruether, Rosemary Radford. *Womanguides: Readings Toward a Feminist Theology*. Boston: Beacon Press, 1985.

Starhawk. *The Spiral Dance: A Rebirth of the Ancient Religion of the Great Goddess*. San Francisco: Harper & Row, 1979/1989.

Warner, Marina. *Alone of All Her Sex: The Myth and Cult of the Virgin Mary*. New York: Knopf/Random House, 1976.

Chapter 8
Jesus the Christ:
Our Elder Brother

Furst, Jeffrey, ed. *Edgar Cayce's Story of Jesus*. New York: Berkeley Books, 1976/1984.

Nolan, Albert. *Jesus Before Christianity*. Maryknoll, New York: Orbis Books, 1978.

Pelikan, Jaroslav. *Jesus Through the Centuries: His Place in the History of Culture*. New York: Harper & Row, 1985.

*Read, Anne. *Edgar Cayce on Jesus and His Church*. New York: Warner Books, 1970.

Robinson, John A. T. *The Human Face of God*. Philadelphia: Westminster Press, 1973.

Smith, Morton. *Jesus the Magician*. New York: Harper & Row, 1977.

*———. *The Secret Gospel: The Discovery and Interpretation of the Secret Gospel According to Mark*. 2d ed. Clearlake, California: Dawn Horse Press, 1982.

Chapter 9
The Word Made Flesh:
Incarnation and Sacrament

Baillie, D. M. *God Was in Christ: An Essay on Incarnation and Atonement*. Boston: Faber & Faber, 1948/1986.

Eastman, A. Theodore. *The Baptizing Community: Christian Initiation and the Local Congregation.* New York: Seabury Press, 1982.

Heyward, Carter. *Speaking of Christ: A Lesbian Feminist Voice.* New York: Pilgrim Press, 1989. Ellen C. Davis, ed.

Porter, H. Boone. *Keeping the Church Year.* New York: Seabury, 1977.

Suchocki, Marjorie Hewitt. *God/Christ/Church: A Practical Guide to Process Theology.* New York: Crossroad, 1989.

Chapter 10
Keeping the Feast:
Celebrating God's Gifts

Boulding, Elsie, and Victor Avila. *From a Monastery Kitchen: A Practical Cookbook.* New York: Harper & Row, 1976.

Capon, Robert Farrar. *The Supper of the Lamb: A Culinary Reflection.* Garden City, New York: Doubleday, 1969.

———. *Food for Thought: Resurrecting the Lost Art of Eating.* New York: Harcourt Brace Jovanovich, 1978.

———. *Capon on Cooking.* Boston: Houghton Mifflin, 1983.

Cox, Harvey. *The Feast of Fools: A Theological Essay on Festivity and Fantasy.* New York: Harper & Row, 1969.

Chapter 11
Righting the Wrongs:
Queer Ethics, Sin, Evil, and Reconciliation

Capon, Robert Farrar. *The Third Peacock: A Book about God and the Problem of Evil.* New York: Doubleday/Image, 1972.

*Fletcher, Joseph. *Situation Ethics: The New Morality.* Philadelphia: Westminster Press, 1966.

Harrison, Beverly Wildung. In *Making the Connections: Essays in Feminist Social Ethics,* edited by Carol S. Robb. Boston: Beacon Press, 1985.

Hick, John. *Evil and the God of Love.* 2d ed. San Francisco: Harper & Row, 1978.

Kushner, Harold S. *When Bad Things Happen to Good People.* New York: Schocken Books, 1981.

*Peck, M. Scott *People of the Lie: The Hope for Healing Human Evil.* New York: Simon & Schuster, 1983.

Pittenger, W. Norman. *Freed to Love: A Process Interpretation of Redemption.* New York: Morehouse-Barlow, 1987.

Sanford, John A. *Evil: The Shadow Side of Reality.* New York: Crossroad, 1982.

Smith, Martin L. *Reconciliation: Preparing for Confession in the Episcopal Church.* Cambridge, Massachusetts: Cowley Publications, 1989.

PART THREE
Finding God in Gay Experience:
The Vocation of Queer Christians

Chapter 12
Coming Out:
Responding to God's Call

Boyd, Malcolm. *Take Off the Masks*. Philadelphia: New Society Publishers, 1984.
Boyd, Malcom and Nancy L. Wilson, ed. *Amazing Grace: Stories of Lesbian and Gay Faith*. Trumansburg, New York: Crossing Press, 1991.
*Eichberg, Rob. *Coming Out: An Act of Love*. New York: Plume/Penguin, 1991.

Chapter 13
I Am What I Am:
Claiming Gay Pride

Marotta, Toby. *The Politics of Homosexuality: How Lesbians and Gay Men Have Made Themselves a Political and Social Force in Modern America*. Boston: Houghton Mifflin, 1981.
McNaught, Brian. *On Being Gay: Thoughts on Family, Faith, and Love*. New York: St. Martin's Press, 1988.

Chapter 14
Sex:
Eros as Vocation

Annand, Margo. *The Art of Sexual Ecstasy: The Path of Sacred Sexuality for Western Lovers*. Los Angeles: Jeremy P. Tarcher, Inc., 1989.
Garrison, Omar. *Tantra: The Yoga of Sex*. New York: Julian Press, 1964.
*Heyward, Carter. *Touching Our Strength: The Erotic as Power and the Love of God*. San Francisco: Harper & Row, 1989.
Johnson, Edwin Clark. *In Search of God in the Sexual Underworld: A Mystical Journey*. New York: Quill, 1983.
Kelsey, Morton, and Barbara Kelsey. *Sacrament of Sexuality: The Spirituality and Psychology of Sex*. Warwick, New York: Amity House, 1986.
*Kramer, Joseph. *Ecstatic Sex, Healthy Sex: A Seminar for Gay and Bisexual Men* (Audiotapes). Oakland, California: Body Electric Publishing Company, 1988.
Loulan-Gardner, Jo Ann. *Lesbian Passion: Loving Ourselves and Each Other*. San Francisco: Spinsters/Aunt Lude, 1987.

*Nelson, James B. *Between Two Gardens: Reflections on Sexuality and Religious Experience.* New York: Pilgrim Press, 1983.

———. *The Intimate Connection: Male Sexuality, Masculine Spirituality.* Philadelphia: Westminster Press, 1988.

Patton, Cindy. *Sex and Germs: The Politics of AIDS.* Boston: South End Press, 1985.

*Ramer, Andrew. *Two Flutes Playing. Spiritual Love/Sacred Sex. Priests of Father Earth and Mother Sky.* Oakland, California: Body Electric Publishing, 6527A Telegraph Ave., Oakland, CA 94609.

*Weinrich, James D. *Sexual Landscapes: Why We Are What We Are, Why We Love Whom We Love.* New York: Scribners, 1987.

Woods, Margo. *Masturbation, Tantra, and Self Love.* San Diego: Omphaloskepsis Press/Mho and Mho Works, 1981.

Chapter 15
Lovers:
The Vocation of Commitment

*Berzon, Betty. *Permanent Partners: Building Gay and Lesbian Relationships That Last.* New York: Dutton, 1988.

Boswell, John. "Rediscovering Gay History: Archetypes of Gay Love in Christian History." The Fifth Michael Harding Memorial Address. London: Gay Christian Movement, 1982/1985.

Butler, Becky, ed. *Ceremonies of the Heart: Celebrating Lesbian Unions.* Washington: Seal Press, 1990.

McWhirter, David P., and Andrew M. Mattison. *The Male Couple: How Relationships Develop.* Englewood Cliffs, New Jersey: Prentice-Hall, 1984.

Sanford, John A. *The Invisible Partners: How the Male and Female in Each of Us Affects our Relationships.* New York: Paulist Press, 1980.

Tanner, Donna M. *The Lesbian Couple.* Lexington, Massachusetts: Lexington Books, 1978.

Uhrig, Larry J. *The Two of Us: Affirming, Celebrating, and Symbolizing Gay and Lesbian Relationships.* Boston: Alyson Publications, 1984.

Williams, Robert. "Toward a Theology of Same-Sex Marriage." *Anglican Theological Review* 72, no. 2 (Spring 1990).

Another excellent resource is *Couples: A Gay & Lesbian Newsletter on Coupling,* TWT Press, P.O. Box 253, Braintree, MA 02184.

Chapter 16
Holy Anger:
Protest as Vocation

Berryman, Phillip. *Liberation Theology.* New York: Pantheon Books, 1987.

Heyward, Carter. *Our Passion for Justice: Images of Sexuality, Power, and Liberation.* New York: Pilgrim Press, 1984.

Lorde, Audre. *Sister Outsider: Essays & Speeches.* Trumansburg, New York: Crossing Press, 1984.

Solle, Dorothee. *The Window of Vulnerability: A Political Spirituality.* Minneapolis: Fortress Press, 1990.

Chapter 17
Being a Berdache:
The Vocation of Being Queer

Blackwood, Evelyn, ed. *The Many Faces of Homosexuality: Anthropological Approaches to Homosexual Behavior.* New York: Harrington Park Press, 1986.

Downing, Christine. *Myths and Mysteries of Same-Sex Love.* New York: Continuum, 1989.

Evans, Arthur. *Witchcraft and the Gay Counter Culture: A Radical View of Western Civilization and Some of the People It Has Tried to Destroy.* Boston: Fag Rag Books, 1978.

*Grahn, Judy. *Another Mother Tongue: Gay Words, Gay Worlds.* Boston: Beacon Press, 1984.

Hopcke, Robert H. *Jung, Jungians and Homosexuality.* Boston: Shambhala, 1989.

Plaskow, Judith, and Carol Christ, eds. *Weaving the Visions: New Paths in Feminist Spirituality.* San Francisco: Harper & Row, 1989.

*Thompson, Mark. *Gay Spirit: Myth and Meaning.* New York: St. Martin's Press, 1987.

Williams, Walter L. *The Spirit and the Flesh: Sexual Diversity in American Indian Culture.* Boston: Beacon Press, 1986.

See also: Andrew Ramer (Chapter 14).

PART FOUR
The Resurrection of the Body:
Life, Death, and Healing

Chapter 18
Letting God Be God:
Addiction and Recovery

Alcoholics Anonymous ("The Big Book"). 3d ed. New York: AA World Services, 1976.

Crawford, David. *Easing the Ache: Gay Men Recovering from Compulsive Behaviors.* New York: Dutton, 1990.

Katz, Stan J., and Aimee E. Liu. *The Codependency Conspiracy: How to Break the Recovery Habit and Take Charge of Your Life.* New York: Warner Books, 1991.

*May, Gerald G. *Addiction and Grace.* San Francisco: Harper & Row, 1988.

Chapter 19
Trusting the Great Physician:
AIDS and Christian Healing

*Asistent, Niro Markoff. *Why I Survive AIDS*. New York: Simon & Schuster/Fireside, 1991.

*Bird, Christopher. *The Persecution and Trial of Gaston Naessens: The True Story of the Efforts to Suppress an Alternative Treatment for Cancer, AIDS, and Other Immunologically Based Diseases*. Tiburon, California: H. J. Kramer, Inc., 1991.

*Callen, Michael. *Surviving AIDS*. New York: HarperCollins, 1990.

*Kelsey, Morton T. *Psychology, Medicine, and Christian Healing*. San Francisco: Harper & Row, 1988.

McNutt, Francis. *Healing*. New York: Ave Maria/Bantam, 1974/1977.

———. *The Power to Heal*. Notre Dame: Ave Maria Press, 1985.

Neal, Emily Gardiner. *The Healing Power of Christ*. New York: Hawthorn, 1972.

Olsen, Kristin Gottschalk, ed. *The Encyclopedia of Alternative Health Care*. New York: Pocket Books/Simon & Schuster, 1989.

Puryear, Meredith Ann. *Healing Through Meditation and Prayer*. Virginia Beach: ARE Press, 1978.

Sanford, Agnes. *The Healing Light*. St. Paul, Minnesota: Macalester Press, 1947. Rev. ed., New York: Ballantine, 1972.

*Siegel, Bernie S. *Love, Medicine and Miracles: Lessons Learned About Self-Healing from a Surgeon's Experience with Exceptional Patients*. New York: Harper & Row, 1986.

*Serinus, Jason, ed. *Psychoimmunity and the Healing Process: A Holistic Approach to Immunity and AIDS*. Berkeley, California: Celestial Arts, 1988.

Chapter 20
Sure and Certain Hope:
Death and Afterlife

Boerstler, Richard W. *Letting Go: A Holistic and Meditative Approach to Living and Dying*. South Yarmouth, Massachusetts: Associates in Thanatology, 1985.

Humphry, Derek. *Let Me Die Before I Wake: Hemlock's Book of Self-Deliverance for the Dying*. Eugene, Oregon: Hemlock Society, 1981/1988.

Kelsey, Morton T. *Afterlife: The Other Side of Dying*. New York: Crossroad, 1982.

Mitford, Jessica. *The American Way of Death*. New York: Simon & Schuster, 1963.

*Moody, Raymond A. *Life After Life: The Investigation of a Phenomenon—Survival of Bodily Death*. New York: Bantam, 1976.

———. *The Light Beyond*. New York: Bantam Books, 1988.

Pike, James A., with Diane Kennedy. *The Other Side: An Account of My Experiences with Psychic Phenomena*. New York: Doubleday, 1968.

ACKNOWLEDGMENTS

Some of the ideas in this book are reincarnations of what I have said or written in other places. In a Palm Sunday sermon at the Church of St. John the Evangelist in Boston, I presented some of the material that is in Chapter 8 about Jesus and the Beloved Disciple. In another sermon in St. John's Chapel at Episcopal Divinity School (my "senior sermon"), I used some of the ideas about the vocation to the sensuous life found in Chapter 10. The idea of the God who brings us out in Chapter 12 was first "play-tested" at a retreat I conducted for the Dignity/Integrity chapter of western Massachusetts. Much of the material in Chapter 15 on queer marriage appeared, in a different form, in the Spring 1990 issue of the *Anglican Theological Review,* under the title "Toward a Theology of Lesbian and Gay Marriage." Parts of Chapter 17, on the vocation of being queer, originally appeared in an article in *Christopher Street* magazine (issue 145) titled "Re-Visioning Christianity for Radical Gay Men and Lesbians." Much of the information in Chapter 19 on healing is from a sermon I preached at the Church of St. Mary of the Harbor in Provincetown in May 1991, which sermon has subsequently been published in *Chrism,* the journal of the Guild of St. Raphael, and also in the *TBS Newsletter,* a publication dealing with gay male spirituality. And finally, some of the ideas in Chapter 20 on death and afterlife were previously presented in a workshop on preparing for death I presented in the winter of 1988 under the sponsorship of Interfaith Provincetown.

Many of my friends, associates, and former professors helped me check and track down quotations and references; these helpers include John Skinner, Don Winslow, Brad Carter, Arthur Pike, Chris Bull of *The Advocate,* and Bob Kazmayer of the TBS Network. Malcolm Boyd and John Westerhoff III were kind enough to correct my misquotations of their words.

I also want to thank the friends who read and commented on chapters in progress, including Jackie Lapidus, Kitty Dewey, Kathy Ganim, John Merschtina, Larry Meilleur, Jim Skelly, Roger Warren, and Margaret Erhart.

It was my late professor and mentor Bill Wolf who first urged me to write a book of gay theology. Although the current book is considerably less formal and academic than what he had in mind, to a large extent this is the book Bill nagged me to write.

Both my agents and my editor deserve special thanks, for their involvement in this book and in my life goes beyond the usual professional relationship. The editor, David Groff, is the one person really most responsible for this book, for in a sense, it was his idea. My agents, Sydelle Kramer and Frances Goldin, not only figuratively held my hand through the writing and publishing of this book, but literally held my hand and brought me chicken soup when I was in the hospital.

I am always, at the very least, amused, and at most, offended, by sports figures (especially wrestlers and boxers) who, when interviewed on television, attribute their victories to Jesus. I question whether Jesus favors one boxer or wrestler over another, even if one is "born again" and the other is an atheist, and I seriously doubt Jesus is on call to help anyone knock an opponent unconscious. My revulsion at that sort of mentality makes me hesitate to say what I am about to say, but my passion wins out: Most of all, I want to thank my Lord and Savior Jesus Christ, for giving me life and for giving my life meaning and adventure.

INDEX